IMAGES
of America

DELAVAN

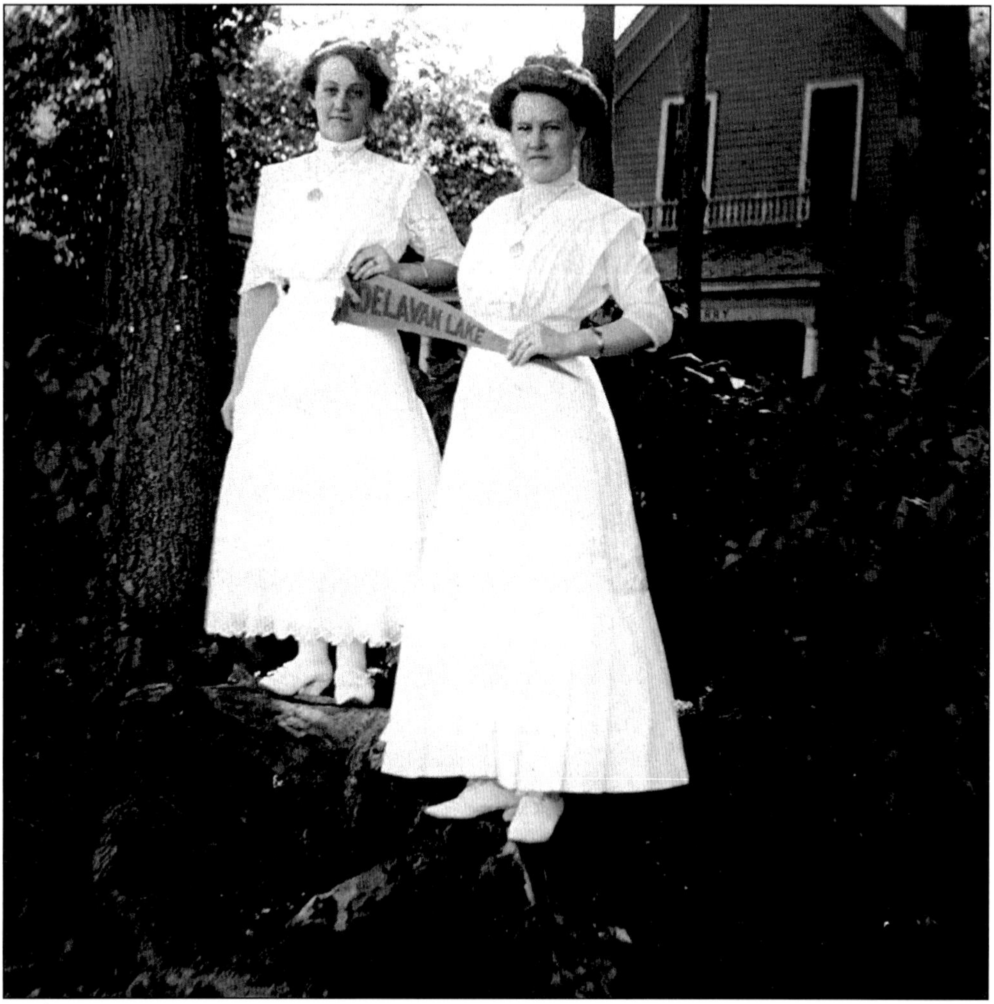

For over a century, Delavan Lake has been a popular tourist destination. Generation after generation of family members have spent summers enjoying the fishing, swimming, boating, and sailing. Whether staying at one of the area's hospitable resorts or bringing the family up to the cottage, time at Delavan Lake was always relaxing and well spent. These ladies pictured here at the turn of the century were probably not born in Delavan, but they got here as fast as they could.

IMAGES *of America*

DELAVAN

Patricia Ruth-Marsicano

ARCADIA PUBLISHING

ISBN 978-0-7385-3311-7

Published by Arcadia Publishing
Charleston, South Carolina

Printed in the Unites States of America

Library of Congress Catalog Card Number: 2004112010

For all general information contact Arcadia Publishing at:
Telephone 843-853-2070
Fax 843-853-0044
E-mail sales@arcadiapublishing.com
For customer service and orders:
Toll-Free 1-888-313-2665

Visit us on the Internet at www.arcadiapublishing.com

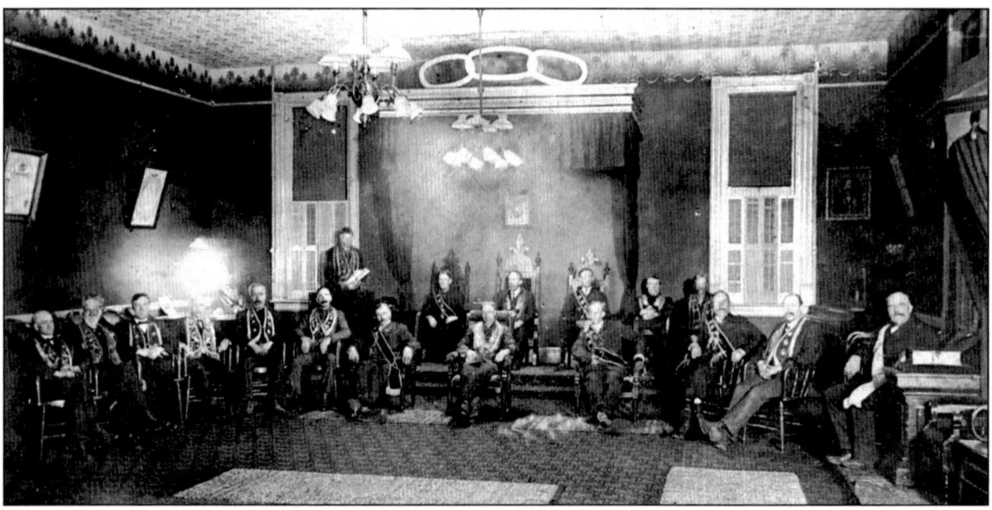

The Independent Order of Odd Fellows was chartered in Delavan in 1871. For many years, they met in various locations until they purchased the former Park Hotel in 1918. This photograph shows their meeting room inside the building in 1916, before they purchased it. The charter still exists, although the organization has not been active for many years.

Contents

ACKNOWLEDGMENTS

Thanks to the generosity of others, this volume contains some interesting views of Delavan and Delavan Lake over the span of a century. I'd like to extend my appreciation to the following people for opening up their collections and sharing their photographs, art, permission, knowledge, and generosity: Franklin Stoneburner, Gordon Yadon, Charles Spooner, Allen Buzzell, John Buckles, Bette Cameron, Bill McKoy, Peggy Murphy, Hazel Williamson, Joan Sullivan, Dorothy Radford, Babs Walsh, John and Barbara Stevenson, Charma Davies Lepke, George Bashaw, Dave Austin, Greg Grether, Jan Bores, Jack and Lois Stritt, Janice Watts, John McClellan, Ed and Linda Siert, Margaret Kaye, Dave and Debbie Marsicano, Patti and Larry Rosencrans, Mary Begun, Marybell Cooper Seeber, Pat Morelli, Peggy Rockwell Gleich, Steve Carlson, Bob Lywellyn, Helen Carlson, Nancy Nugent, Sean Everette, Joe and Julie Zagone, East Delavan Baptist Church, the Wisconsin Historical Society, Wisconsin School for the Deaf, Aram Public Library, Sta-Rite Industries, and the Burlington Historical Society.

I am deeply indebted to Gordon Yadon, Franklin Stoneburner, Charles Spooner, and John Buckles for sharing their vast knowledge of Delavan's history and taking time to make sure it was written acceptably. My appreciation and respect know no end.

I would like to thank my husband Chris for his unfailing endorsement and support, along with my family, my niece Nina Piolatto, my good friend Charlie Gardes, and those close to me for their encouragement and help in making this book a reality.

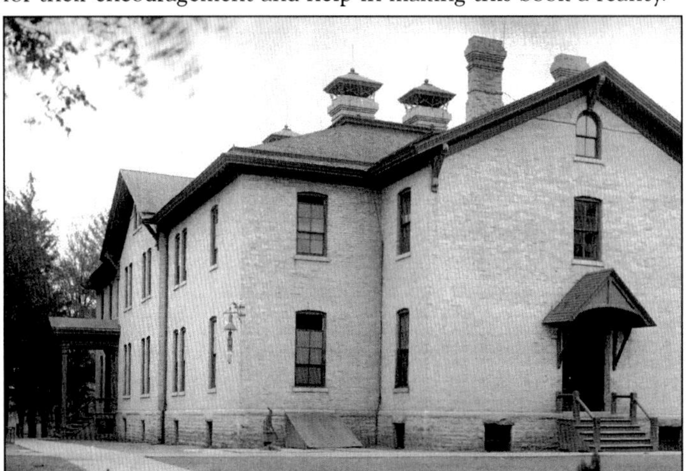

Phoenix Hall at the Wisconsin School for the Deaf was formerly located at 309 West Walworth Avenue and aptly named for the man who donated the land. The building was utilized as a dormitory since its completion in 1867. It was placed on the National Register of Historic Places in 1987, but sadly razed in approximately 1998.

Introduction

Effigy mounds found today around Delavan Lake, near the lake's northeast-shore outlet and in Assembly Park, indicate pre-historic Woodland Indians were the first known inhabitants of the Delavan area. First realized in the early 1800s, the mounds and former Indian Village locations were studied and reported in the December 1936 edition of *The Wisconsin Archeologist*, volume six, number one. Through settlement and growth around the lake, many of these mounds have been lost forever.

After the Late Woodland era, the Winnebago and Pottawatomie tribes inhabited the area when the first white settlers arrived. Other explorers had traveled through Delavan, but not until 1836, when Col. Samuel Phoenix came, was Delavan's potential realized. Phoenix spent his first night in a deserted wigwam on the shore of Swan Lake, which would be renamed Delavan Lake after he chose this site for a new temperance colony. His vision was to build a virtuous God-fearing community that would abide by Christian principles. Phoenix would fight to have this new colony bear the name of temperance leader and abolitionist Edward C. Delavan.

Colonel Phoenix immediately set to work on building his community and in March 1837 he moved his family to Delavan, followed in 1838 by the family of his brother, Henry. By 1846, Delavan was a thriving village and was growing as a trade center. Although founded on strict temperance principles, the first tavern opened in Delavan in 1845.

Delavan's early settlement in the 1830s developed into its incorporation into a village in 1856. During this period, the entire township functioned under one government. It wasn't until 1897, when Delavan became a city, that the town and the city governments first functioned independently.

In 1847, Jeremiah and Edmund Mabie, of Brewster, New York, were searching for a location to better centralize their circus during the winter months when they came across Delavan Lake. They immediately recognized the advantages of the lush unspoiled land and purchased what is now Lake Lawn property and its adjacent areas for their U.S. Olympic Circus. The Mabie Brothers became prominent business men in the community, raised their families here, and were instrumental in Delavan's growth.

Other circuses would soon follow, and between 1847 and 1894, 28 different circuses wintered in Delavan. During this time, it was a normal to see elephants or camels being walked about town. It was in Delavan, during the winter of 1870–71, where William Coup and Dan Castello organized the P.T. Barnum Circus. Delavan would later be recognized as the "19th Century Circus Capitol of the Nation."

The American railroads were rapidly expanding westward, making transportation easier, faster and more convenient. Recognizing this, the circuses no longer needed winter quarters here and the last circus left in 1894.

Ebeneezer Cheseboro came to Delavan from New York in the late 1830s, bringing his family, including his daughter Ariadna, who was deaf. Delavan had no facility for teaching a deaf child, but the Cheseboros still wanted their daughter educated. A former New York Institute for the Deaf graduate lived nearby and was hired to school their daughter and a neighbor boy who was also deaf. In 1852, with the help of family and friends, they petitioned the state legislature to establish a school for the deaf in Delavan. Franklin Phoenix, a family friend and son of Col. Samuel Phoenix, offered to donate land to the state for the school.

The petition succeeded and on April 19, 1852, the governor signed the law appropriating funds for the Wisconsin School for the Deaf and Dumb, now called The Wisconsin School for the Deaf. Thousands of students have since graduated from the school, which has continued to uphold a high standard of education for over 150 years.

The 1880s saw an explosion of summer cottages and resorts popping up along the lake's shoreline. Some residents of the village of Delavan had a cottage at the lake where they could escape the summer heat. Prosperous Chicago area residents built summer retreats here. Visitors were serviced by the many resorts and hotels that sprang up toward the turn of the 19th century. In the summer months, both the south and north shores of the lake came alive with activity and soon the railroad depot had as many as six passenger trains a day transporting vacationers to Delavan.

The influx of visitors caused many resorts to erect dance pavilions on their grounds and hire bands, thus giving birth to Delavan's Ballroom Era. Ballrooms would be built large enough to attract prominent entertainers in the music world who would perform before as many as 2,000 patrons a night. Dancing to the music of nationally known bands in Delavan would continue until the 1950s.

Between 1892 and 1910, the Art Institute of Chicago held summer classes in Delavan on the shores of Lake Comus, which assisted in developing some of the local talent. These summer classes attracted several prominent artists to move to Delavan and maintain art studios here.

The industrial boon started in the 1910s with Bradley Knitting Company. During World War I, the company had government contacts to make sweaters for the Army, providing an economic boost for the community during the war. The 1930s saw the beginning of the George W. Borg Company and Sta-Rite, in the 1940s the T.B. Gibbs Company, and later in the 1950s, Ajay. Delavan's industrial growth kept the area economy moving during the Depression and World War II.

Delavan's history had been shaped by ordinary individuals who had a vision and desire to make their lives and the lives of their neighbors better. Through religion, education, industry, art, and entertainment, Delavan's history is a part of its present and its future.

One

DOWNTOWN VIEWS ON WALWORTH AVENUE

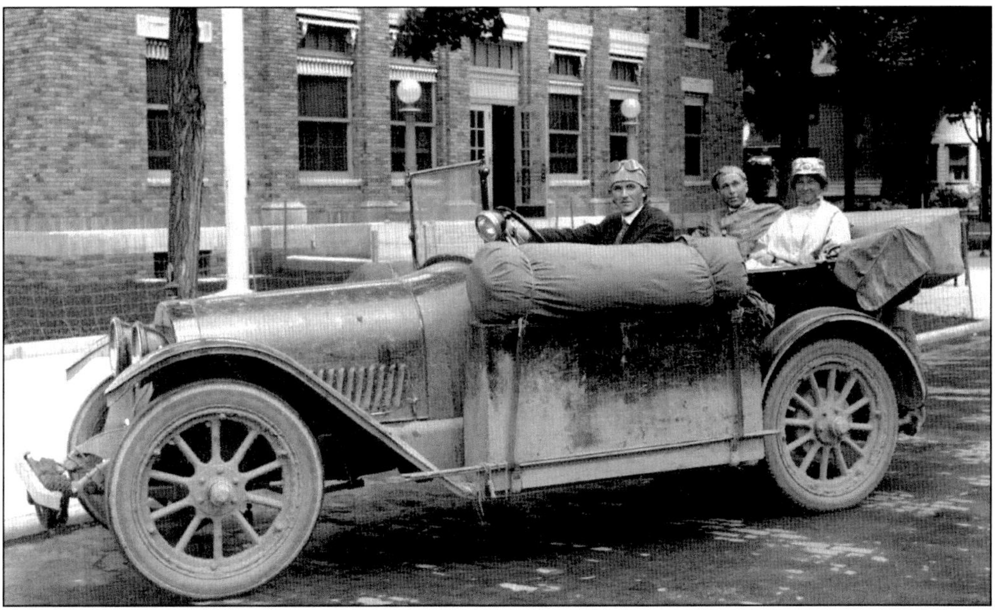

This adventuresome trio has just returned from an exciting day of motoring, c. 1920. The Delavan Post Office, shown in the background and located at 333 East Walworth Avenue, was dedicated in 1914 and placed on the National Register of Historic Places on October 24, 2000. Also visible in this photograph is Delavan's Vitrified Brick Street, located in the 100–300 blocks of Walworth Avenue. It was constructed in 1913 to keep the dust from the road out of the shops along the street. Delavan's Vitrified Brick Street was entered on the National Register of Historic Places on March 7, 1996. The house visible further right of the post office belonged to John and Peg Lynch. The Lynch Family owned and operated Lynch & Son clothing store from 1906 to 1960 in Delavan.

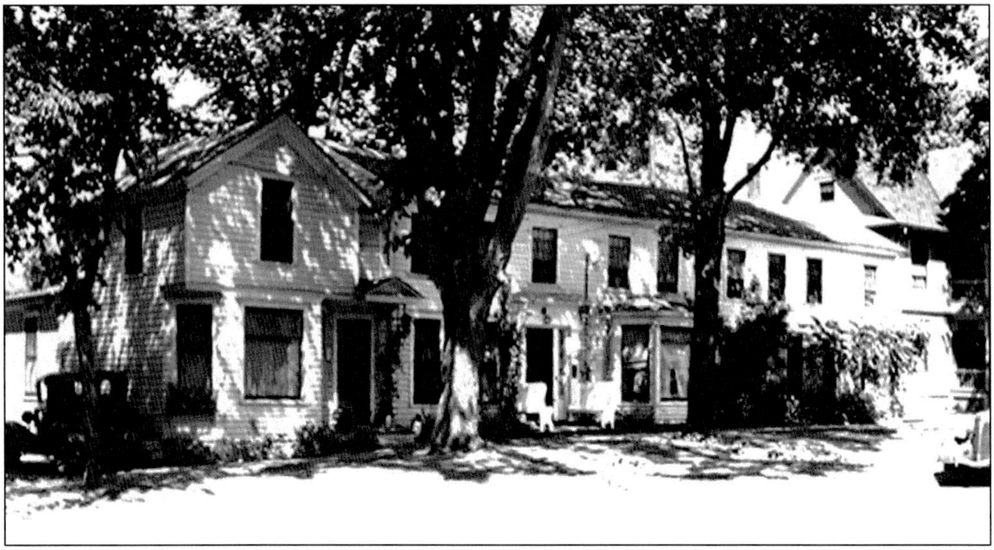

The Temperance Inn, at 61–65 East Walworth Avenue, was built by Israel Stowell in 1840 under the strict specifications of the Phoenix brothers. The building was used as a lodging facility for only about 15 years, as the Park Hotel was opened in 1847, followed by the White Hotel in about 1850; both offered larger rooms. To stay at the inn, one had to be of high Christian caliber and no alcohol was allowed. It was later turned into a residence and been home to several businesses. It was listed on the National Register of Historic Places as the Israel Stowell Temperance House in 1978.

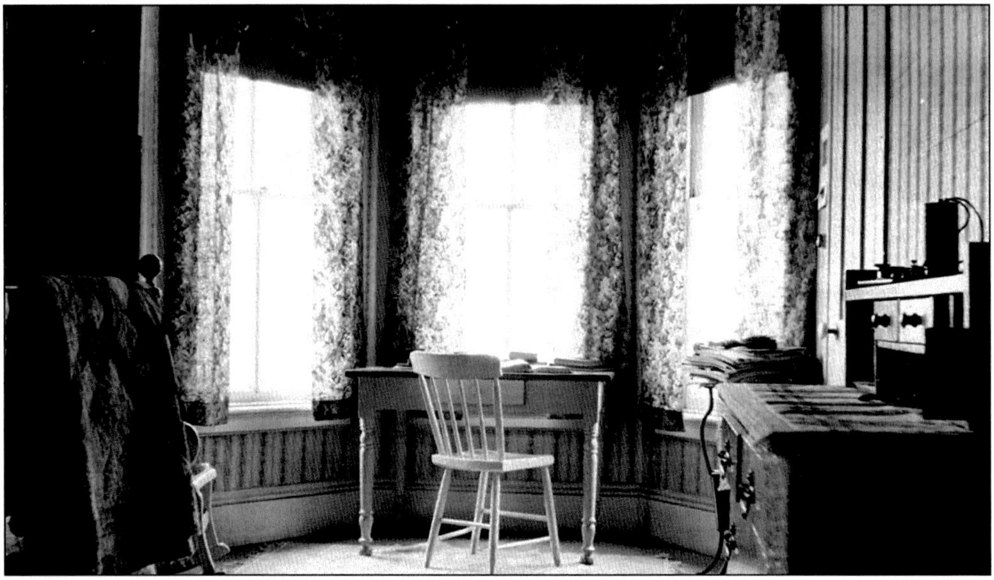

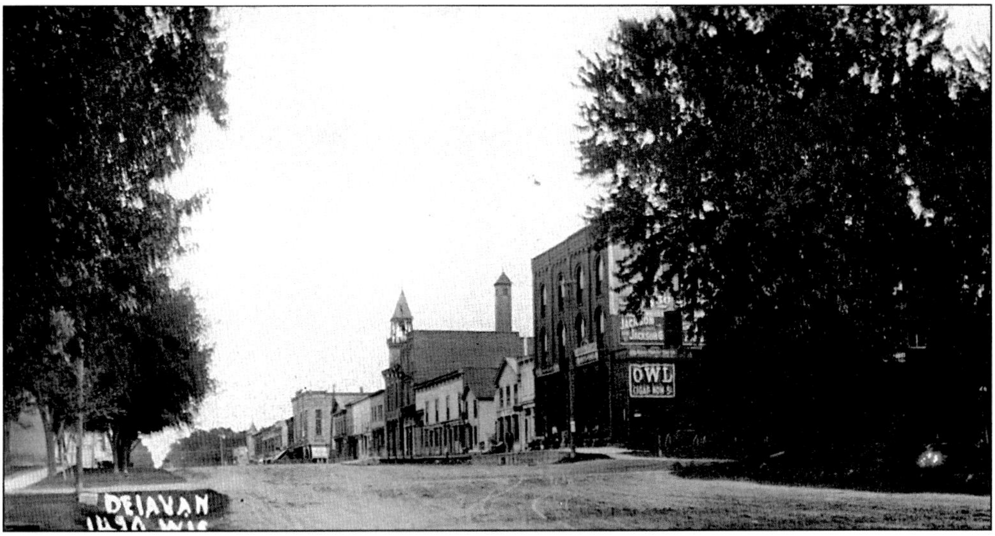

This is a 1910 view of the south side of the 100 block of West Walworth Avenue, looking east. Noticeable in the foreground is the Jackson Building, formerly called the Hollister Building. To the east of the Jackson Building is where the VanVelzer building would be constructed in 1914.

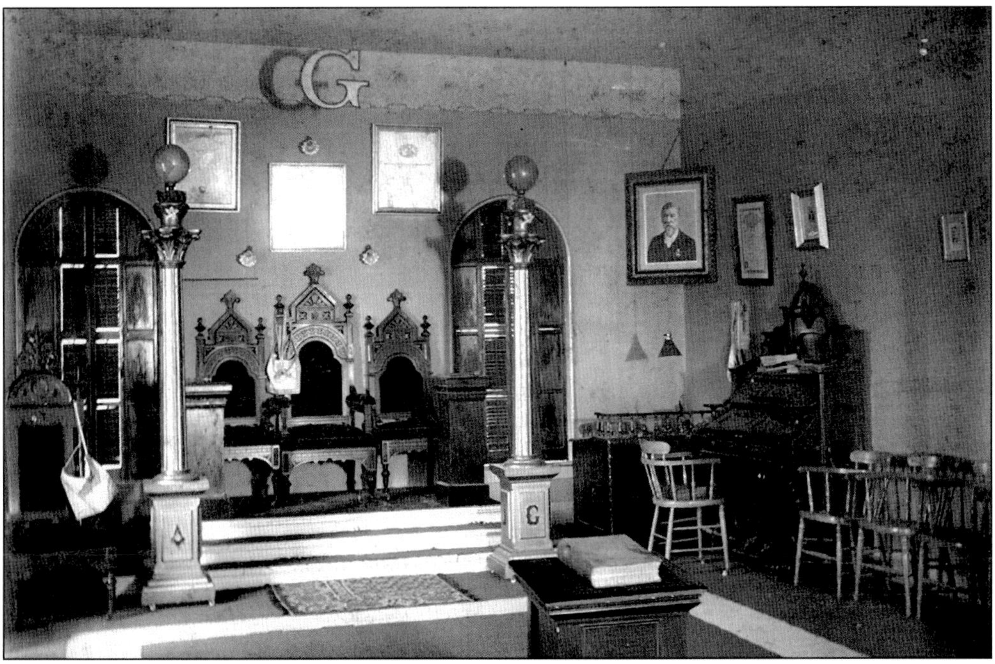

The Masonic Lodge No. 12 AF&AM has had several homes over the years. After they organized on August 12, 1860, they met in the room pictured here, located in the Jackson Building on the corner of South Main and Walworth until 1909. During 1909–1969 they met at 313 Walworth Avenue, after which they built a lodge located south of Delavan on County Trunk O.

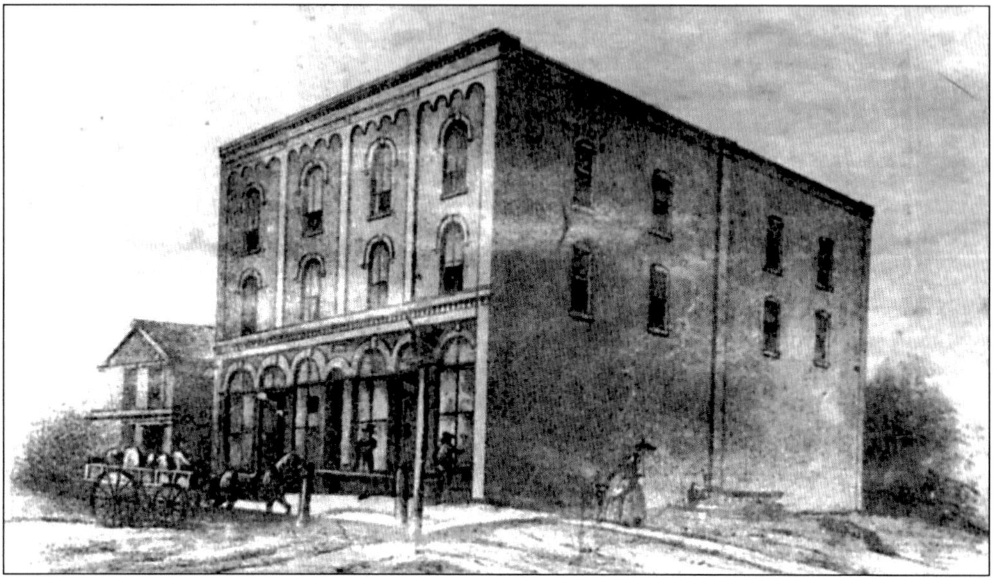

The Delavan Exchange Building was built on the southeast corner of Main and Walworth in 1851. It was home to numerous businesses, the largest was a grocery store run by K.N. Hollister and later his partner, Stedman L. Jackson. By 1900, Jackson was operating his retail grocery business with his son Arthur under the name Jackson & Jackson Co. His former partner K.N. Hollister had a store a few blocks away. In 1914, they converted the upper floors into apartments, adding balconies and room for two more small shops on both the east and west side. More recently referred to as the Jackson Flats, the building is currently under renovation.

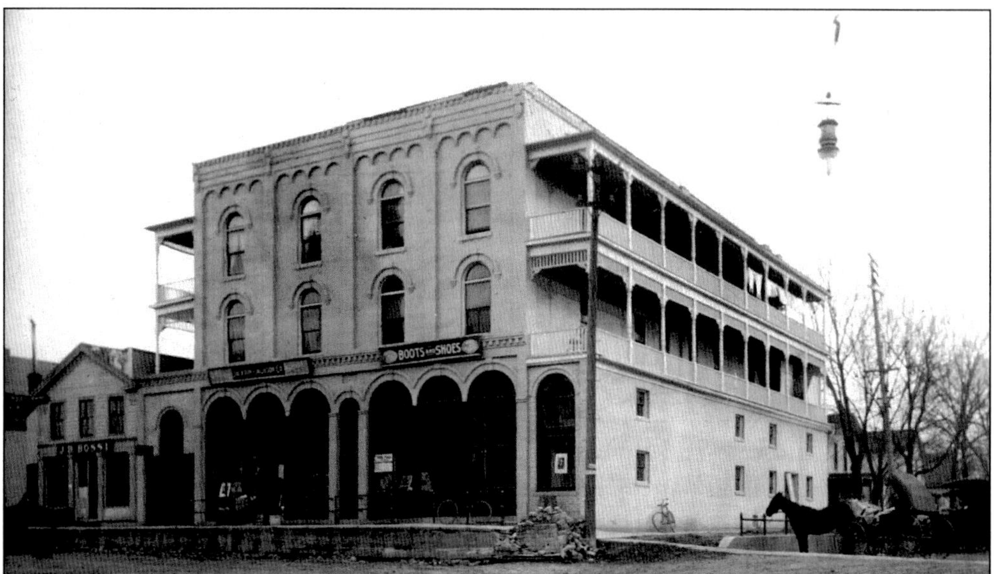

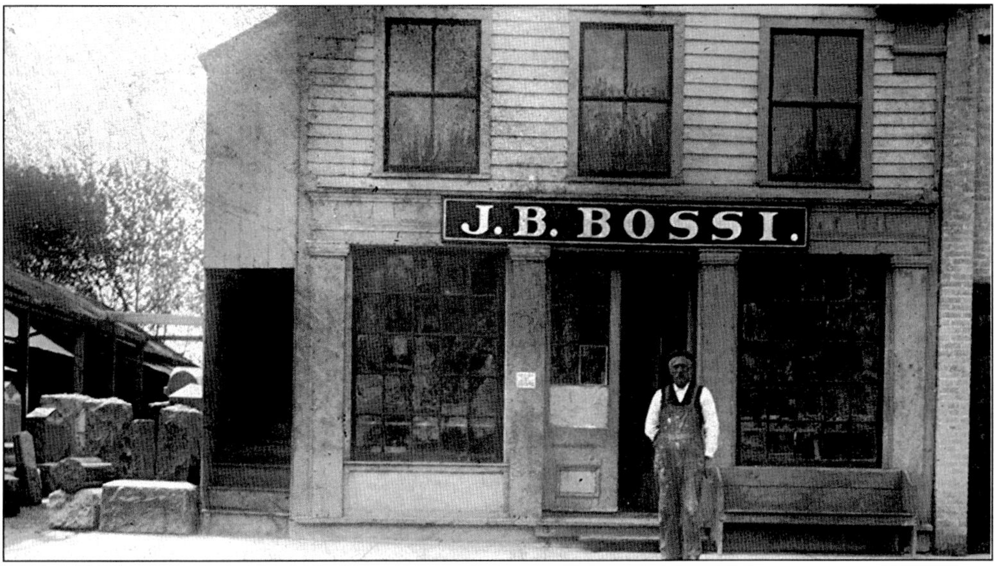

John Bossi had his monument business at 106 East Walworth Avenue from about 1868 to 1914. He came from Italy as an experienced marble cutter, and his assistant, Italian-born Paul Turri, was a very talented marble cutter who had worked in many of the beautiful cathedrals throughout Europe. John Bossi and Paul Turri can be credited with many of the beautiful old monuments at Spring Grove and St. Andrew's cemeteries.

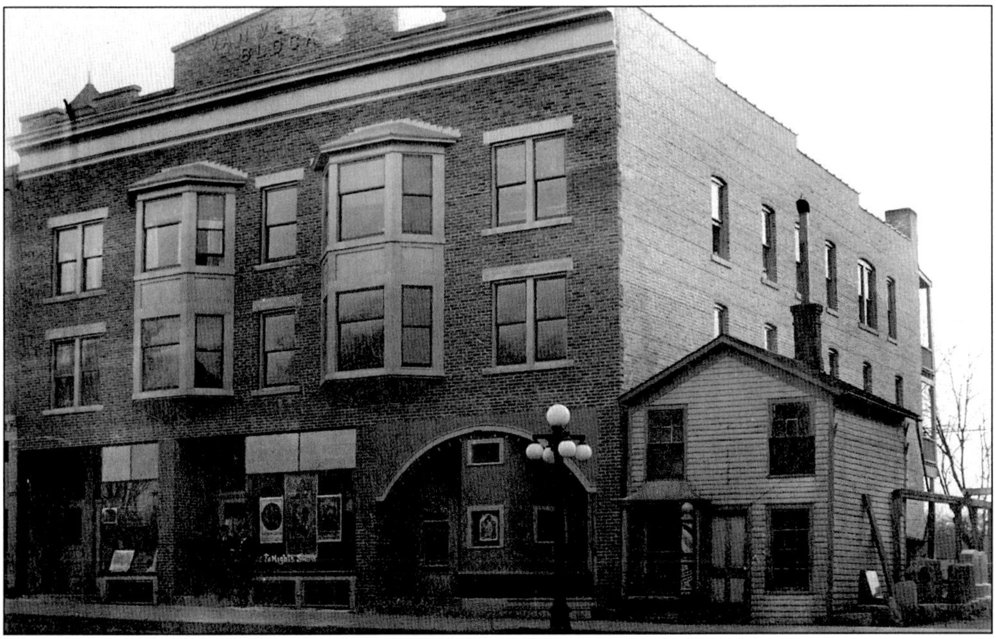

The building that stood between 110–118 East Walworth Avenue was razed to make room for the VanVelzer building, erected in 1914. Designed by William Rothering of Burlington, the main floor housed a movie theater and two stores, with the second and third floors divided into flats. Next to the VanVelzer building on the right is a barbershop and part of Bossi's monument yard is visible.

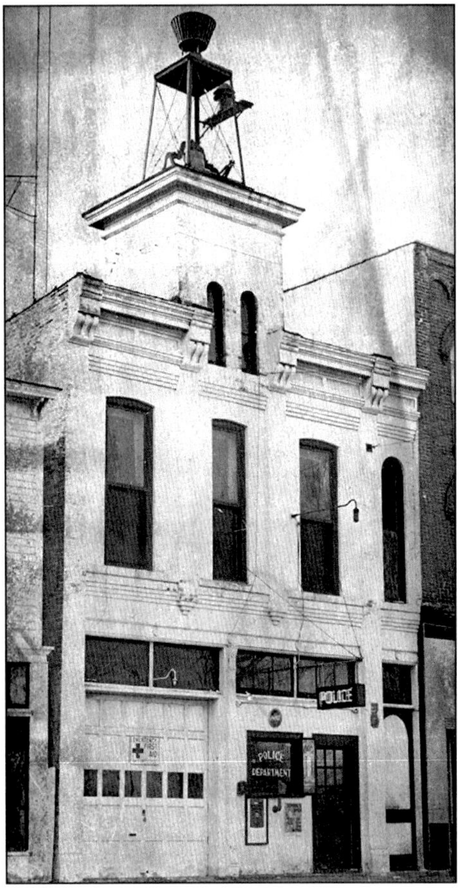

This photograph taken about 1950 shows the police station located at 126 East Walworth. It was built in 1878 and remained in use until 1968, when the police department was moved to the new municipal building constructed on Second Street. The siren was added to the roof after World War II. This building is now Ron's Barber Shop. The structure to the immediate right was the fire station.

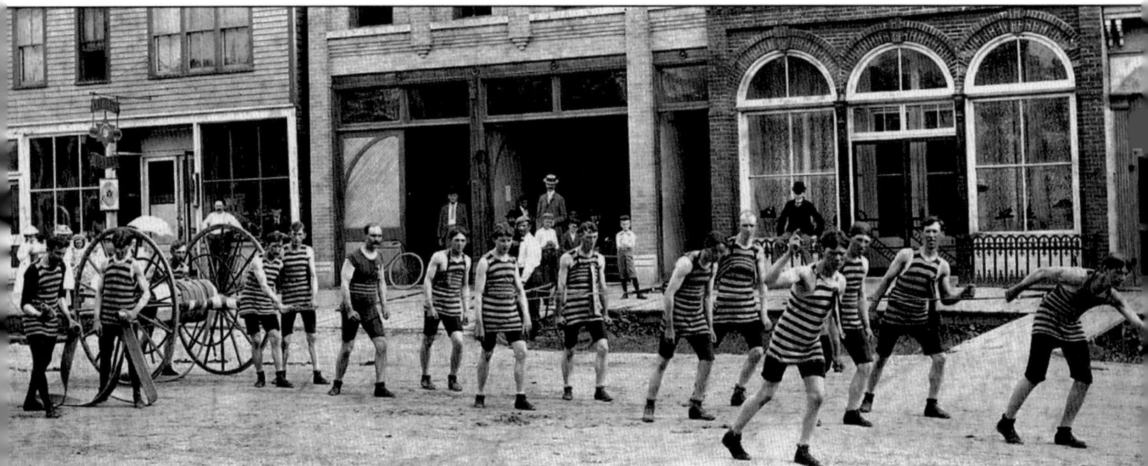

The members of the 1901 Delavan Fire Department, shown here from left to right, are Charles Sturtevant, John Burke, Frank Gray, Harry Nichols, Will Doyle, Arden Brown, Will Baumeister, Peter Chesire, Will Keefe, Roy Thomas, Lew Heir, Al Flitcroft, Bert Christian, and Adolph Fenn. Fire Chief William Passage is wearing the straw hat in the center of the fire station door.

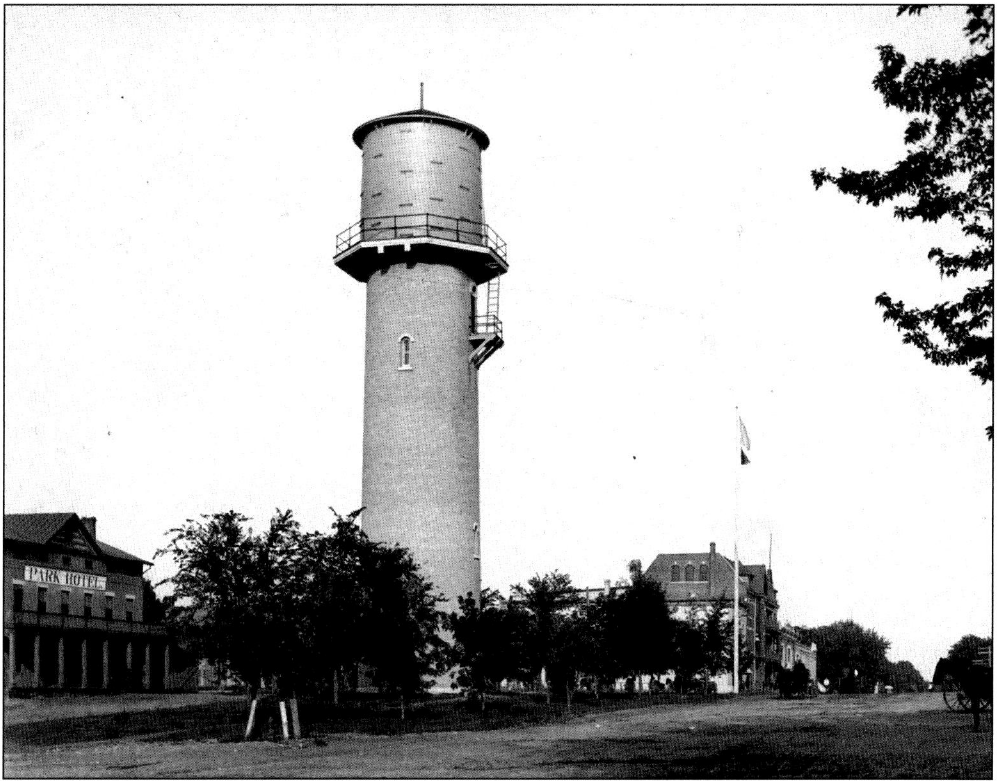

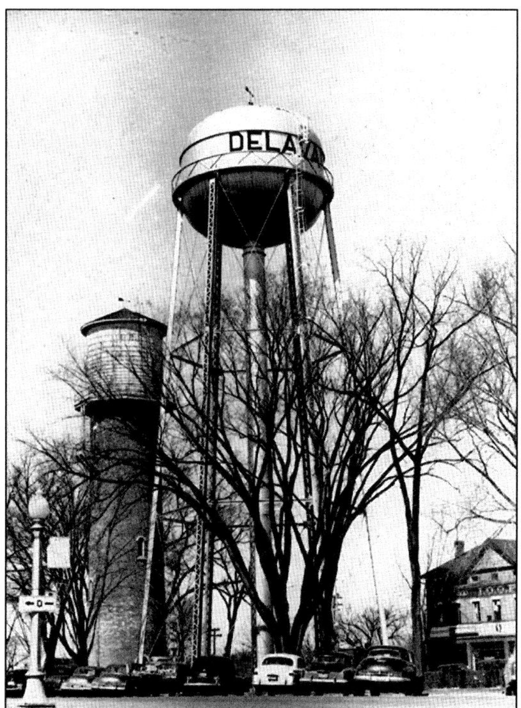

The original water tower shown above was built in 1893. It was a 90 foot high brick tower with the water tank at the top. Behind the water tower is a good view of the Park Hotel. In 1951, a new, more modern tower was erected. The two towers stood side by side for a few years before the old one was torn down in 1954. You can just catch a glimpse of the former Park Hotel beyond the tower, then being utilized by the International Order of Odd Fellows (IOOF) in the 1950s.

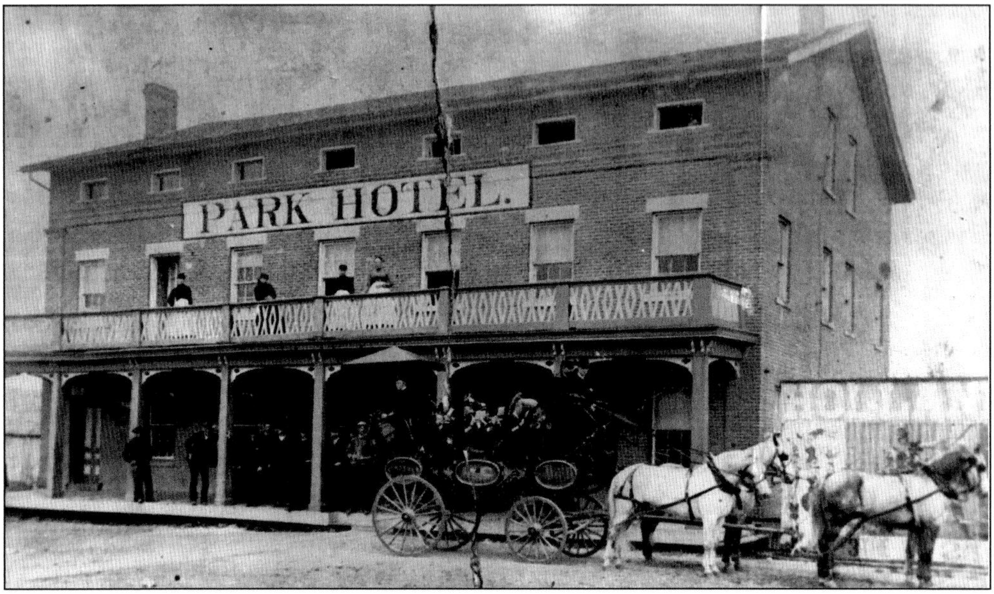

The Park Hotel, pictured here with the Holland and Gormley Circus bandwagon in 1889, was dedicated on July 4, 1848, and functioned as a hotel until 1904. Located on the north side of Tower Park, it had a reputation for attracting a rough crowd in the 1890s, forcing it to lose favor to the newer White Hotel. It was sold to the IOOF in the early 1900s.

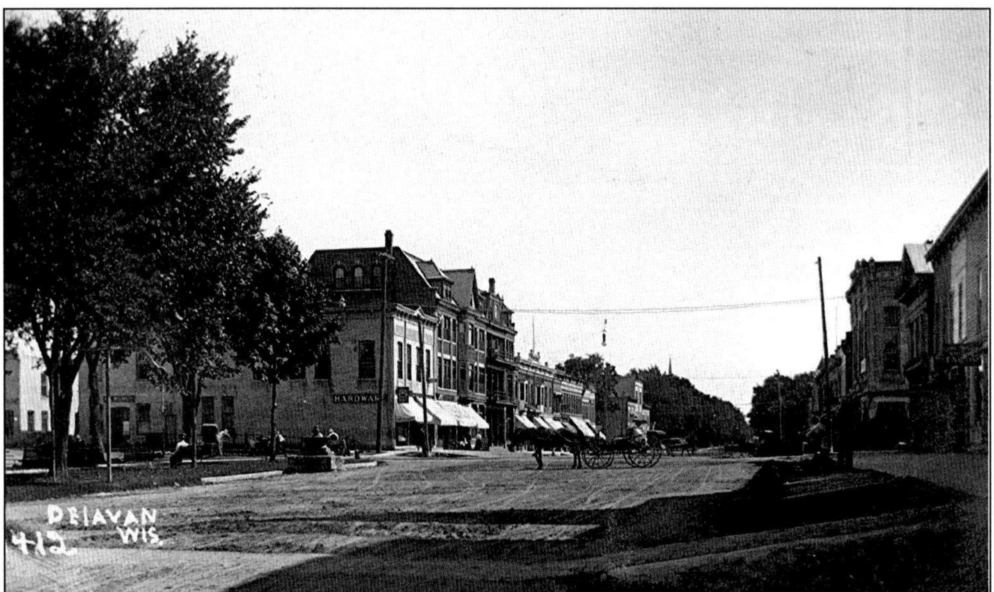

This 1910 image shows the far east edge of Tower Park on the left. The intersection is Second and Walworth looking east. Visible on the corner of the park is a water fountain for the horses.

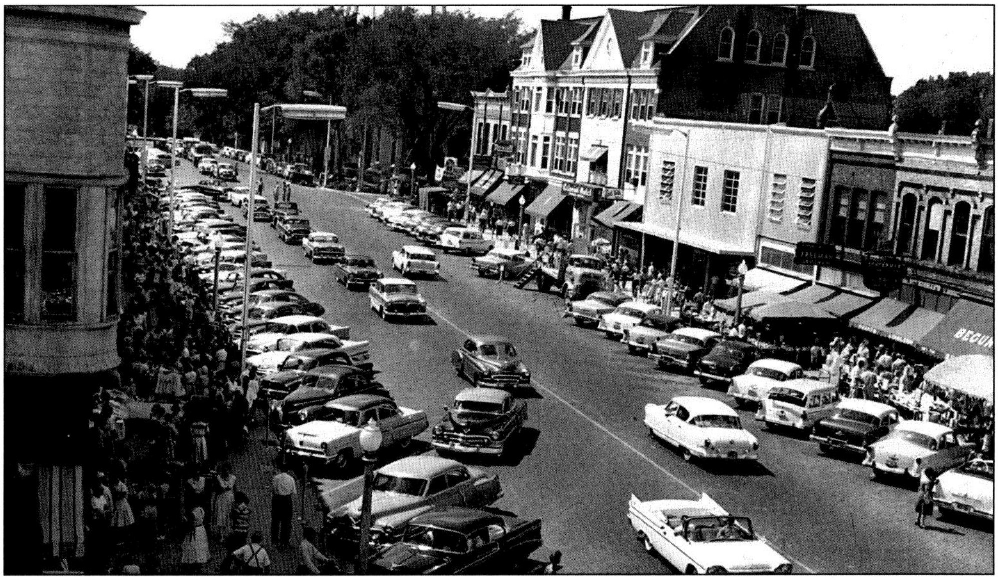

Maxwell Street days is a longtime tradition in Delavan. Shop owners take their wares out to the sidewalk to sell. Usually held in August, Maxwell Street days were very popular, as shown here in 1958. This was a good time for merchants to move discontinued items to reduce their inventory, with the sidewalks crowded with shoppers searching for bargains.

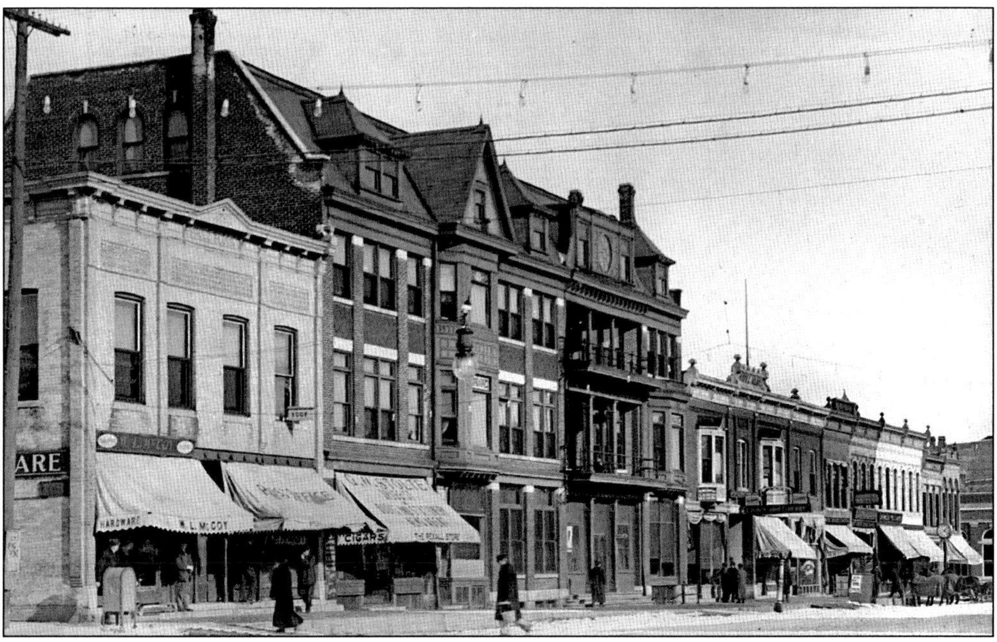

This photo, taken about 1910, shows the north side of Walworth Avenue, looking east in the 200 block. Visible are William McKoy's Hardware Store, the post office, and, above the post office, the meeting place of the IOOF, George Shulte's Drug Store, and the Delavan Hotel. Further at right in the photo you can just make out a cigar shop and livery. The clock of H.H. Williams stands further down the block.

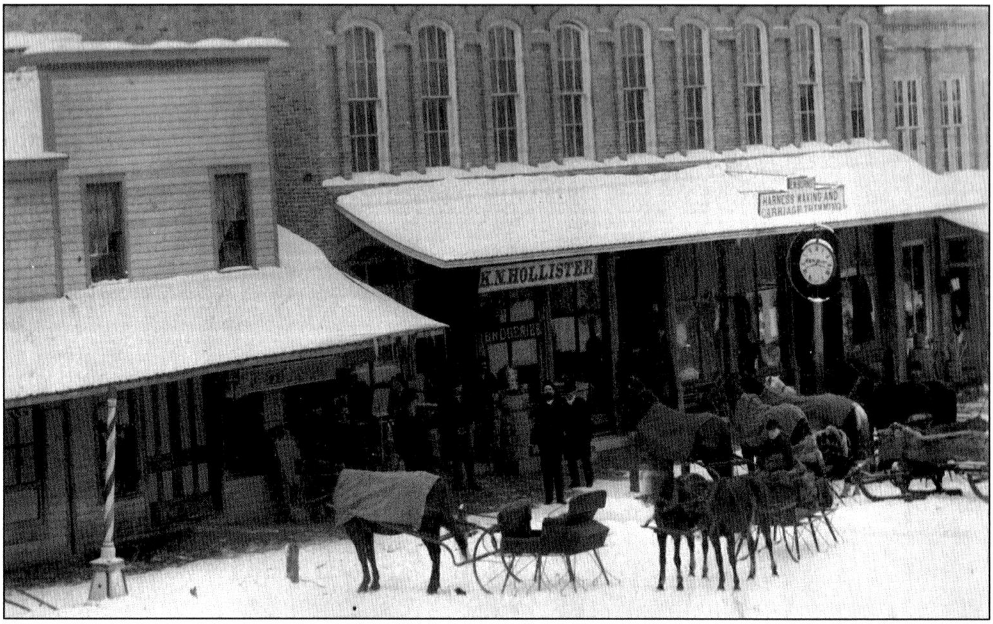

This pre-1900 view on a cold winter day shows the north side of the 200 block of Walworth Avenue. This picture shows the barbershop, post office, K.N. Hollister's Retail Store, and, beyond the clock and shop of H.H. Williams, Jeweler, is E.M. Burns' Harness Making Shop.

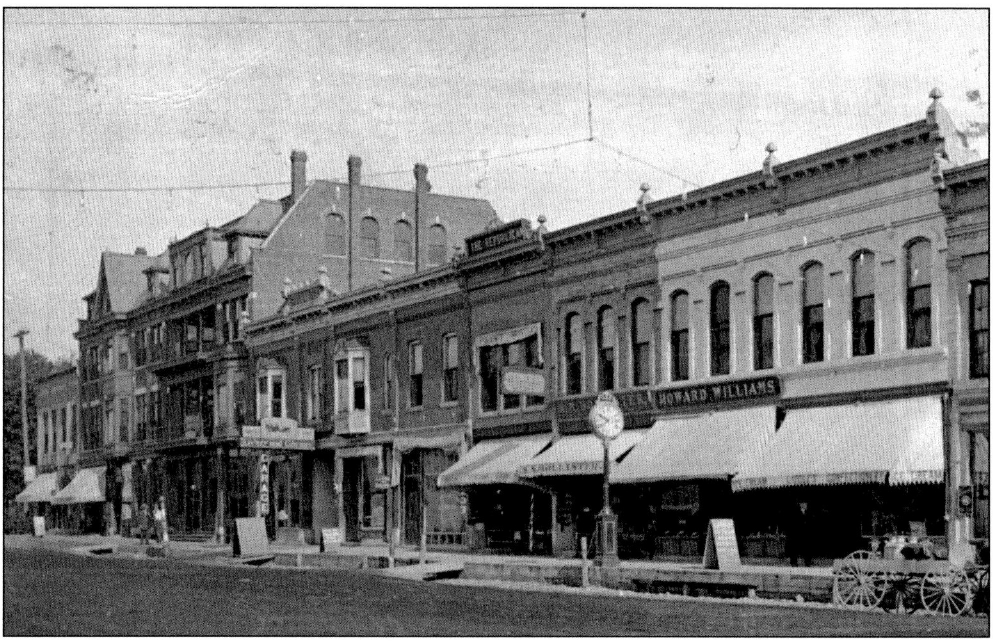

Another view of the north side of the 200 block of Walworth Avenue, looking west from Third Street in 1910. Buildings visible from left to right are the Delavan hotel; the livery and garage; the *Republican* newspaper office; K.N. Hollister's retail store; H.H. Williams, Jeweler; Liddle's Confectionary and Ice Cream Shop; and D.E. Cannon, Grocer. Notice the wooden sidewalks and the horse and wagon carrying milk cans.

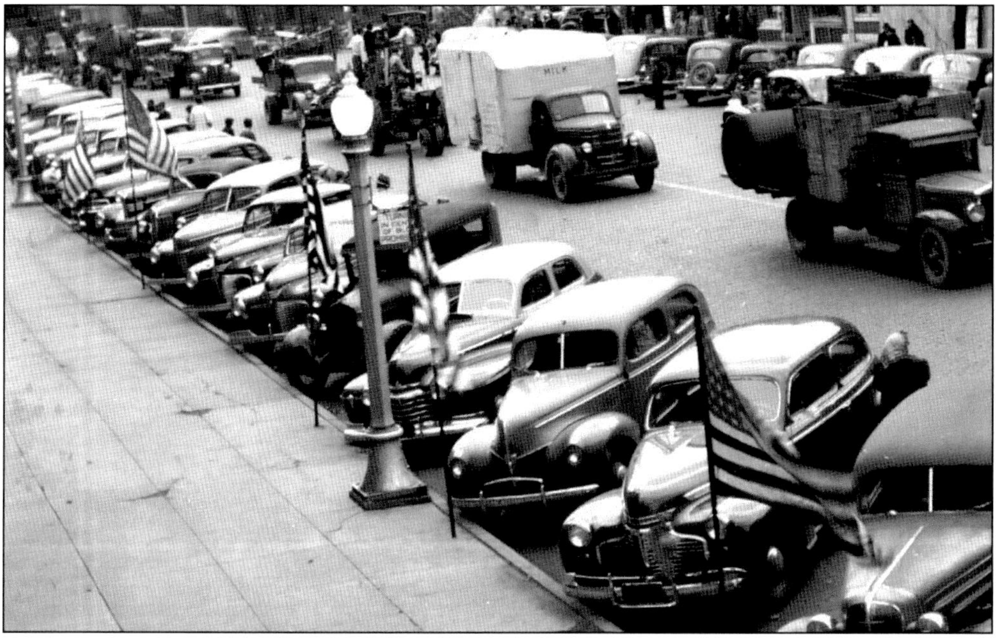

The scrap metal drive in Delavan in the 1940s during World War II became a way for the citizens to participate in the war effort. No one threw a tin can in the garbage, they would flatten it and it would be collected along with other things like old ice skates, aluminum pots, tin type photographs, guns, and even cars. Delavan had three old cannons, one in Flat Iron Park, now called Triangle Park, and two in Tower Park along with a World War I mobile artillery gun. Pictured here are some ladies posing with a cannon in Tower Park. All of these, the cannons and artillery gun, were honorably donated to the cause and never replaced.

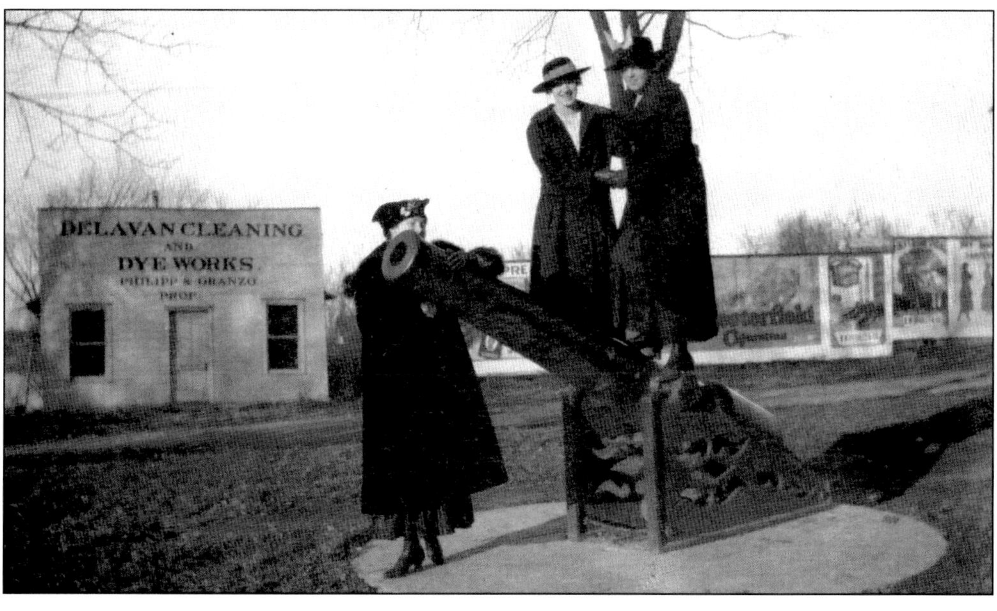

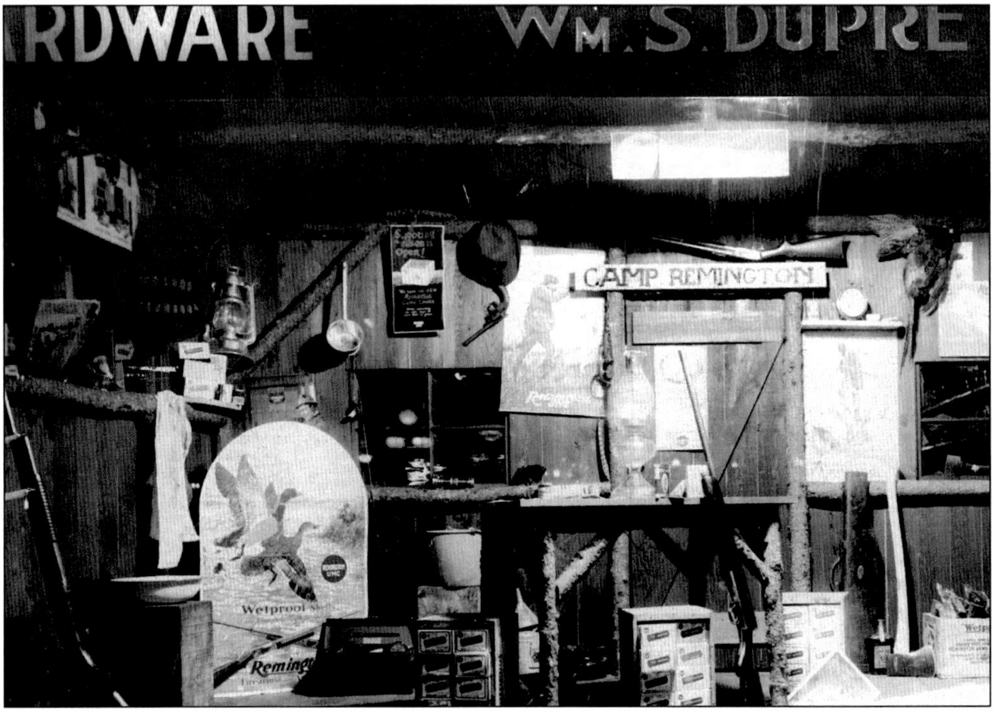

The Dupre Hardware Store was located at 231 East Walworth Avenue. William Dupre started doing business in this location in 1920. This was the oldest, continuously operating hardware store in Walworth County for many years. Preceding owners were K.N. Hollister (1871–1910) and K.L. Hollister (1910–1920). Shown here is a creative display from Remington rifles.

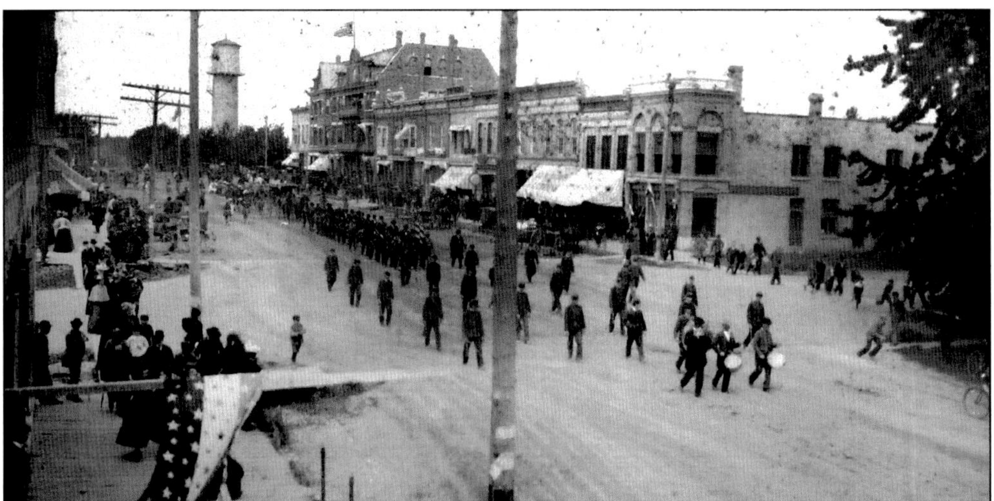

The 1900 Memorial Day parade down Walworth Avenue in Delavan was a well-attended event. This old, but important view of downtown reveals a good look at the sidewalks and hitching posts in front of the shops. It was taken from an upper floor on the south side of the 300 block of Walworth Avenue. Looking to the west, you can see the hotel and water tower in the distance.

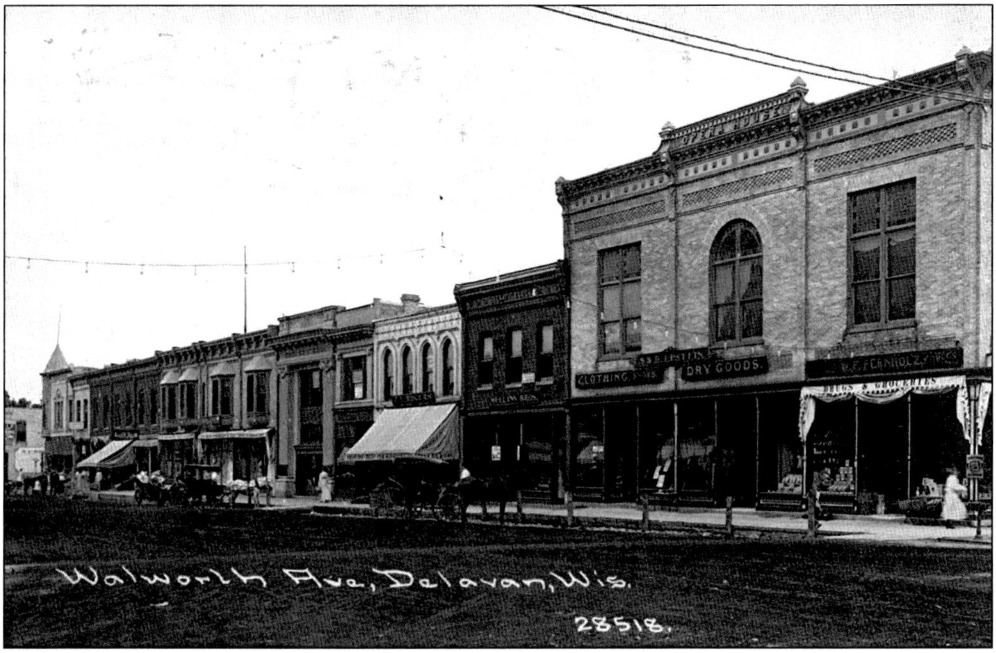

This 1910 view is the south side of the 200 block of Walworth Avenue. The building all the way to the left was a millinery shop. The next shops continuing west are W.W. Bradleys; Citizen's Bank; F.W. Rogers, Grocer; Mullins Bros. Saloon; S&D Epstein Clothing & Dry Goods; and Fernholz Drugs. The Opera House occupied the entire floor above the dry goods store and the drug store.

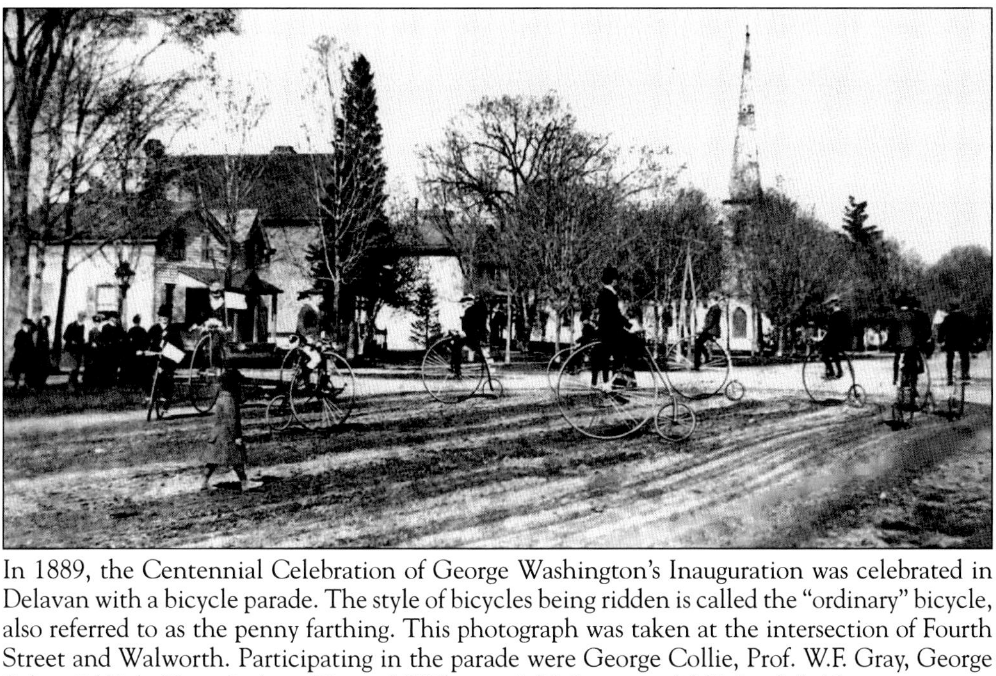

In 1889, the Centennial Celebration of George Washington's Inauguration was celebrated in Delavan with a bicycle parade. The style of bicycles being ridden is called the "ordinary" bicycle, also referred to as the penny farthing. This photograph was taken at the intersection of Fourth Street and Walworth. Participating in the parade were George Collie, Prof. W.F. Gray, George Baker, Ed Fisk, Harry Judson, Howard Williams, A.H. Lowe, and S.D. Littlefield.

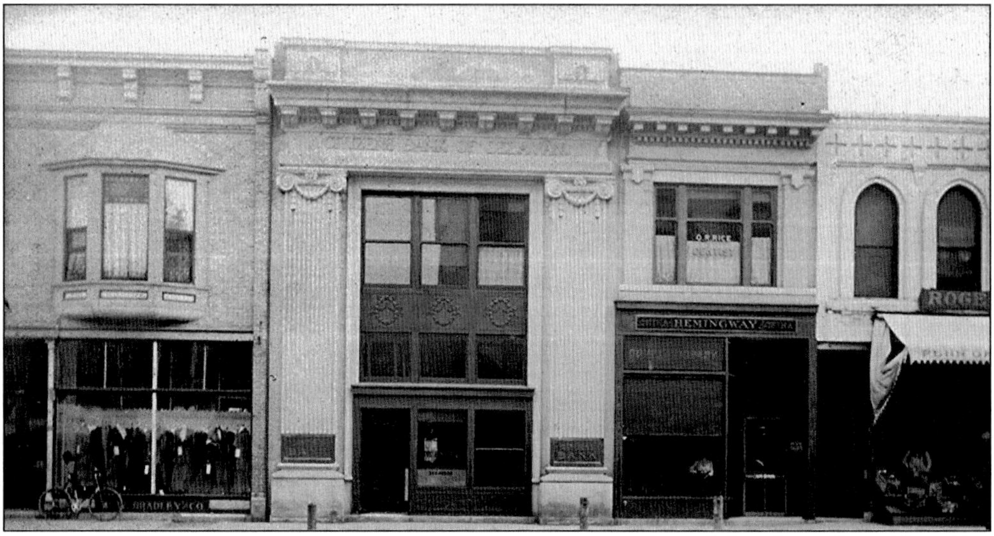

The Citizen's Bank was founded in 1875 and played a significant role in Delavan's financial and trade businesses. Taken in 1912, this photograph also captures W.W. Bradley & Company at left and to the right are the Hemingway China Shop and the dental office of Dr. O.R. Rice. The Citizen's Bank functioned at this location, 218 East Walworth, for several decades before moving to the corner of Fifth and Walworth.

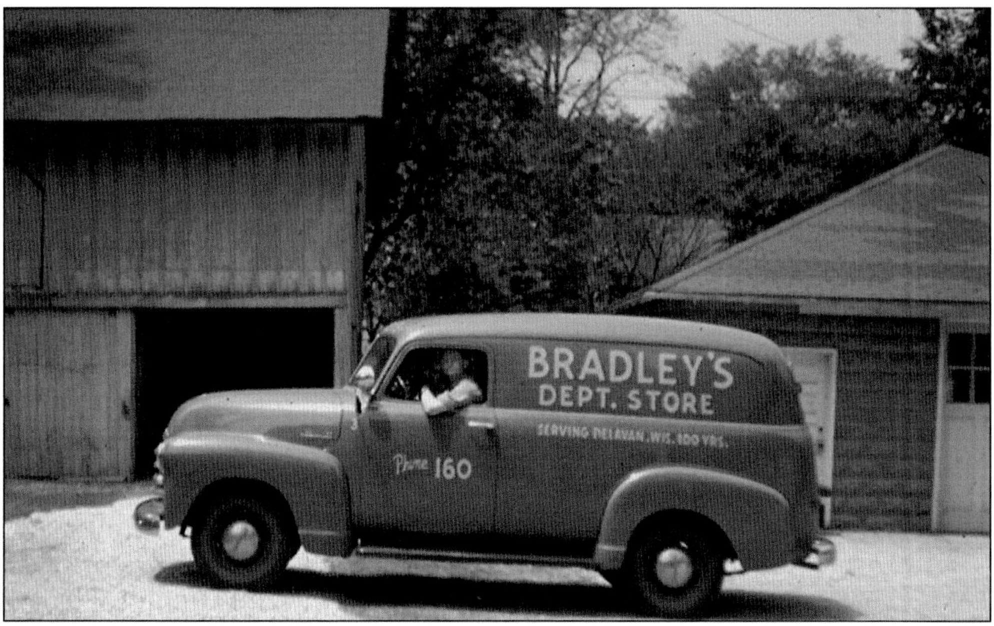

Since the 1940s, the McKoy family has owned the Bradley's Department Store, conducting business in the same location as its forerunner, W.W. Bradley & Company. Promoting the same strong business philosophy of its predecessors, operations at this location have been continuous since 1874. This photograph from the 1960s shows George Bashaw in the Bradley's Department Store delivery truck.

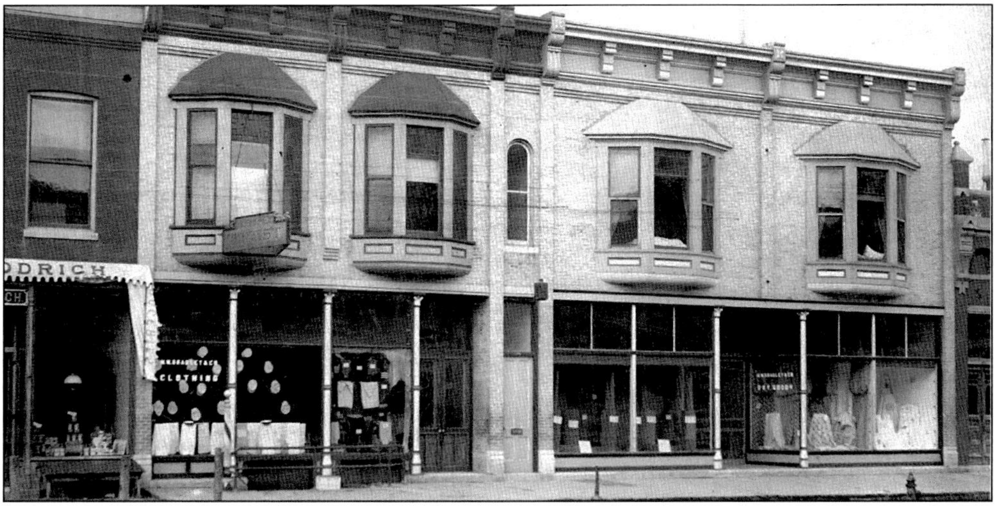

In about 1874, William Wallace Bradley purchased the stock and store of C.M. Sturtevant Dry Goods, located at 222 East Walworth Avenue, after already running a merchant tailor business in Delavan for 20 years prior. In 1886, his business became incorporated under the name W.W. Bradley Company, with Bradley, W.H. Tyrell, and J.J. Phoenix as owners and incorporators. It wasn't until 1887, when the old building was torn down, that the one standing today was constructed; shown in the above photograph about 1905. Below is a Sweet-Orr pants tug-of-war demonstration, taking place about 1910 in front of W.W. Bradley & Company on a stage erected in the middle of Walworth Avenue.

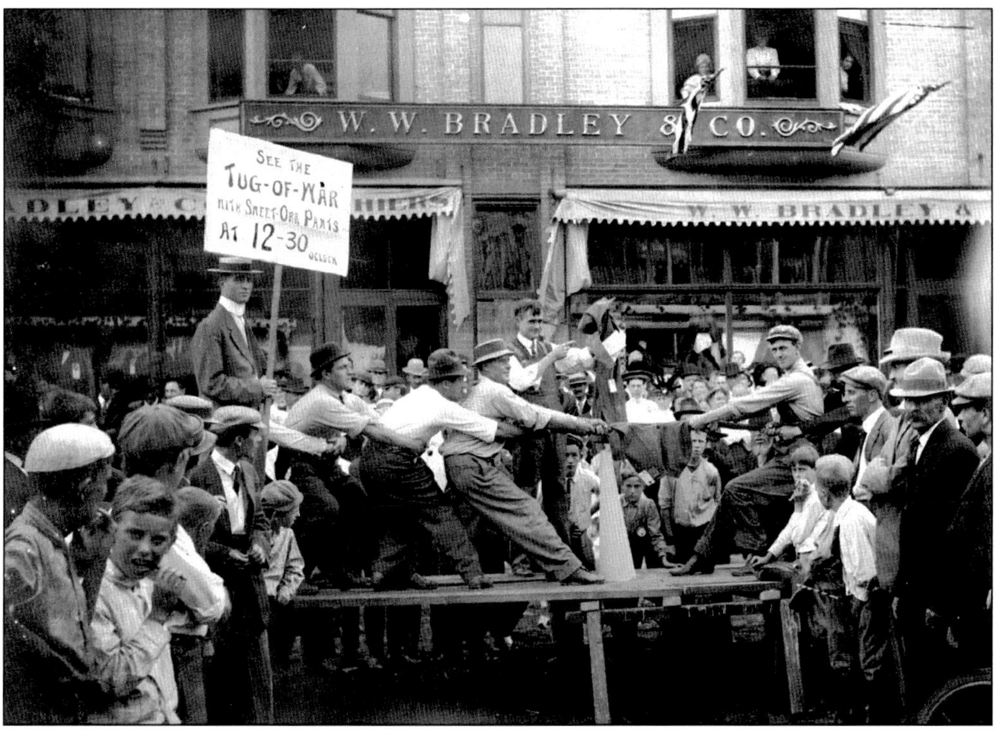

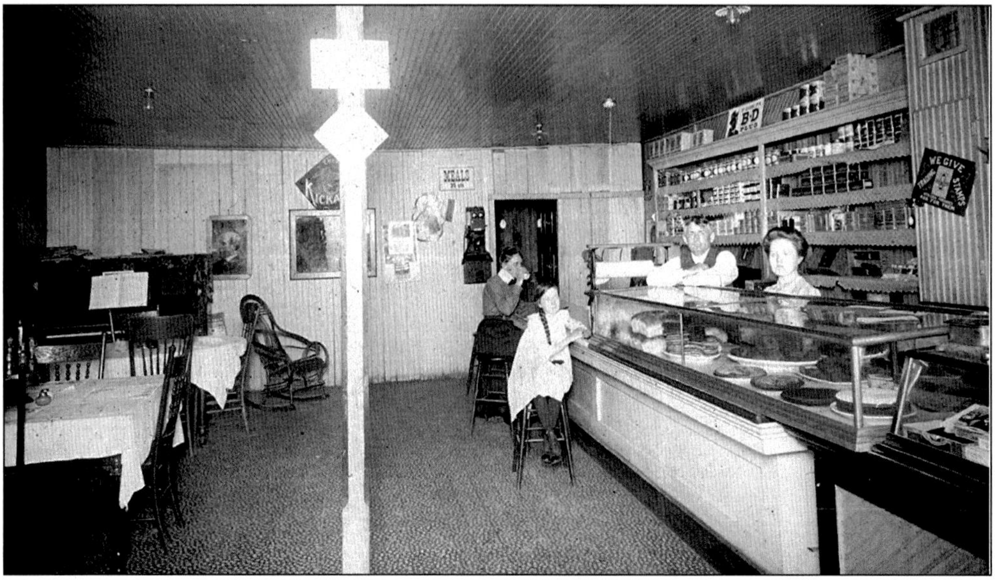

This restaurant was located at 312 East Walworth Avenue in 1902. This homey little restaurant has a piano visible in the back left corner and a sign on the wall advertising meals for 35¢. The glass case holds some wonderful looking baked goods. While the name of the restaurant remains unidentified, it was located next to McSorley & Son Market at 314 East Walworth Ave.

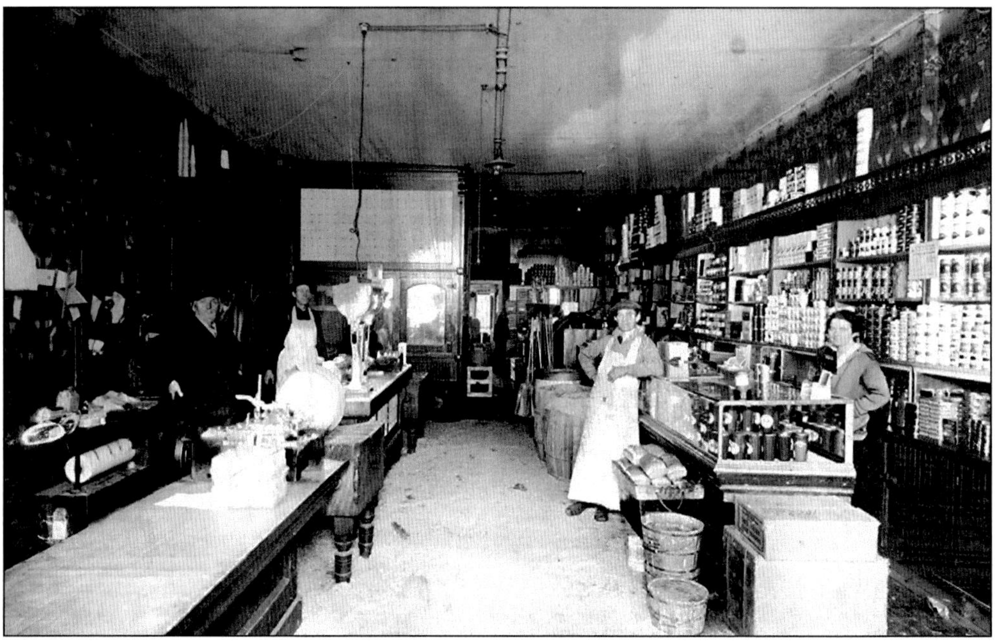

J.B. McSorley & Son started a small restaurant with his wife doing the baking, which gradually evolved into a meat market and grocery store. He brought his son Ben into the business and occupied his daughter Mary as bookkeeper. J.B. McSorley retired in 1922 due to illness, and in 1932, after continuing to acquire experience elsewhere, his son Ben opened McSorley Inc. in the same building.

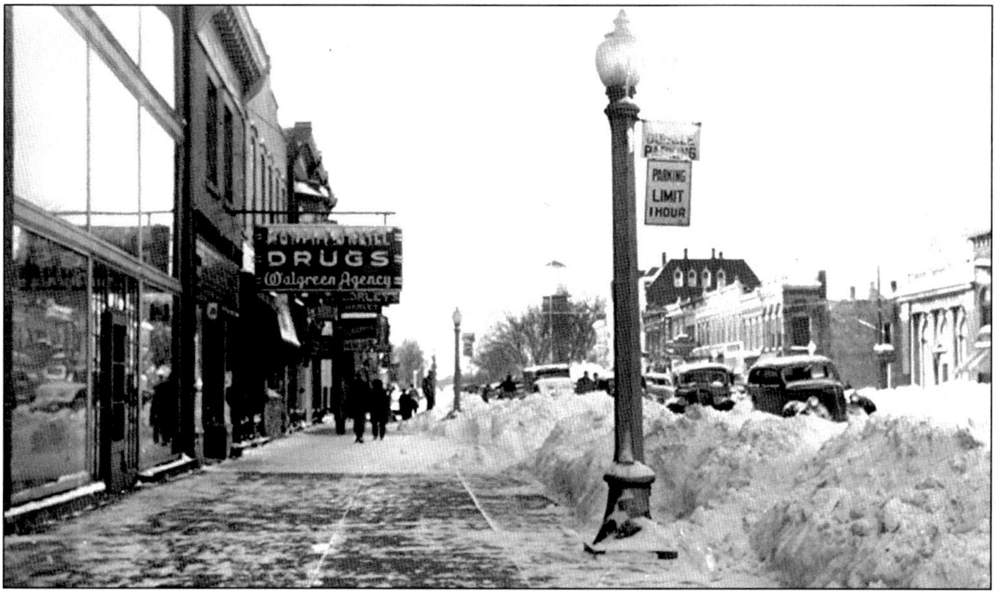

February 1, 1947, left Delavan residents cleaning up after a snowstorm. The shopkeepers on the south side of the street, Murphy and O'Neill's Walgreens Drug Store, and McSorley's Market had their sidewalks clear. Looking west in the distance you can see the hotel and the water tower.

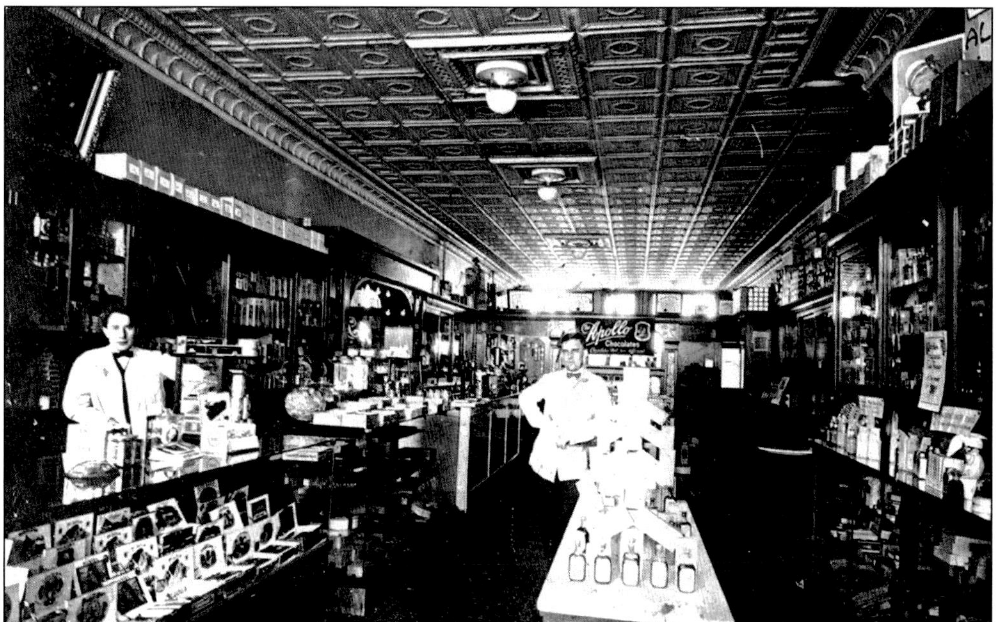

The Murphy and O'Neill Drug Store was started by John "Jack" Murphy and Harry O'Neill in May 1929 at 322 Walworth Avenue, and later moved to 202 Walworth Avenue. The drug store was also known as the Central Drug Store and was part of the Walgreens' company. It's up-to-date soda fountain and booths were real crowd pleasers in the 1930s and 40s. They operated a successful business, later sold to Edward McCullough.

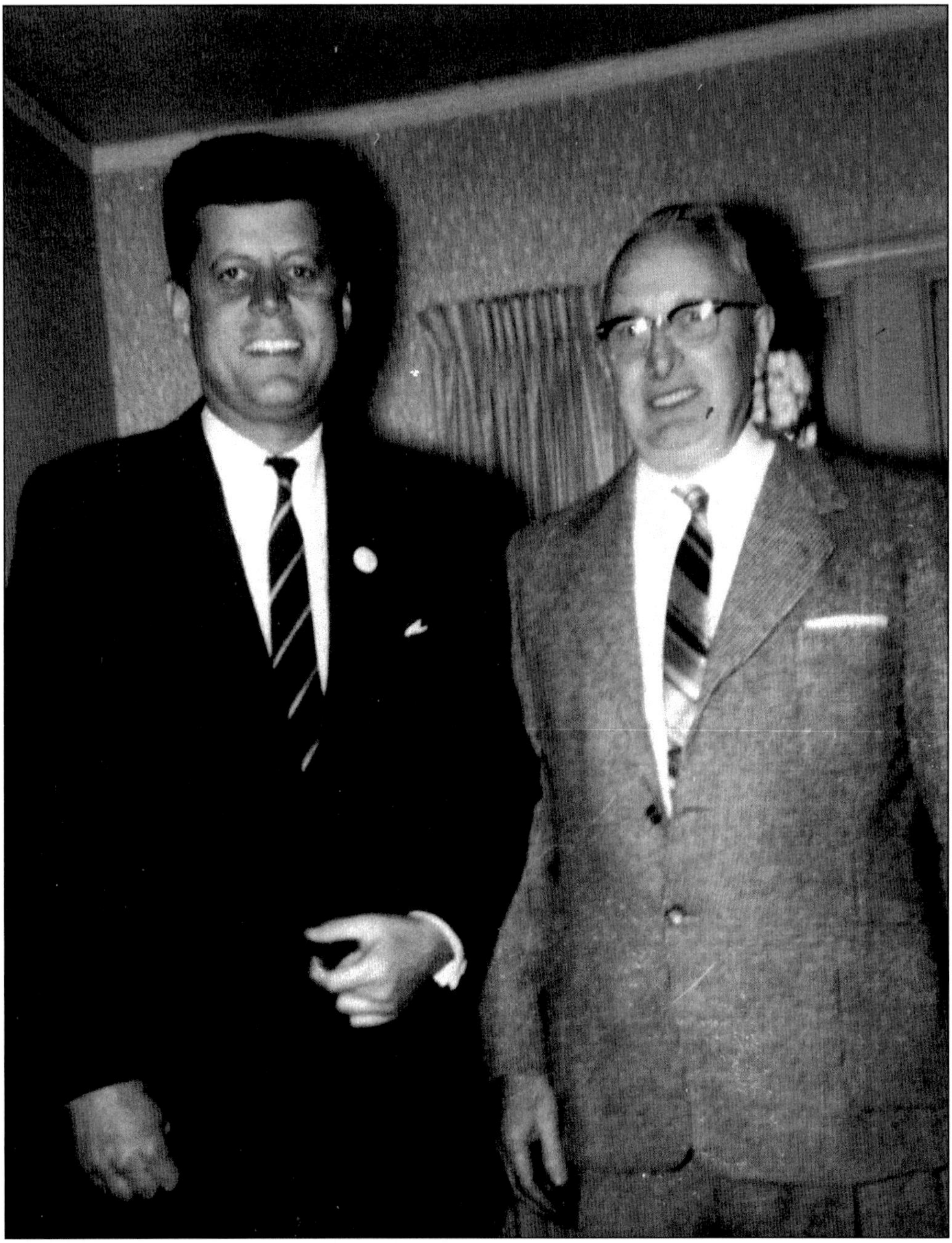

In 1960, Jack Murphy, co-owner of Murphy and O'Neill Drug Store and former Delavan postmaster, had some friends in Boston who knew John F. Kennedy. When Kennedy was scheduled to make a stop in Delavan to speak at the hotel, it was arranged so that Murphy had an opportunity to meet him. Jack Murphy was there, but his wife had to stay home due to a previous commitment. When Kennedy concluded his speech, Jack took the future President Kennedy to his home on McDowell Street to meet Mrs. Murphy. Kennedy accepted the offer of a liver sausage sandwich and a beer "for the road" and took a moment to pose for this photograph with Murphy.

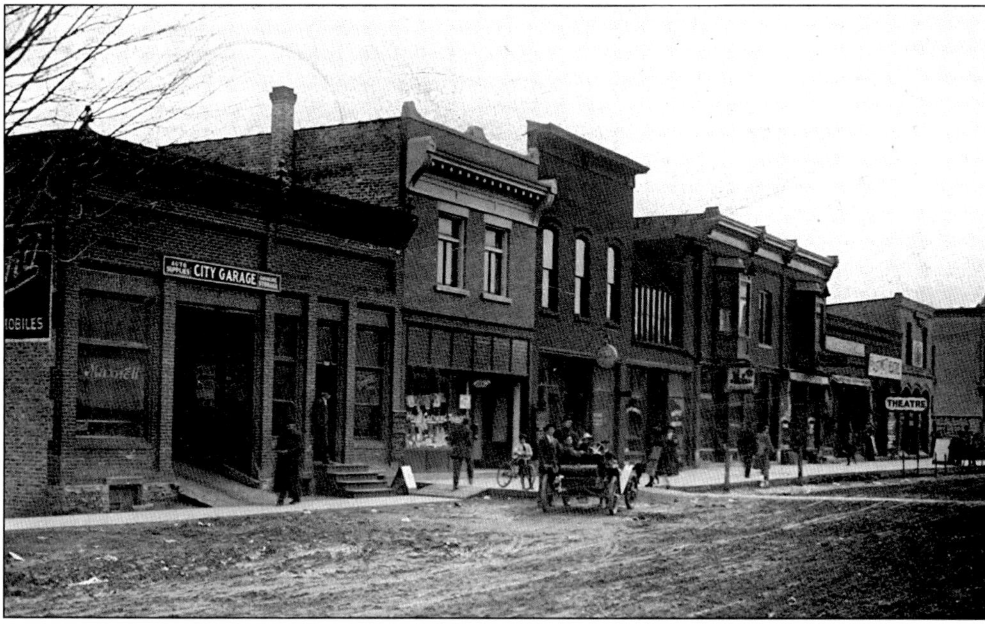

Pictured here is the south side of East Walworth Avenue, looking west in the 300 block. The city garage is visible in the foreground and further down the block, toward the end, is the Pastime Theater. The city garage building, with the later addition of two more floors, now houses Bibliomanics bookstore. This 1910 view shows the dirt street; bricks were laid down in 1913.

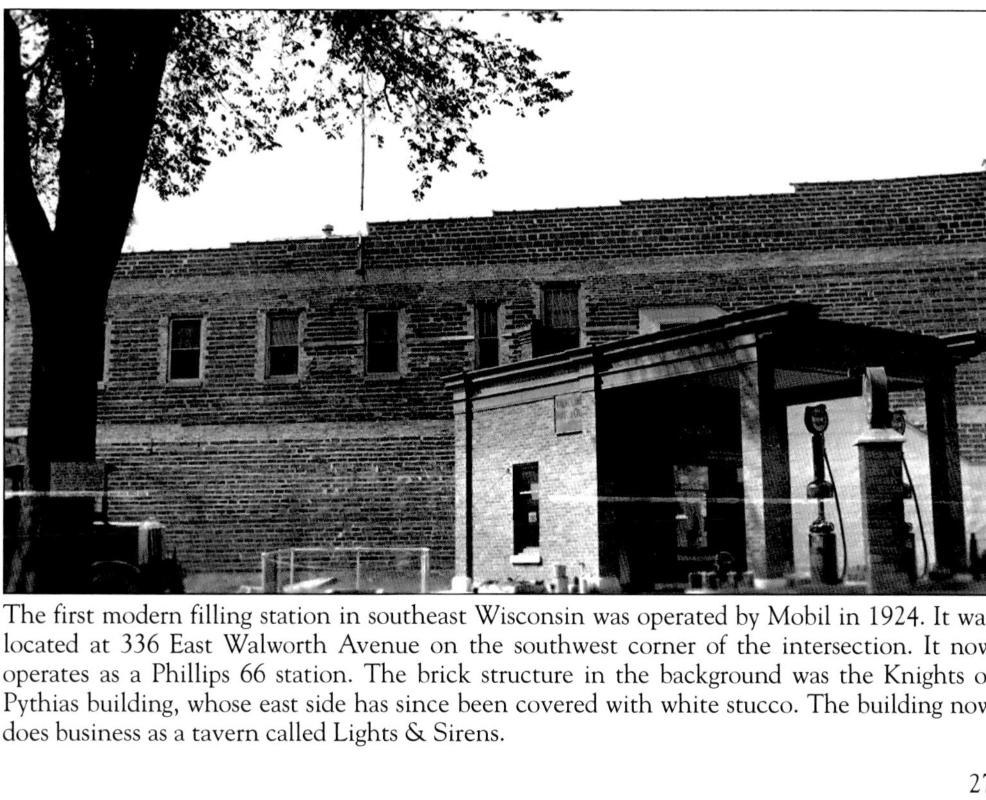

The first modern filling station in southeast Wisconsin was operated by Mobil in 1924. It was located at 336 East Walworth Avenue on the southwest corner of the intersection. It now operates as a Phillips 66 station. The brick structure in the background was the Knights of Pythias building, whose east side has since been covered with white stucco. The building now does business as a tavern called Lights & Sirens.

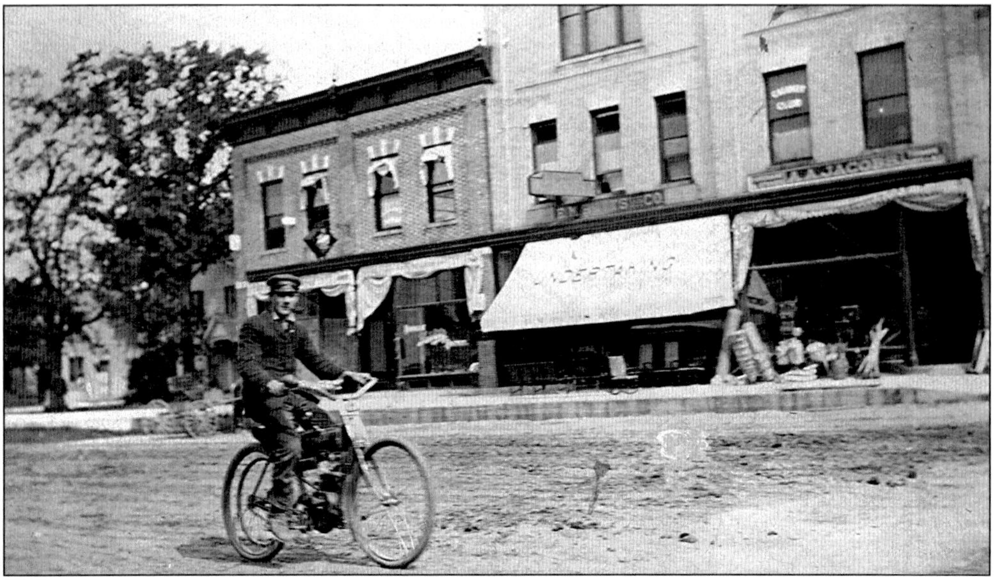

This rare 1904 view of the north side of the 300 block of Walworth Avenue may not look familiar unless you look closely at the building on the left. The buildings further west have not been built yet. In a few years the Latimer Bank would occupy that corner. The shop with the large awning is Butts Undertaking, and to the right A.A. Jacobs. On the motorized bike is Leon Babcock Sr. Today, the following businesses make up the buildings shown: Memories From the Heart, JMJ Trading Co., and Remember When Antiques.

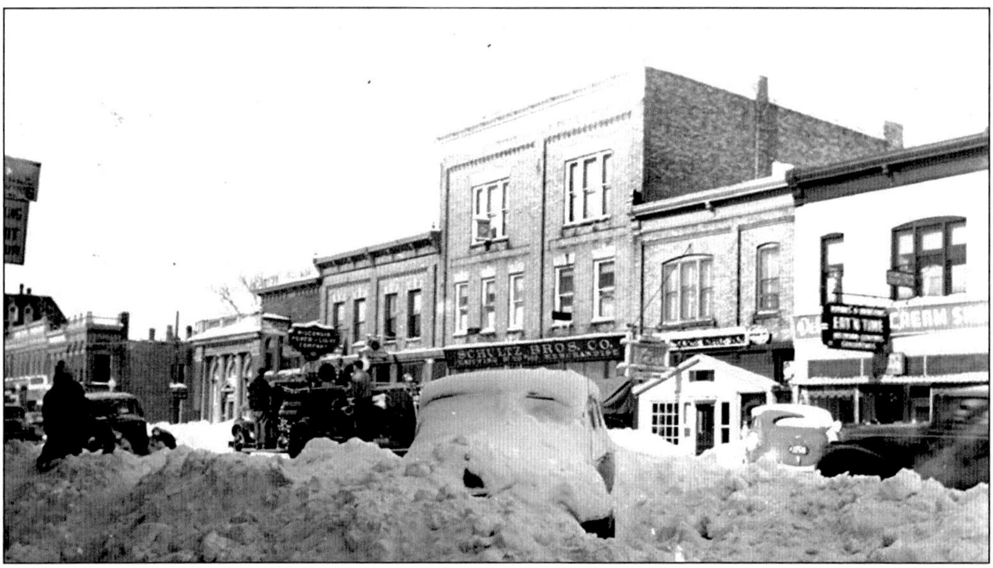

This photograph taken after the snowstorm of 1947 shows some familiar businesses in places that are often forgotten about. This is the north side of the 200 block of Walworth. Schultz Bros. had a location here before they moved across the street, as did Eat-N-Time before they moved to South Seventh Street. And who could forget Dinty Moore's Waffle Shop, where the Traveler Restaurant is now?

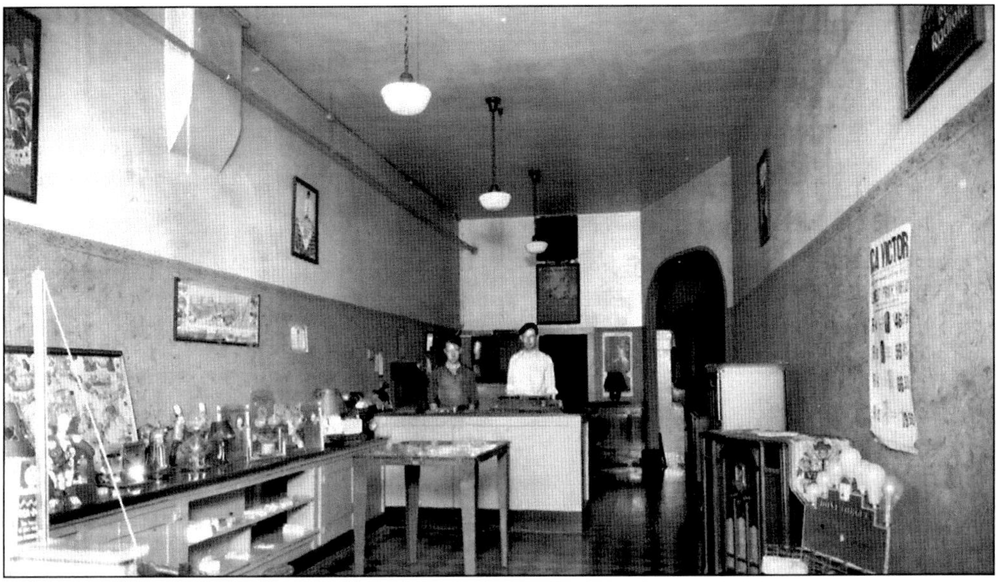

H.C. Dukelow purchased the radio store of Arthur Schumacher in 1932 after graduating from Coyne Electrical School. His store was located in the 300 block of Walworth Avenue, where it occupied half of where the Traveler Restaurant is today. Shortly after this image was taken, he moved to a shop at 106 North Third Street and operated from that location for many years.

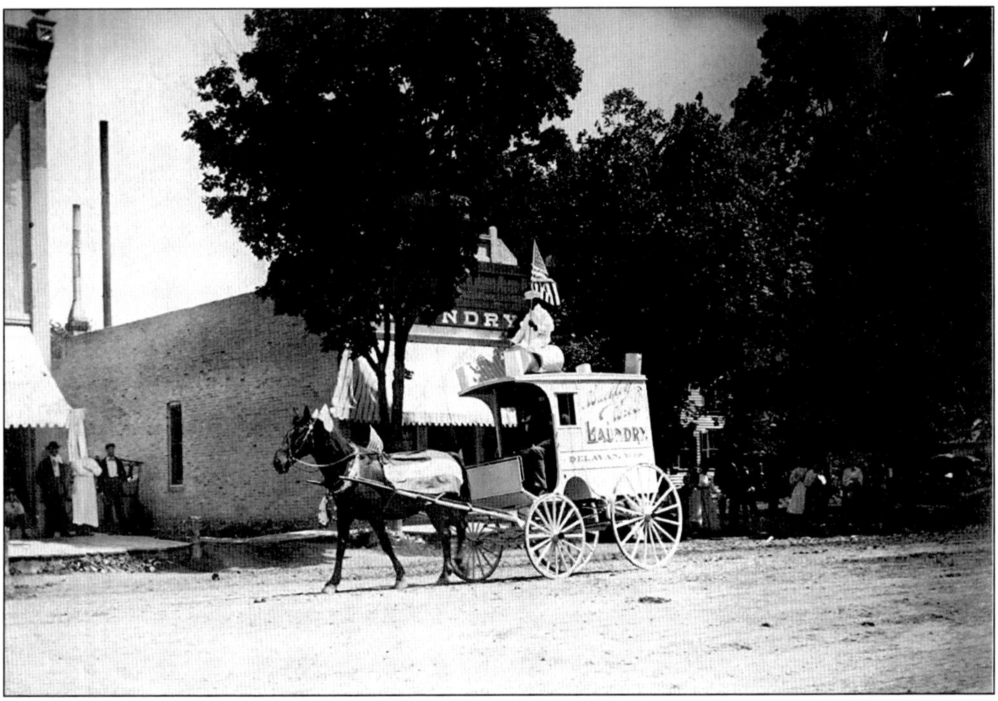

This photo, taken around the turn of the century, shows the Buckley laundry truck outside of the Buckley Laundry Shop at 331 East Walworth Avenue. This location is now the empty lot located west of the post office.

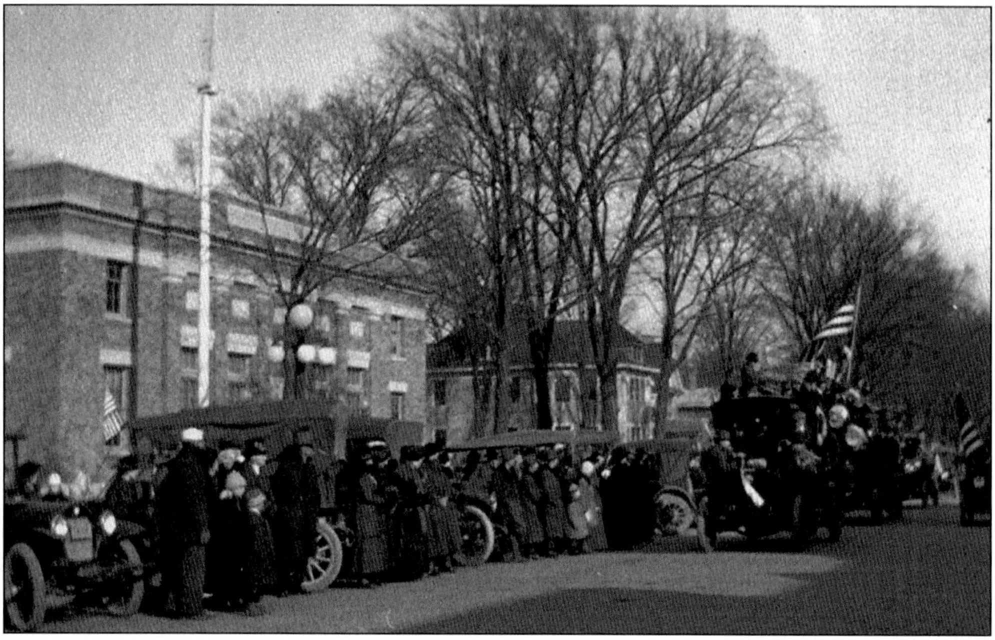

It was a Monday morning when the news reached Delavan that World War I had ended. The war ended with an armistice on the eleventh hour of the eleventh day of the eleventh month. Plans were immediately set in motion for a celebration. Shown here are views of the Peace Parade that took place in Delavan on November 11, 1918. Above, citizens gather in front of the post office to share in the festivities. Below, the Red Cross Ladies join in the parade carrying Red Cross and U.S. flags.

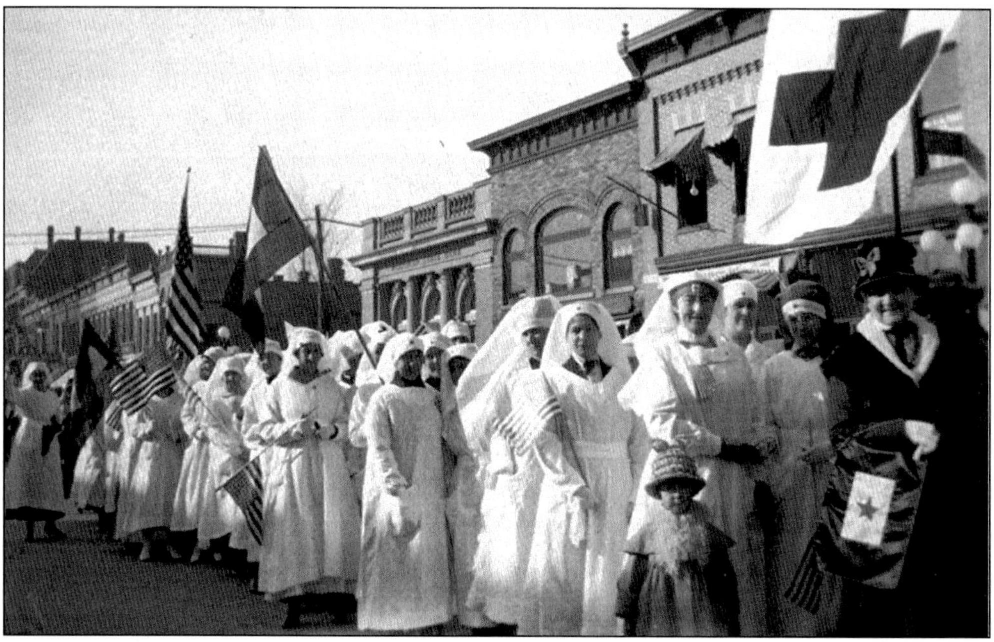

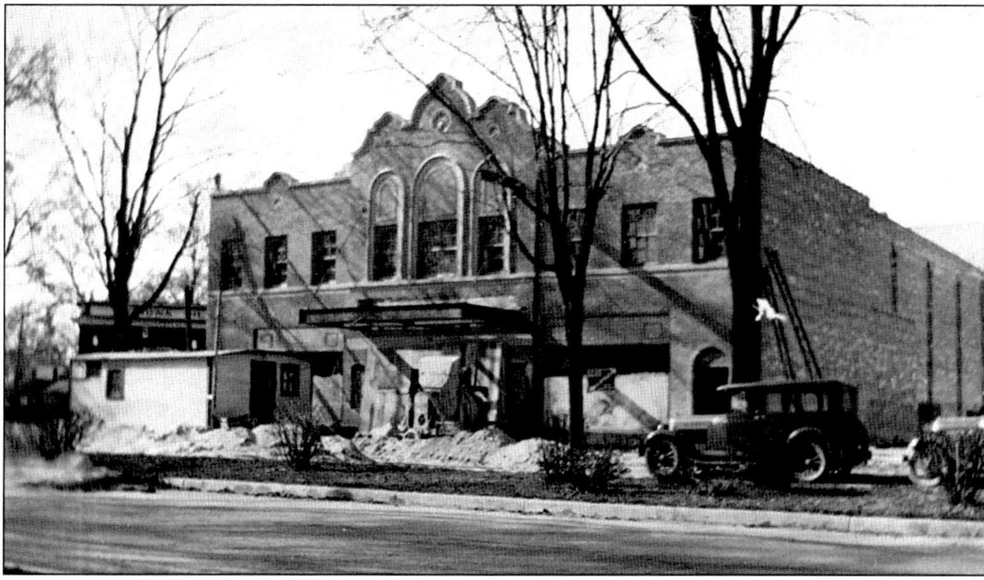

In 1928, the owner of the Pastime Theater wanted a larger facility and decided upon the 400 block of Walworth Avenue for its new home. It was dedicated in 1929 and the name was eventually changed to the Delavan Theater. It was built as the era of silent film was ending and talking movies were the rage. The photograph below shows the beautiful interior of the theater during a W.W. Bradley & Co. fashion show in the 1930s, complete with orchestra pit. The theater now sits quiet and has not been in use for several years.

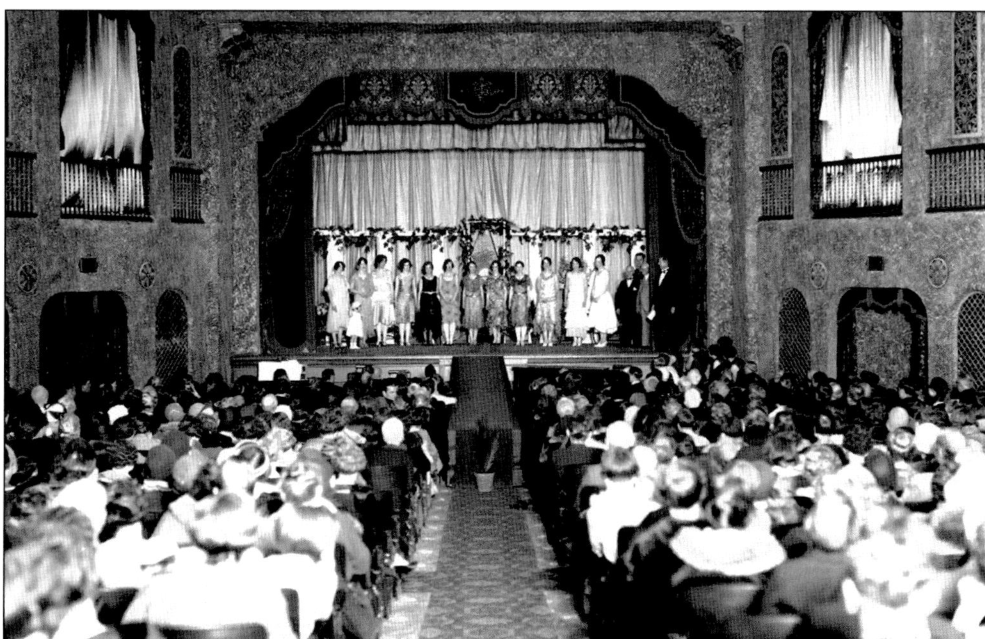

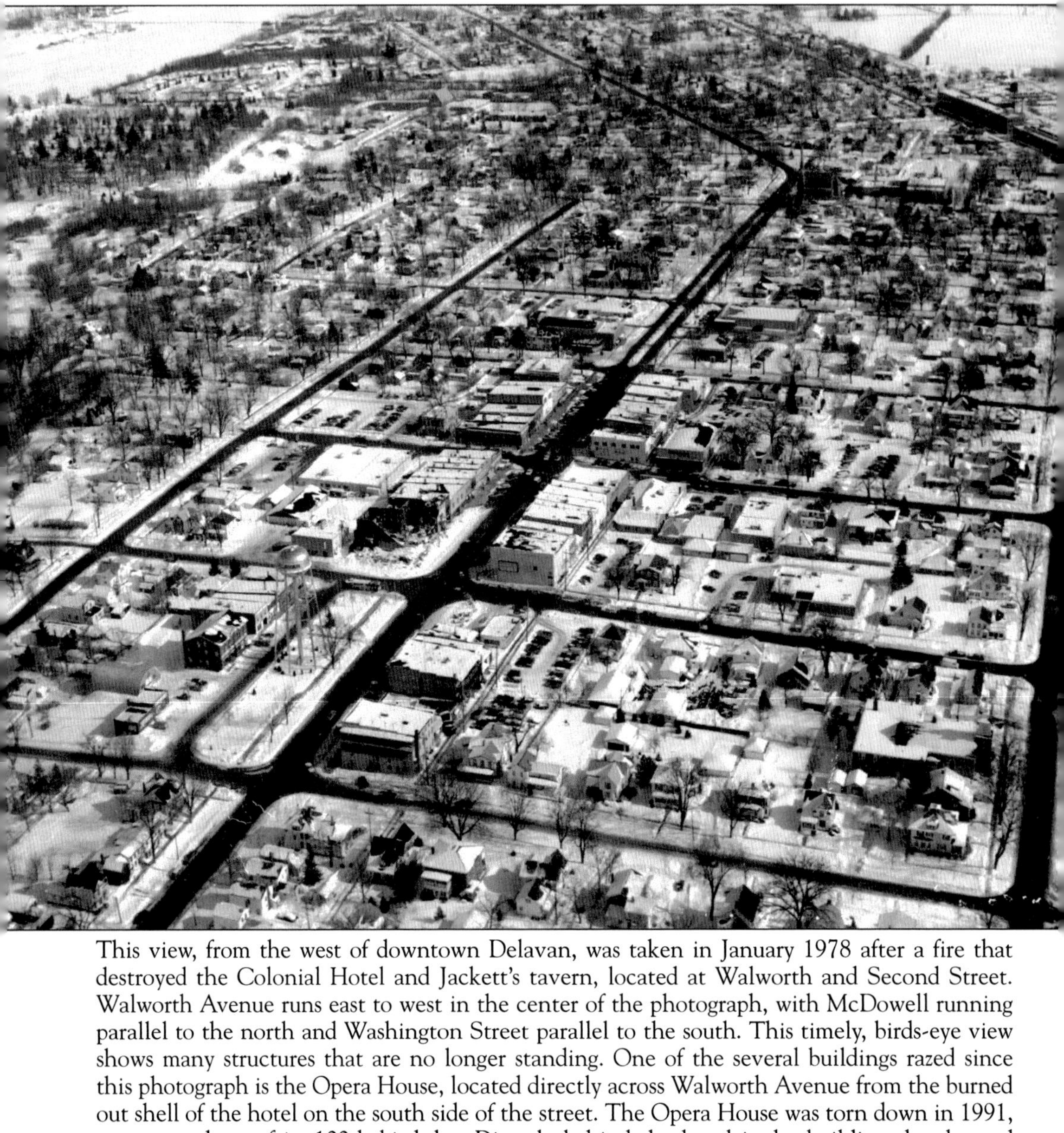

This view, from the west of downtown Delavan, was taken in January 1978 after a fire that destroyed the Colonial Hotel and Jackett's tavern, located at Walworth and Second Street. Walworth Avenue runs east to west in the center of the photograph, with McDowell running parallel to the north and Washington Street parallel to the south. This timely, birds-eye view shows many structures that are no longer standing. One of the several buildings razed since this photograph is the Opera House, located directly across Walworth Avenue from the burned out shell of the hotel on the south side of the street. The Opera House was torn down in 1991, two years short of its 100th birthday. Directly behind the hotel is the building that housed Sturtevant's Blacksmith Shop in 1898. In later years, the Delavan Enterprise had office there, although they vacated the building in 1968. Montgomery Ward also had a sales office in the building, which was razed not long after the fire.

Two

Off Walworth Avenue

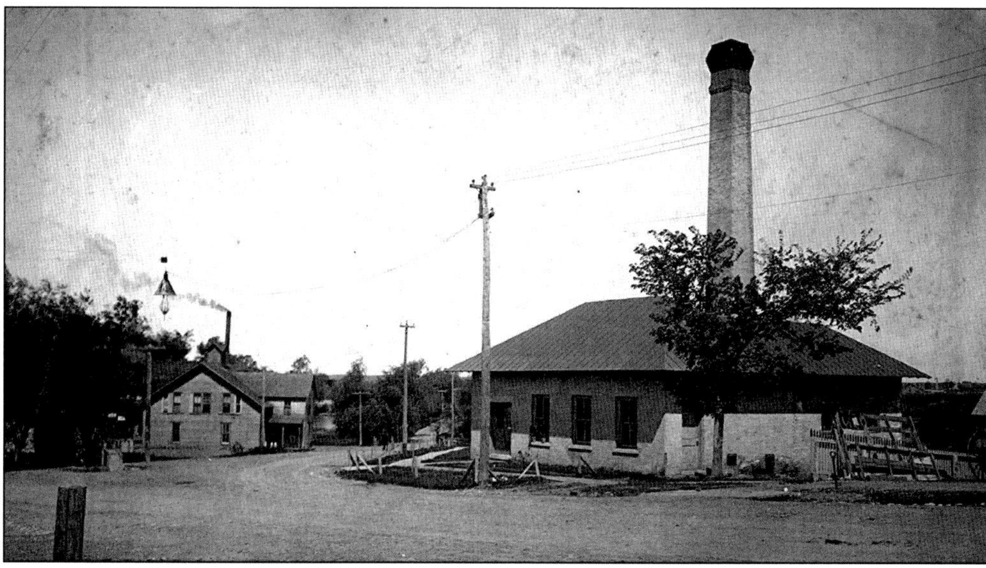

After many devastating fires downtown, the village council was prompted to figure out a way to provide a dependable water source to the community. In 1893, the pumping station, shown on the right, was erected, as was the water tower in Tower Park. The pumping station was operated by steam power with a coal-fired system. The operator lived just up the hill and would run down and stoke the fire if the fire bell sounded. It was put to use a short time after completion when a fire was extinguished at a barn on north Third Street. The spectators cheered as the firemen quenched the flames by using the hydrant at Third and McDowell. The pumping station has undergone some remodeling over the years and the smoke stack has since been removed. Visible on the left is the Cheever Cheese Factory.

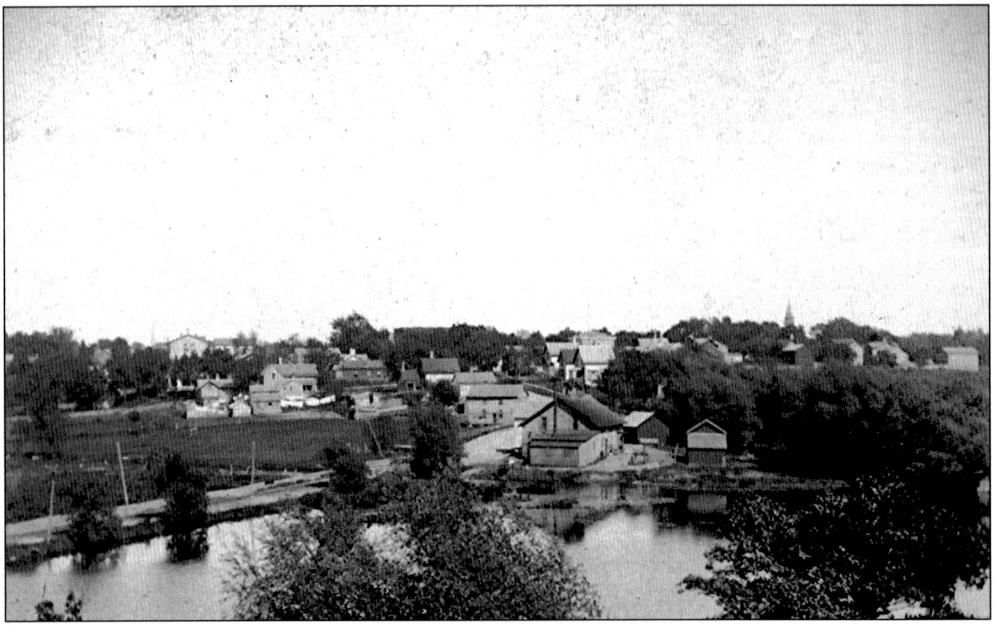

This early view was taken from the State School hill looking east/southeast across the Mill Pond towards Walworth Avenue. Most of the buildings in the foreground have not existed for a long time.

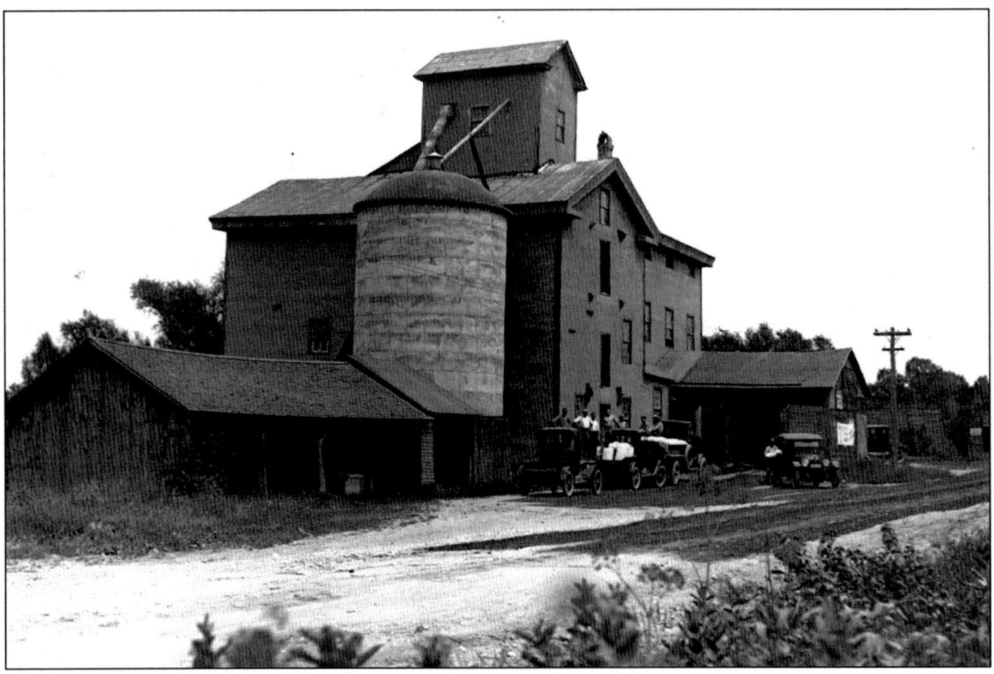

The mill was located at the northwest end of town on what is now County Trunk M. In most pioneer villages, as in Delavan, the grist mill was built as soon as possible. The mill shown here was built about 1839 on Turtle Creek. It was expanded several times, but destroyed by fire in 1927 and rebuilt right away. Part of the mill built in 1928 is still standing in that same location.

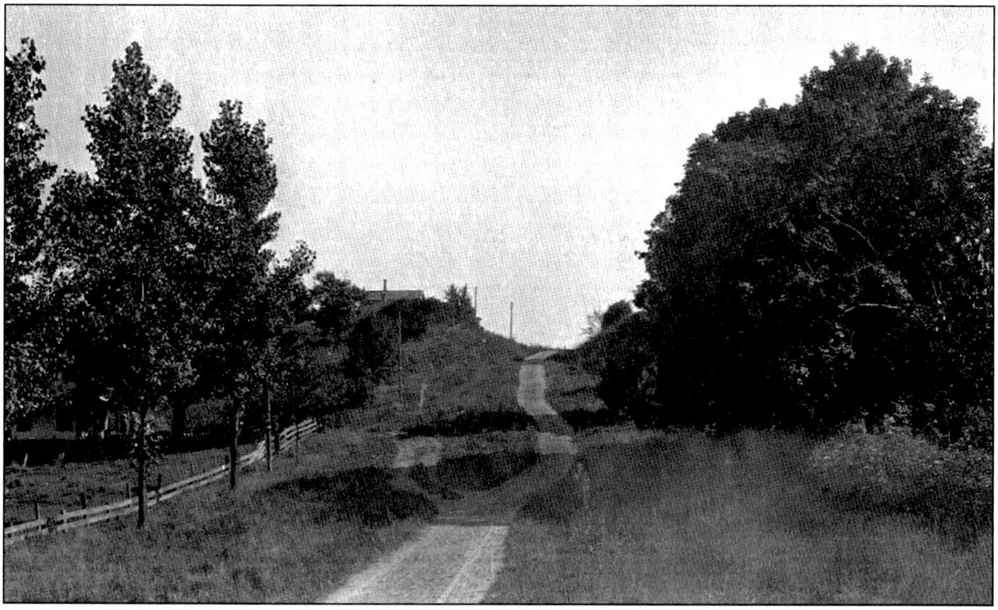

This is a view southward on Vine Street. Located on Vine Street in this general vicinity, possibly even captured in this image, was the "Pest House." It was a time when hospitals would not admit patients with communicable diseases, but because they were highly infectious they needed to be quarantined. Citizens or travelers who were contagious were sent to the Pest House where they would be cared for. Pest Houses were intentionally located in a sparsely populated area of the community. Delavan's Pest House was razed in the 1920s.

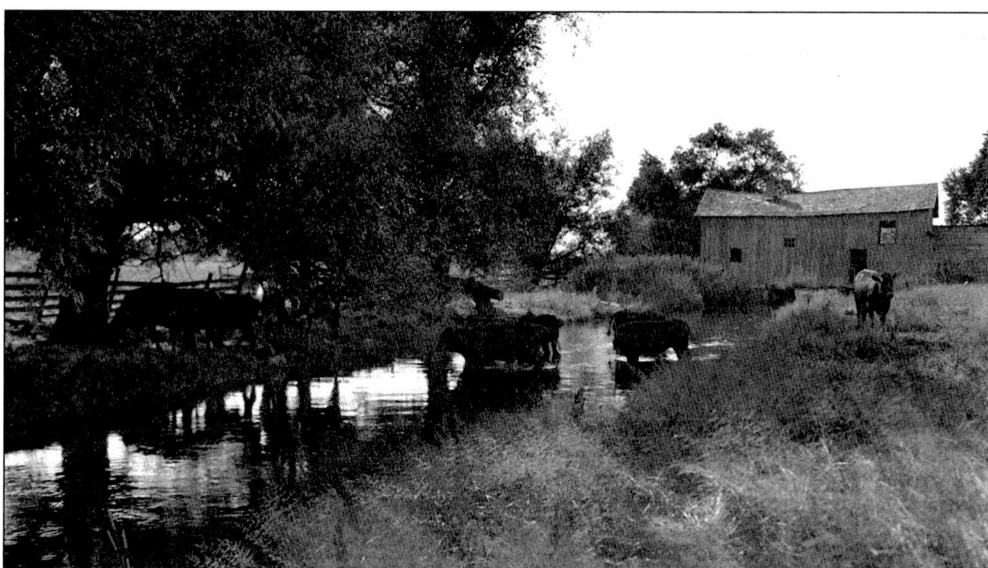

This is the old slaughter house on County Trunk M, north of the Wisconsin School for the Deaf. The cows are peacefully wading in the creek while the slaughter house looms in the distance.

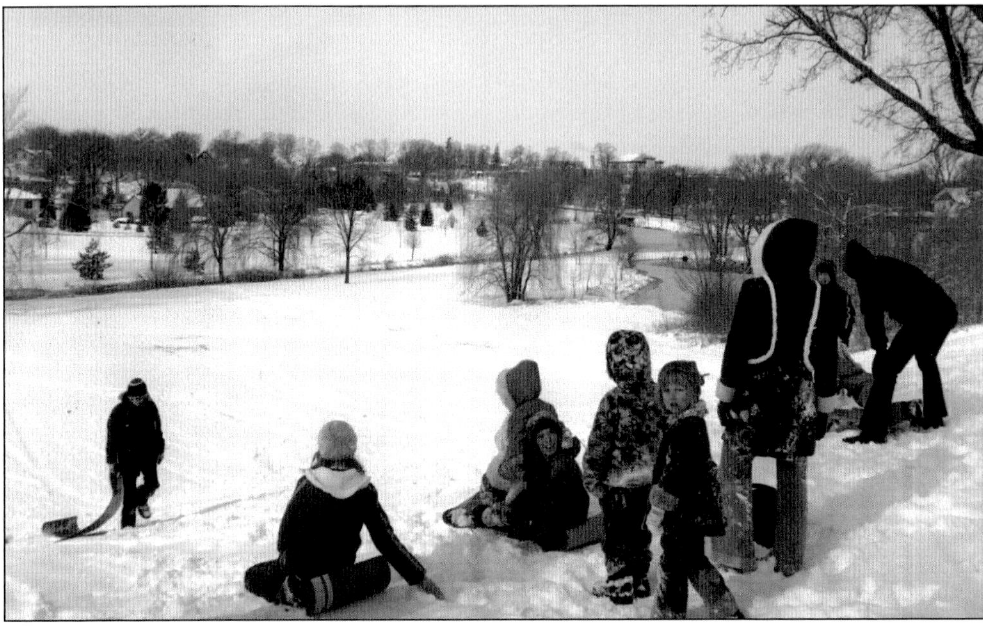

This is a familiar view to everyone who grew up in Delavan, Rudy Lang Sledding Hill. Sledding is enjoyed in the snowy months by kids of all ages and in the spring the graduating class from the high school has a tradition of carving their graduation year into the side of the hill. Shown above are children and adults in the 1970s taking pleasure in winter activities on the hill. The Wisconsin School for the Deaf can be seen in the distance. Below, the hill as it looked in the early 1900s, facing south with the Baptist Church Steeple in the background.

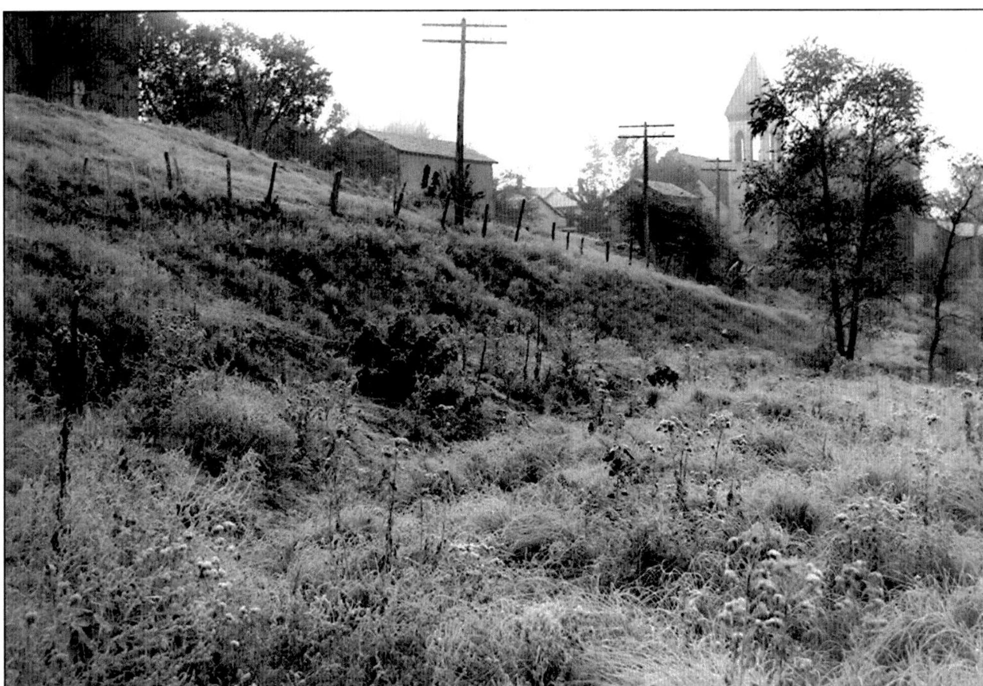

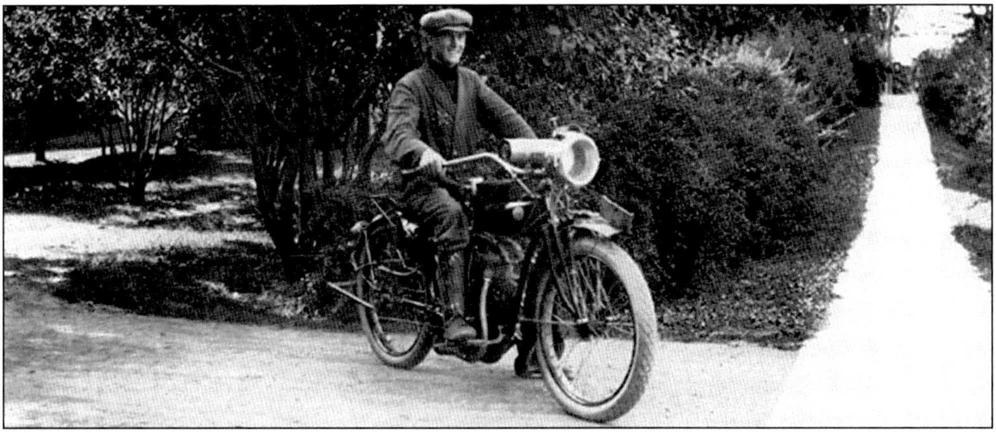

Ernest Franzen was an Indian Motorcycle dealer in Delavan in 1921 by the age of 21. He was also an avid photographer and proudly snapped a photo of his 1916 Indian motorcycle underneath an advertisement for his business. He was hired as a Delavan Motorcycle Policeman in June 1916 to enforce the 15 m.p.h. speed limit. His tour as a motorcycle cop lasted only a few months. In August the owner of a garage in town complained in the newspaper that strict enforcement of the speed limit by motorcycle policemen was a negative way to draw visitors to Delavan.

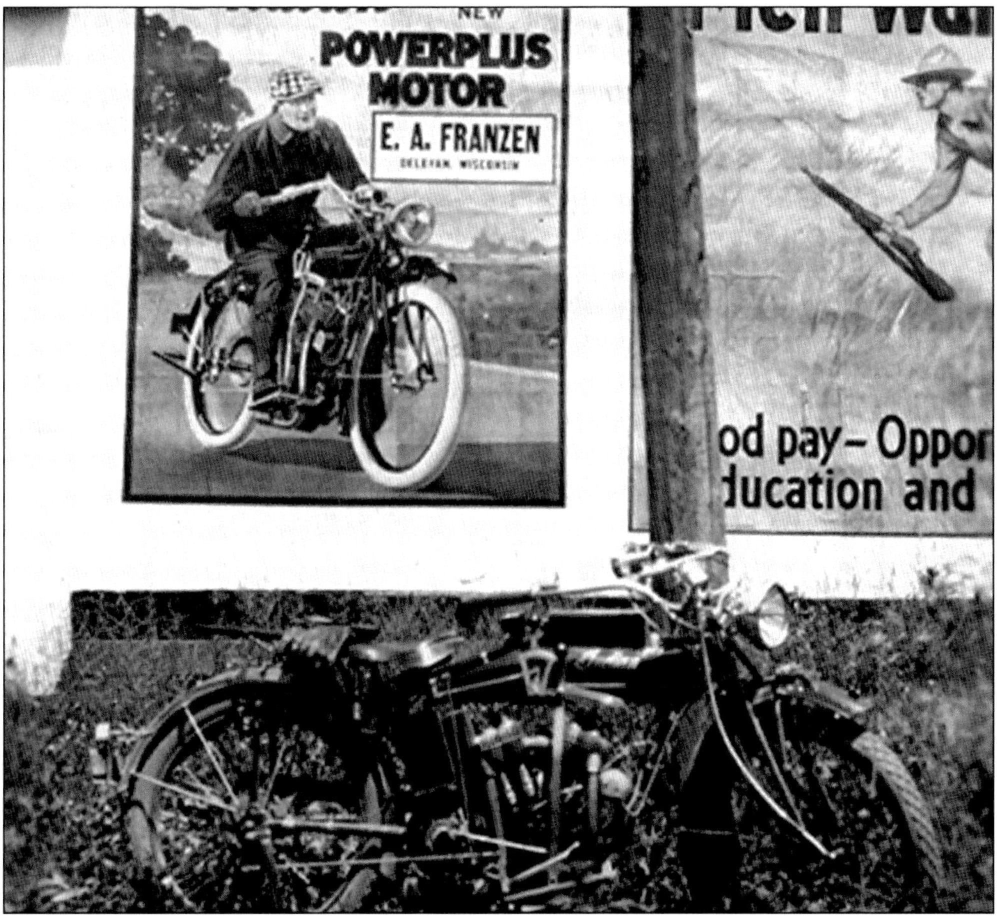

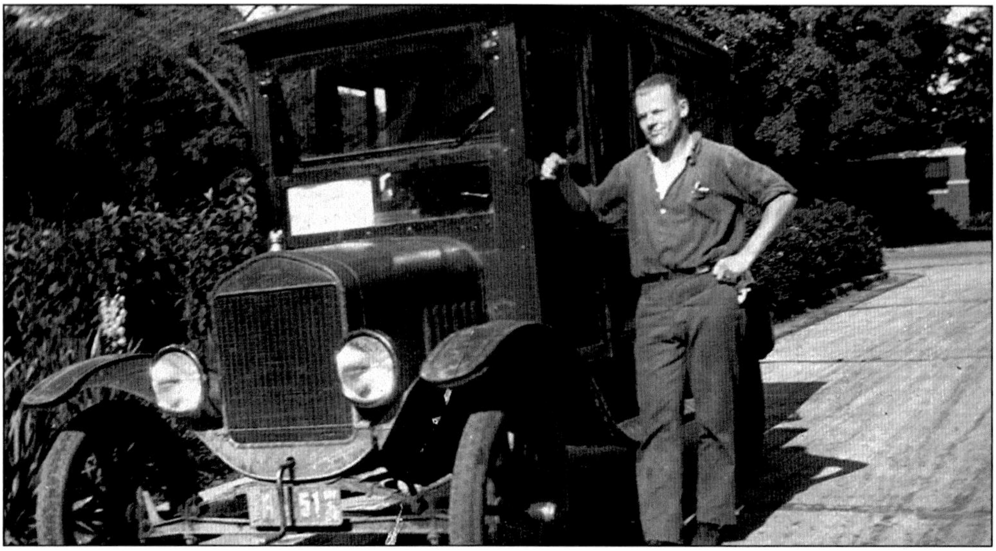

Carl Boutelle was driving the delivery truck for the Delavan Sanitary Bakery, also known as Boutelle's Bakery, in 1924. The bakery was started by his father, Orin Boutelle, at 310 East Walworth Avenue in 1923 and became immediately popular for their fine bakery goods, wedding cakes, and birthday cakes. The business was operated in the same location until 1981, when it was sold to the Shanklins.

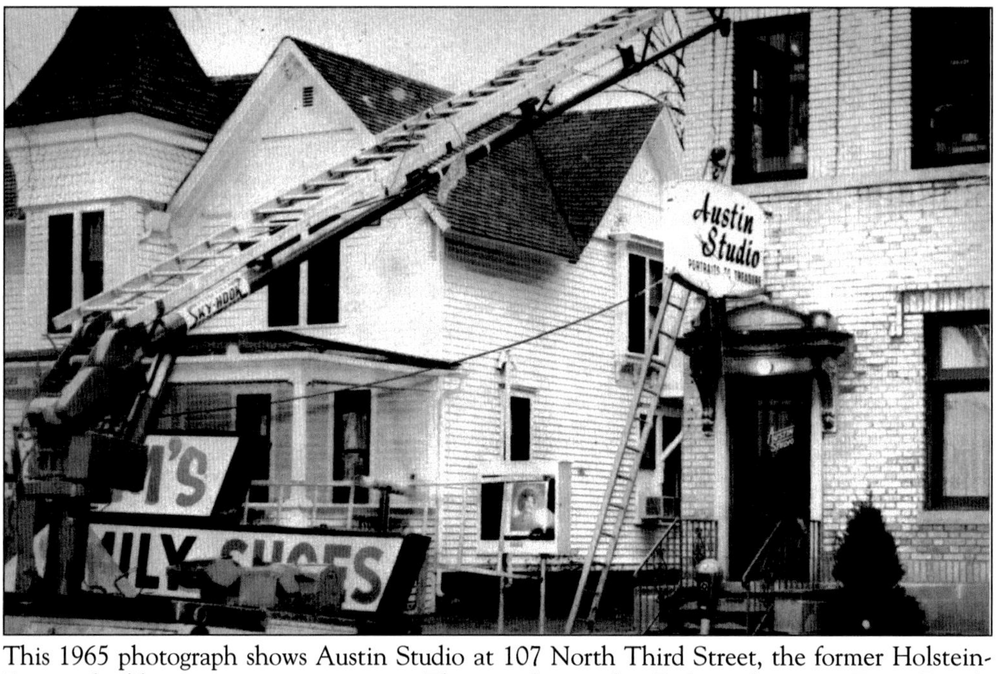

This 1965 photograph shows Austin Studio at 107 North Third Street, the former Holstein-Friesian building, receiving a new sign. The sign for another Delavan business, Tom's Family Shoes, is still in the truck waiting to be delivered. For a short time, the house to the left of Austin Studio housed the city offices while the new municipal building was being constructed. A parking lot is now in that location.

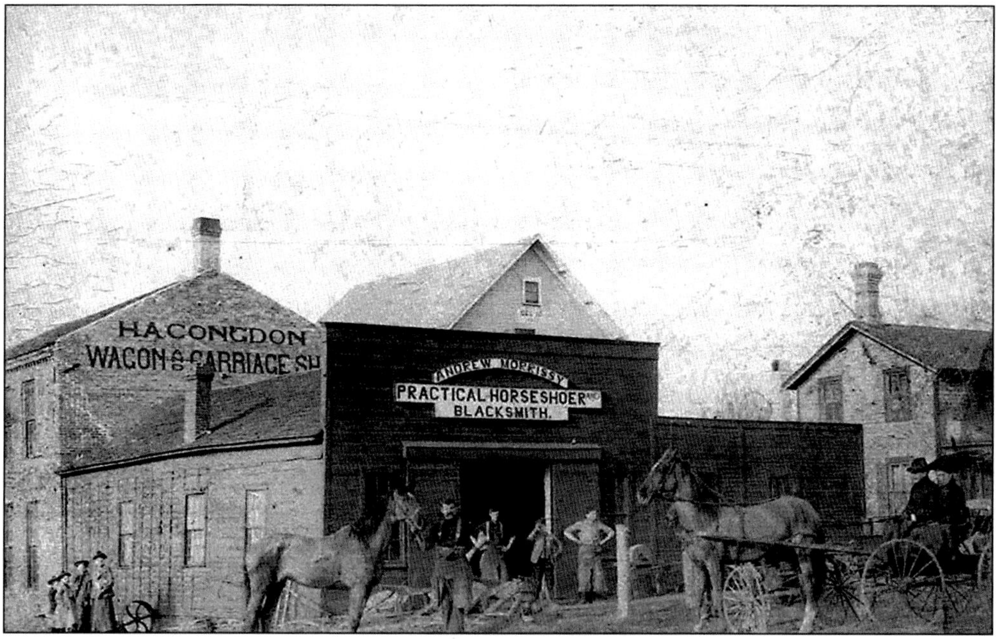

Pictured above is H.A. Congdon's Wagon & Carriage Shop and Andrew Morrissy's Practical Horseshoer & Blacksmith. These businesses were located on the northeast corner of Walworth and Terrace Street and pictured here *c.* 1910. Below is Thompson's Carriage and Wagon Shop, pre-1892. It was located just north of the alley on North Second Street. The building also housed a blacksmith shop and advertisements for house, sign, and carriage painting. It burned down with the rest of the buildings in that downtown vicinity in 1892. This was one of the fires that precipitated the village council providing water to the community.

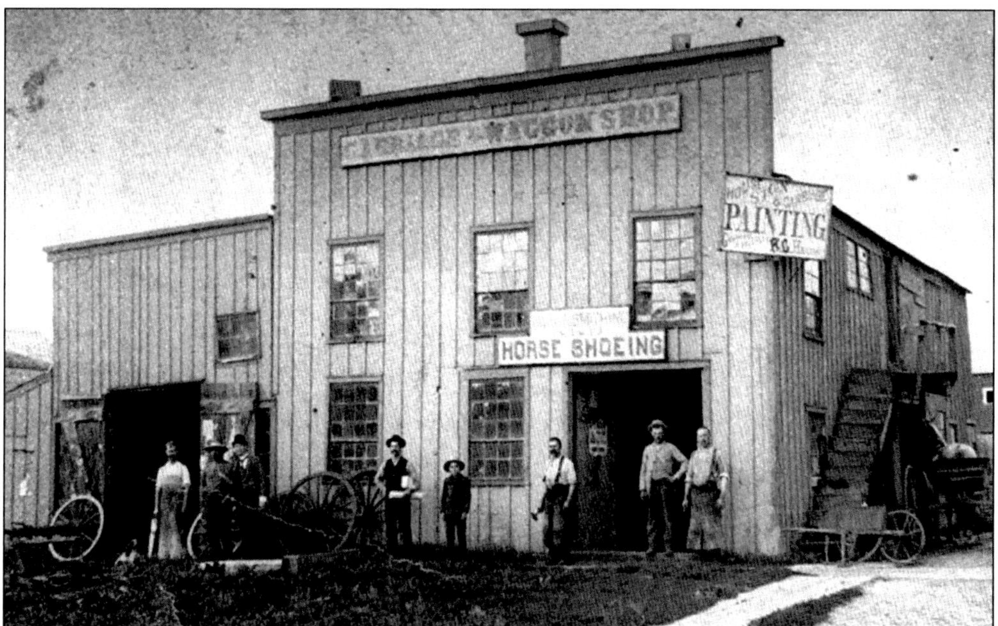

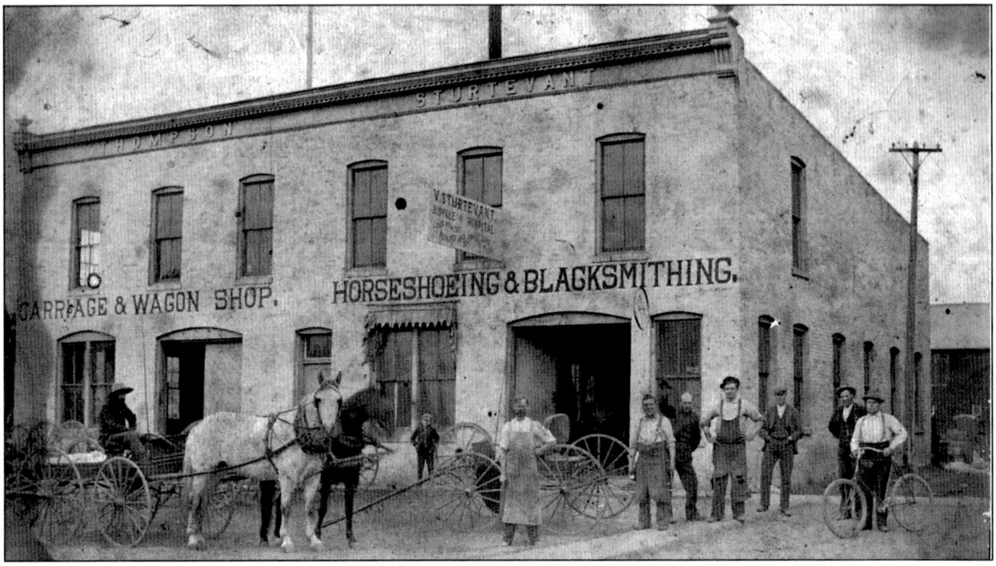

Mr. Thompson bounced back from the fire that destroyed his business in 1892, (shown on preceding page) and by the time these photos were taken in about 1898, he was operating at 112 North Second Street. Shown above is Thompson's Blacksmith & Carriage Shop, sharing the building with Sturtevant Horseshoeing & Blacksmith. The sign above the door advertises a bicycle hospital, lawnmower, and saw sharpening services. The photo below shows George Sturtevant on the left, inside the blacksmith shop.

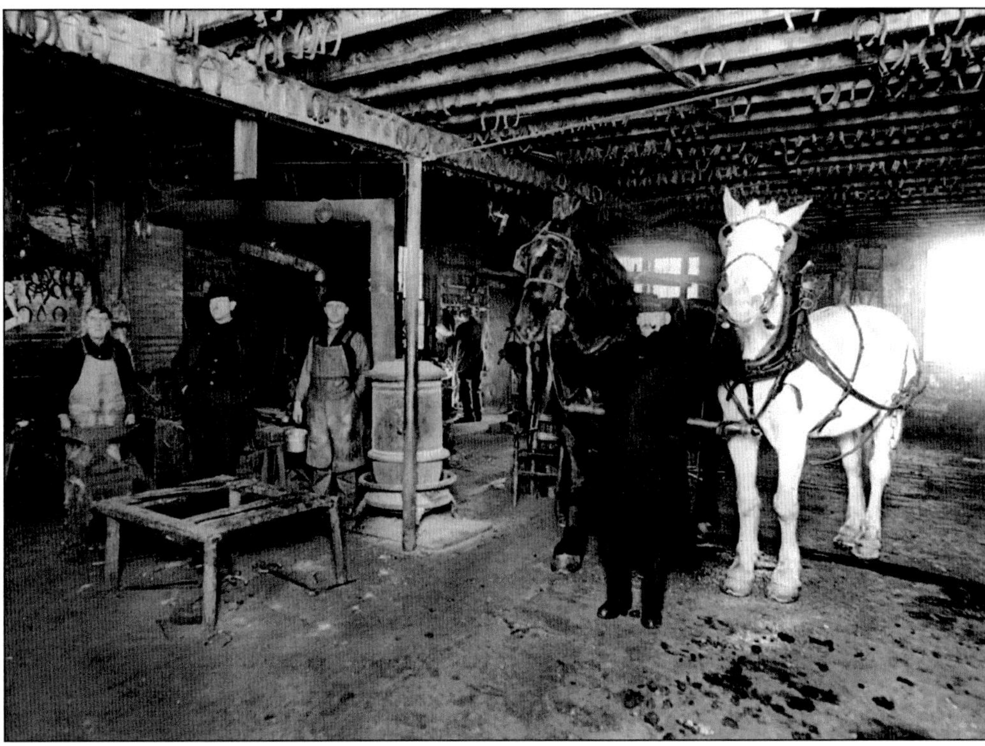

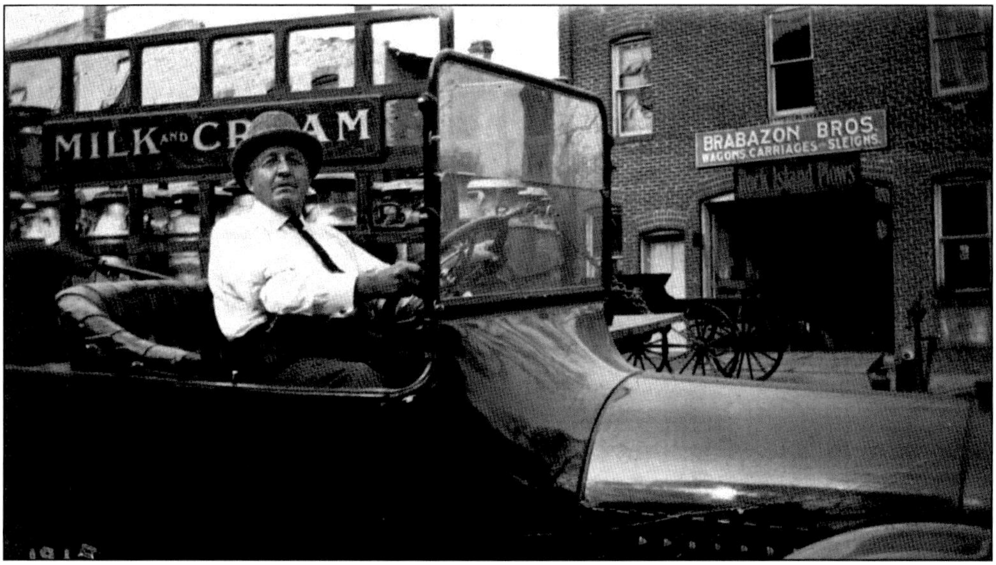

This gentleman is taking a leisurely drive down the 100 block of South Third Street in 1915. Revealed behind him is the Brabazon Brothers wagon, carriage, and sleigh business, and the milk and cream wagon is passing by in the opposite direction. The Brabazon's business was located on the east side of the street, just south of the alley. It was torn down about 1939 to make room for the new Anderson car dealership.

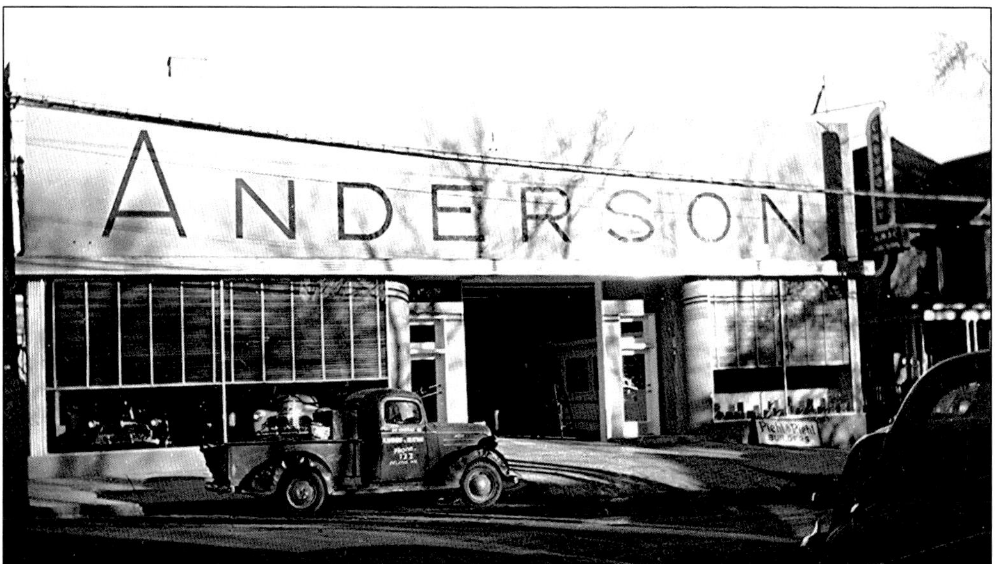

In the 1940s, Clarence Anderson built a new Quonset hut building for his Chevrolet-Oldsmobile dealership, located on the east side of the 100 block of South Third Street. After World War II, the government sold its surplus Quonset huts to the public for $1,000 each. They were well-engineered structures and the ease of assembly made them desirable. Today, this building houses Jan's Hallmark.

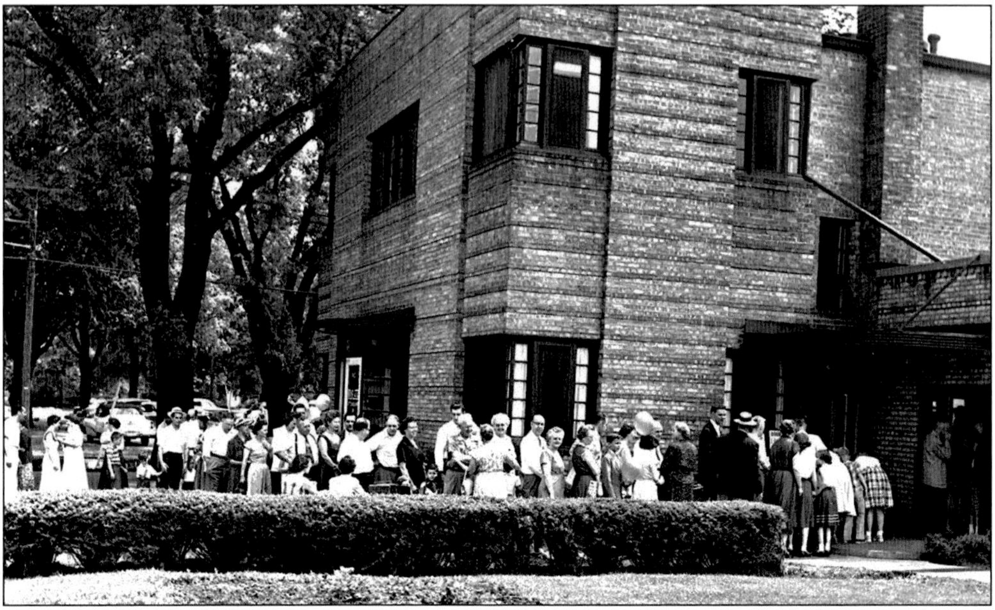

In 1934, a time when unemployment was high, a small firm called Sta-Rite was founded by William C. Heath. The corporation quickly evolved into a major manufacturer of water systems. Sta-Rite's first office occupied space above the Murphy and O'Neill Drug Store, and its earliest manufacturing plant was located at Eighth and Ann Street. Through the World War II era, Heath created landing gears for bombers and one of his earlier designs produced a high speed submersible pump, which later aided the United States in the capture of a German submarine. Shown above is Sta-Rite's open house, which took place after remodeling in 1954. Their fleet of cars from the 1960s are shown below. Henry S. Lauter served as president of Sta-Rite for many years.

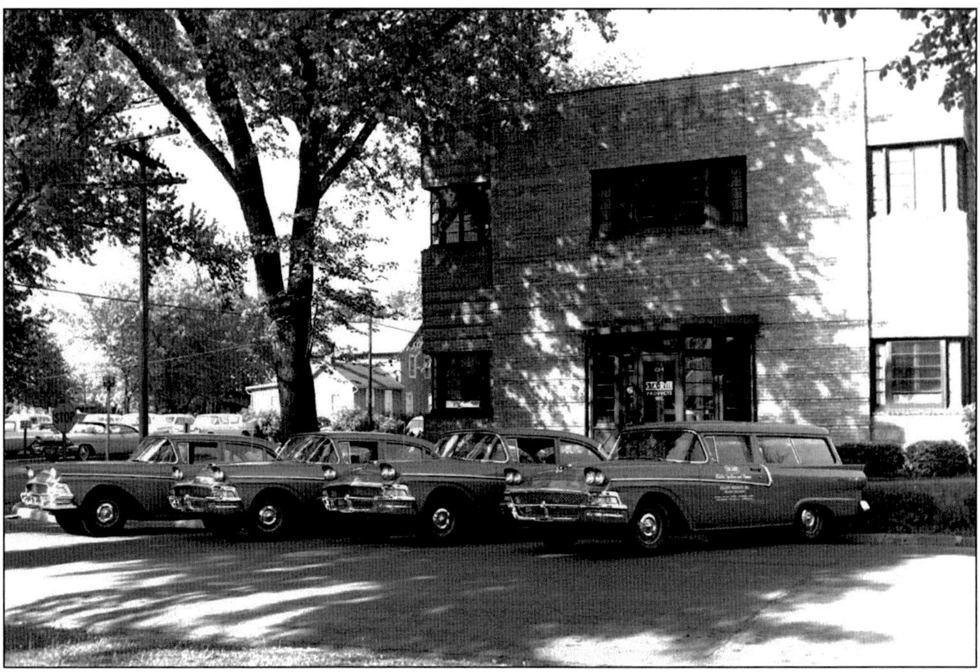

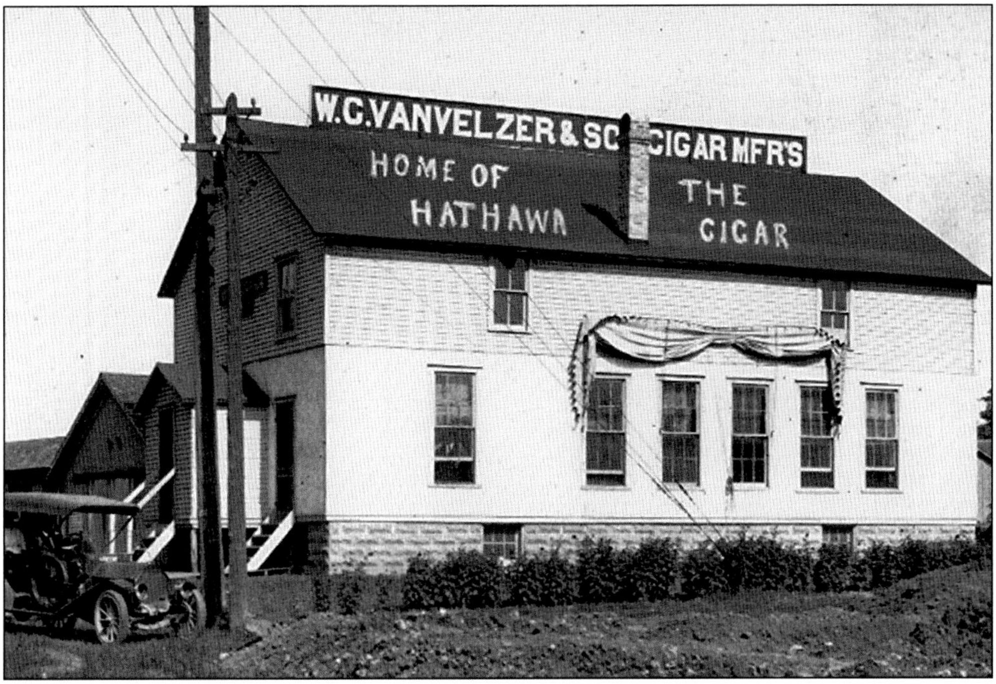

When these photographs were taken, the W.C. Van Velzer Cigar Company was occupying the former Delavan Shoe Company building in the 600 block of East Wisconsin Street. The business got its start in 1877, when Washington and Ferdinand Van Velzer bought the tobacco shop (to which W.W. Bradley would later relocate). In the 1890s, the two dissolved their partnership and W.C. Van Velzer continued the cigar manufacturing alone until his son Fred joined him in 1900. This building is now a private residence.

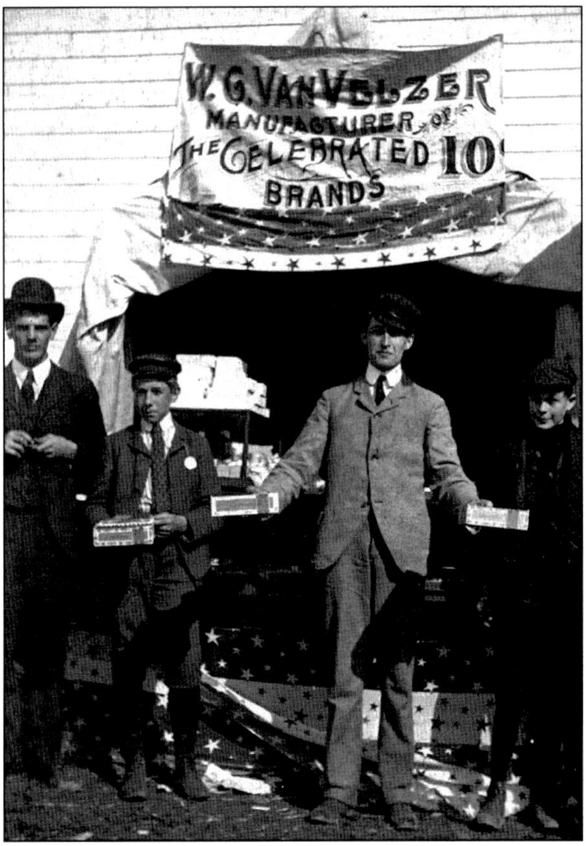

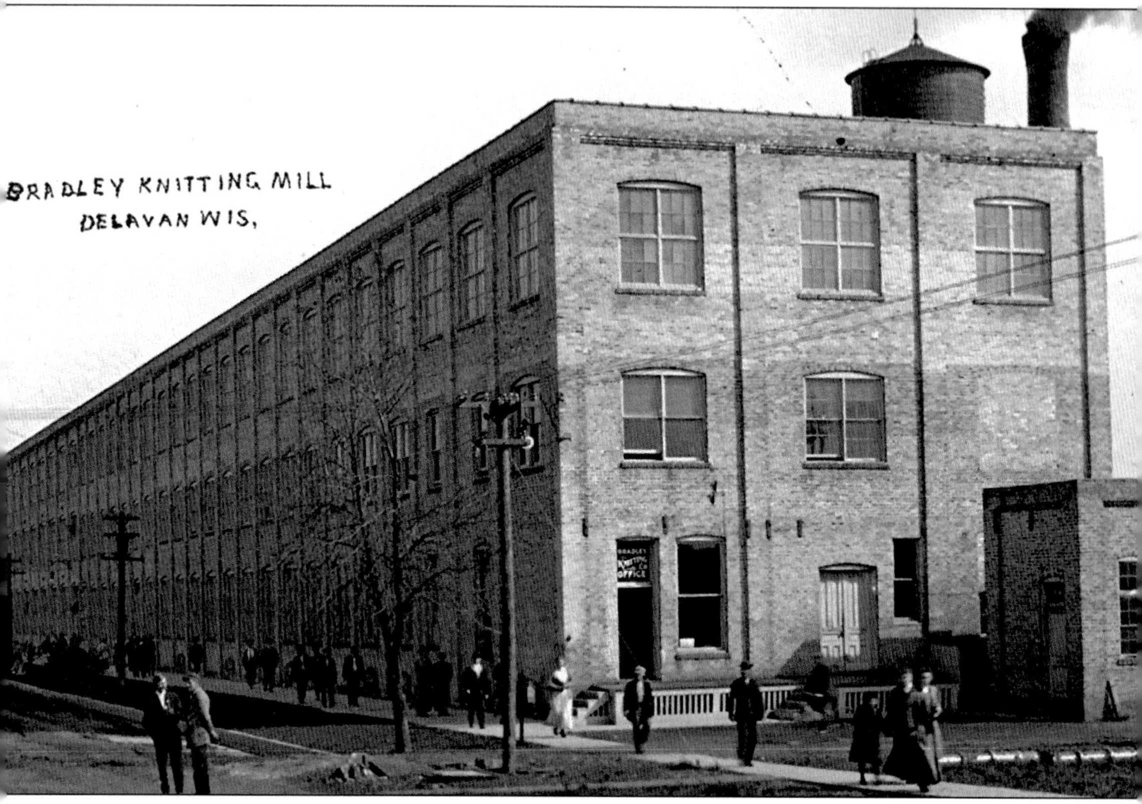

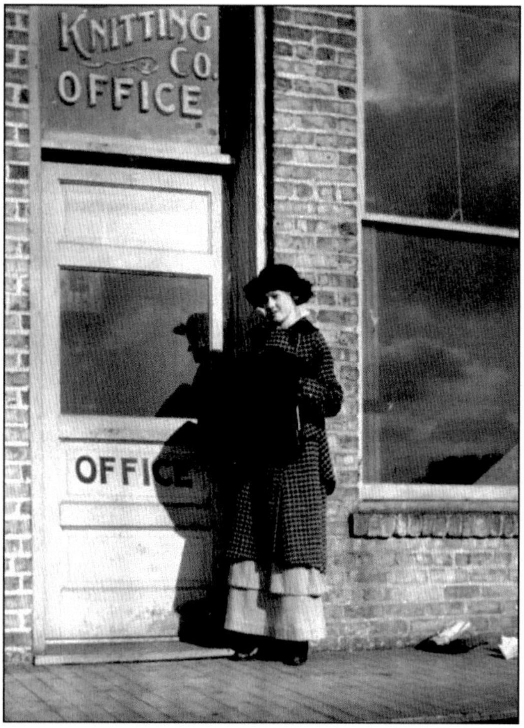

In 1905, Tyrell and Phoenix bought out the Globe Knitting Company that had just started operating the previous year. The Bradley Knitting Company did great business and continued to grow into the 1920s. The stock market crash of 1929 did not show an immediate effect on the company, but in the early 1930s orders were reduced or cancelled. Their business would continue to falter until George Borg and Thomas Gibbs entered the picture in the 1940s. The Bradley Knitting Company is represented here in about 1919.

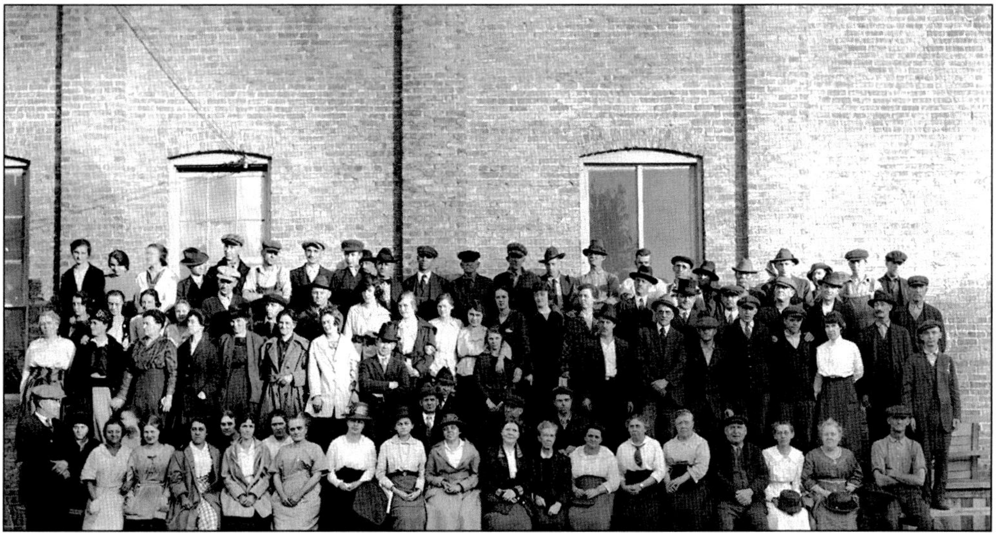

This is the work force of the Bradley Knitting Company about 1909. Some local families can boast several generations of Bradley Knitting Company employees. The Bradley/Borg Building was placed on the National Register of Historic Places in 1992. The building was torn down in 2003 and many bricks and other parts of the Bradley Knitting Company were salvaged by the Delavan Historical Society for future use.

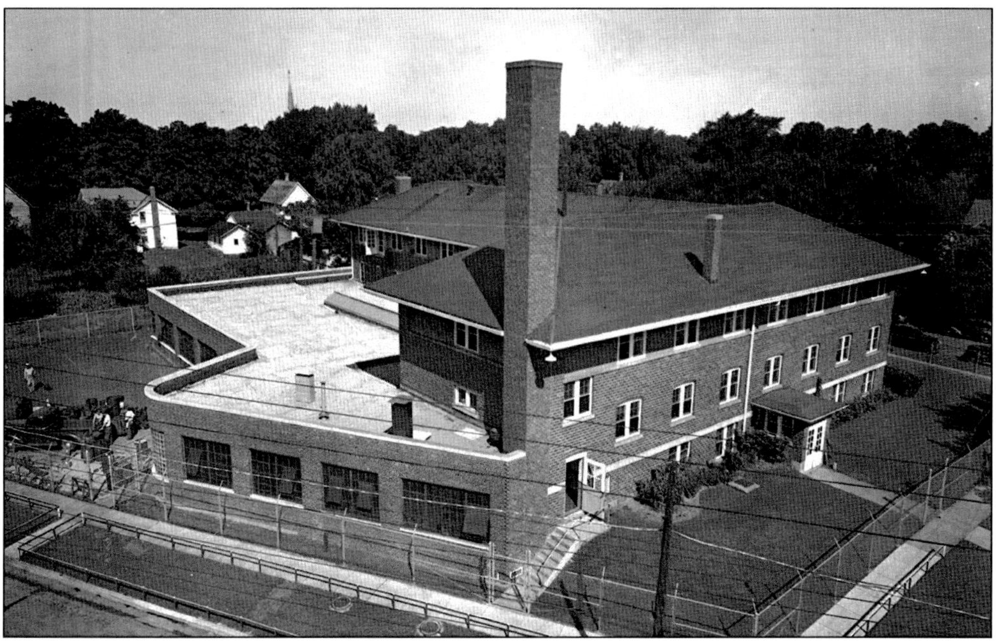

In 1940, Thomas Gibbs began the T.B. Gibbs Company in the former Bradley Dormitory Building on Wisconsin Street. The Gibbs Co. manufactured precision timing and electronic devices. In 1941, operations were expanded and during World War II they were awarded additional contracts. In 1942, Gibbs merged with George W. Borg and in 1943 they erected a new building at 820 East Wisconsin Street. The plant terminated operations in 1950.

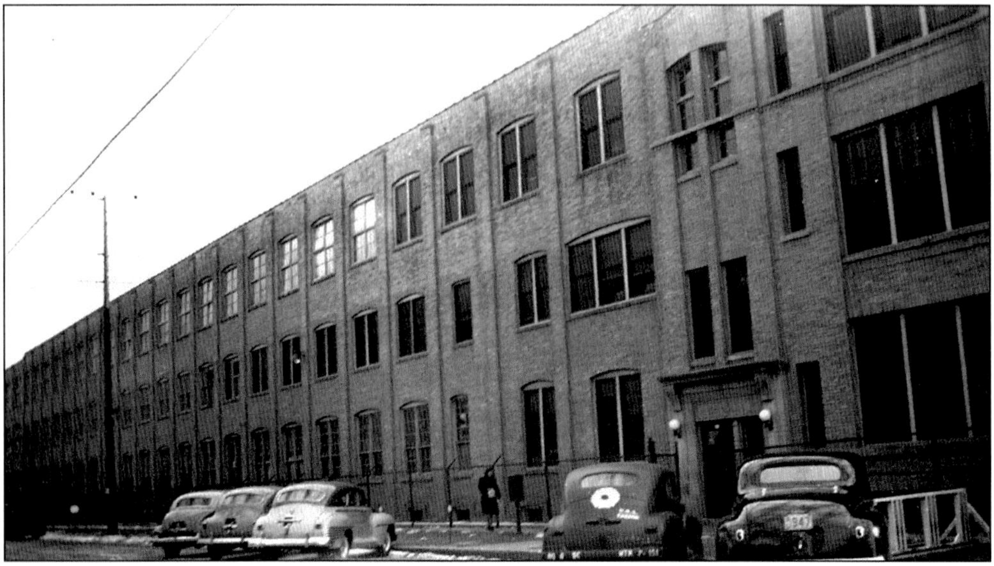

The 1930s saw George W. Borg come to Delavan and lease a portion of the Bradley Knitting Company building to manufacture automobile clocks. He joined forces in 1940 with the man who was manufacturing parts for his clocks, Thomas Gibbs. Borg bought the Bradley Knitting Company in 1941 and received a substantial contract with the government to make knitted goods for soldiers. Automobile clock production was halted when they received contracts from the government during World War II. Borg-Gibbs manufacturing war products placed Delavan on the Department of Defense's top-ten prime sabotage target list, and security was tightened. Shown below are the company buses that traveled to surrounding towns to deliver employees to and from the plant.

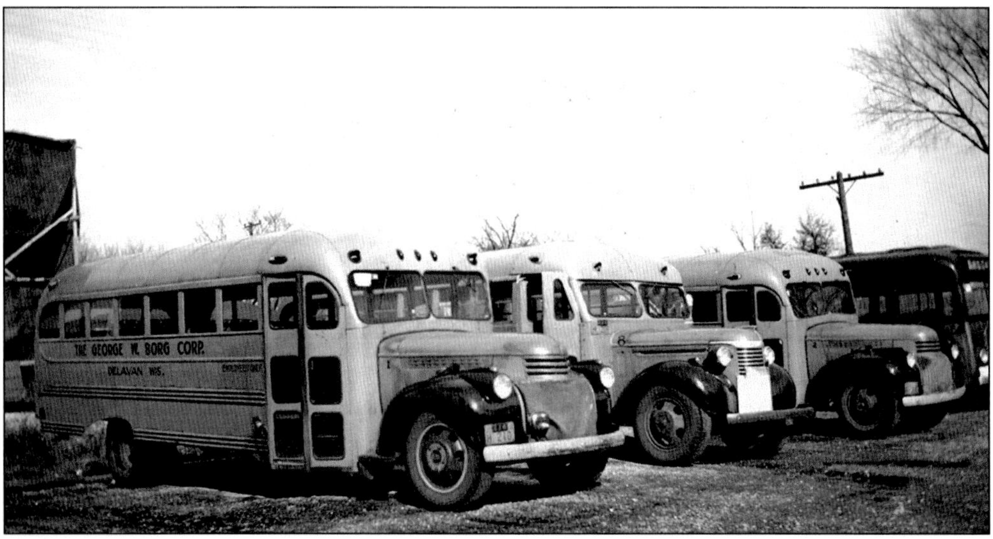

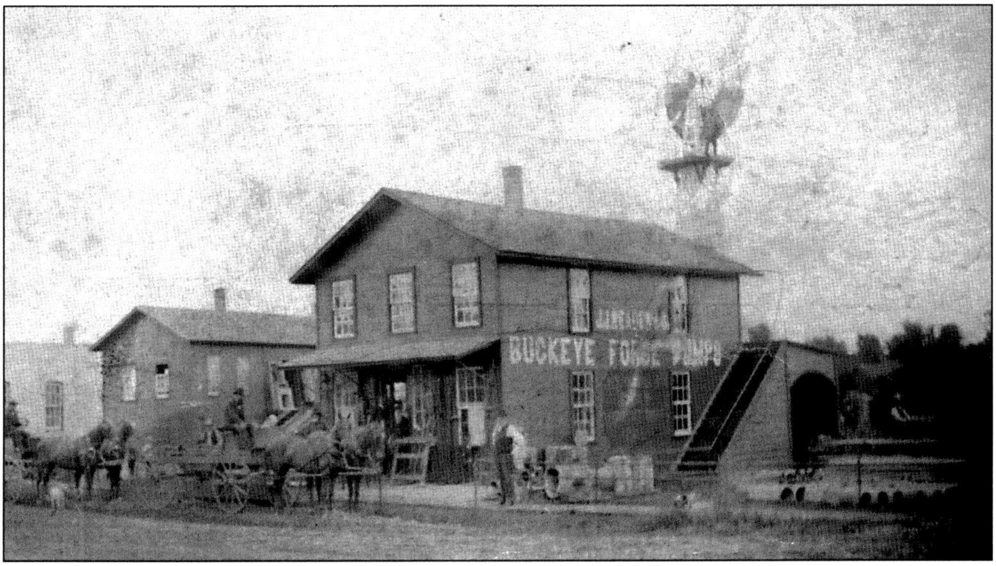

Sometime before 1881, John B. Reader started his windmill business on South Seventh Street in the approximate location of what is now R.A. Carlson Plumbing. His son John J. Reader took over the business and ran his successful J.J. Reader & Co. Buckeye Forge Pump operations. The photograph above shows a view of Seventh Street as it looked about 1890. Below is a side view of his buildings from Washington Street, looking south about 1890. This location was considered the "east end" for many years due to its distance from the downtown area.

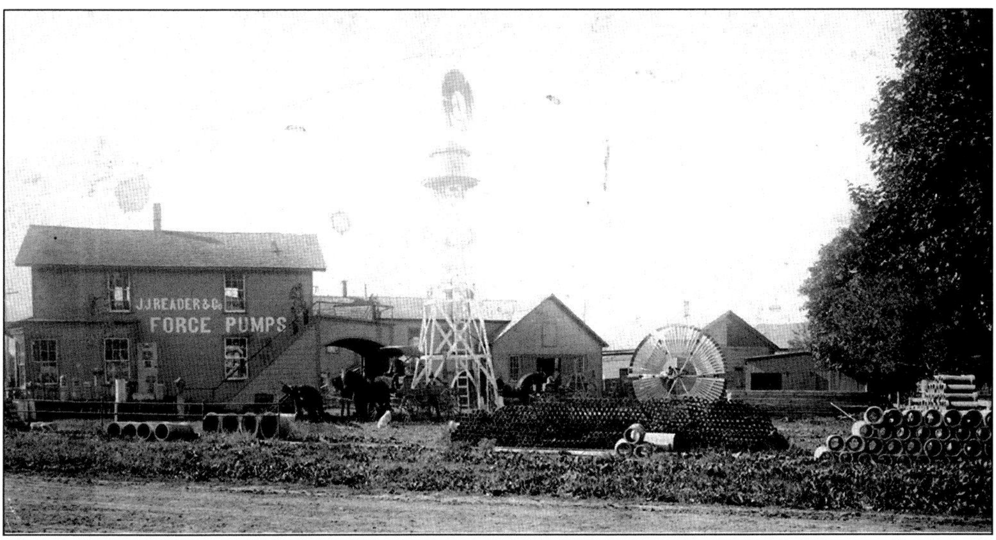

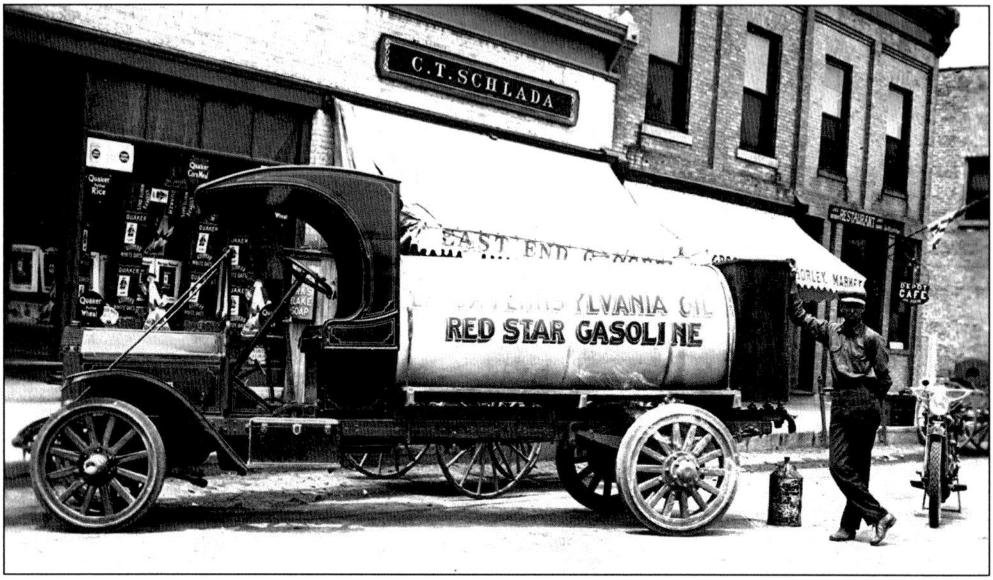

This is a pre-1920s view of the 200 block of South Seventh Street, looking north. The Pennsylvania Oil, Red Star Gasoline Truck is parked in front of the East End Grocery Store owned by C.T. Schlada, which is now New Horizons Sports Bar. The next building to the right is McSorley's Market and the Depot Café, now home to Hernandez Mexican Restaurant.

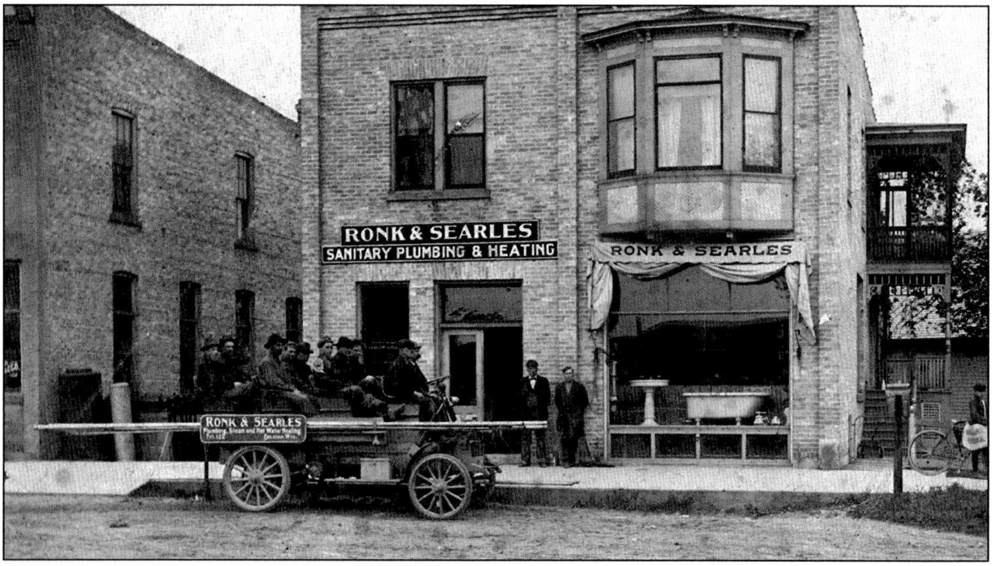

Ronk & Searles Plumbing and Heating was owned by John Ronk and Grant Searles, who started their business in 1896 on the northwest corner of Seventh and Washington. Ronk, who kept working well into his 80s, later went into business with B.W. Christian and ultimately Christian owned the business himself. This photograph was taken about 1905.

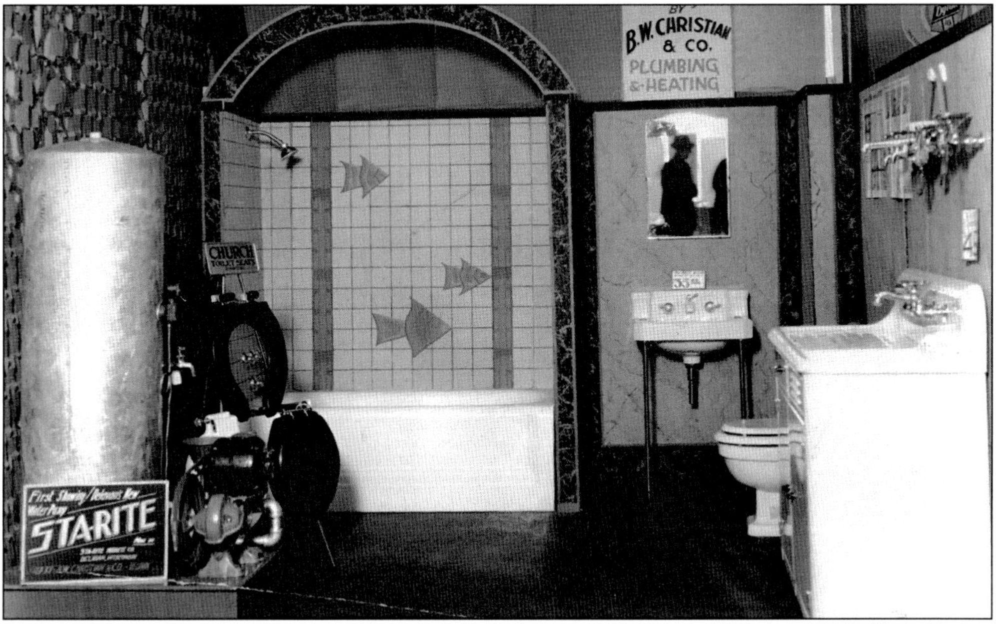

Sta-Rite Manufacturing's first pump order came from Bert Christian, owner of B.W. Christian & Co. The order was filled in March 1935, right around the time Sta-Rite was moving its offices from above Murphy and O'Neill Drug Store to their new building on Eighth and Ann Street. Christian installed the new pumps at Edgar Buzzell's Glen Eyrie Farm at Delavan Lake. The 1959 photograph below is an aerial view looking south at the newly completed Sta-Rite plant on Wright Street. Further south of the new facility is the intersection of Highway 50 and Wright Street.

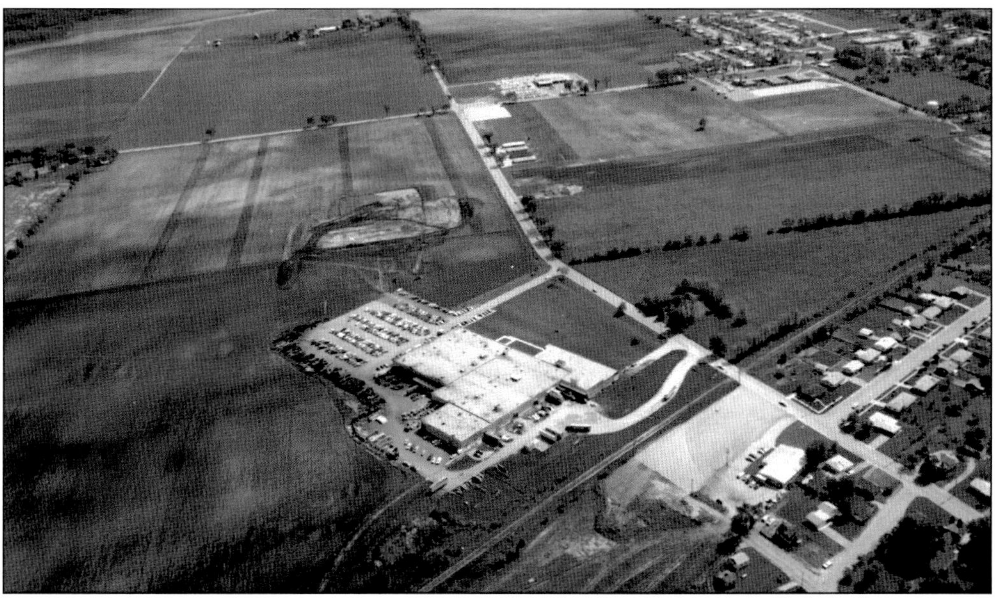

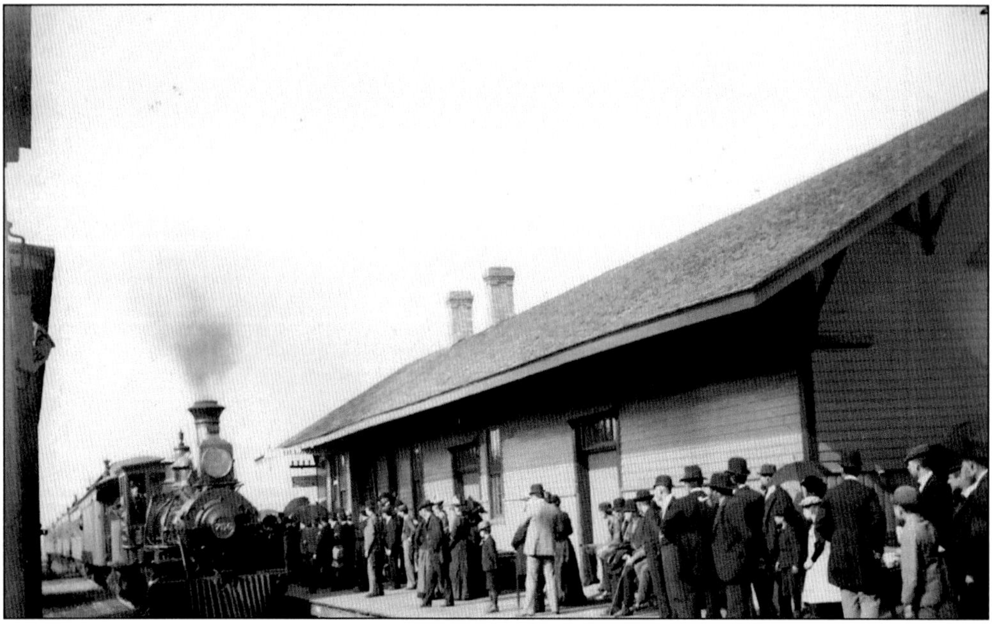

The Delavan Railroad Depot pictured here was constructed in 1912. In 1855, the Racine and Mississippi Railroad Company constructed 46.73 road miles of track from Racine to Delavan. The railroad would help the economy and aid Delavan's industrial future. The line was extended another 22.58 miles from Delavan to Beloit in 1856. The original depot, built in 1856, was moved to a location on Eighth Street and used as a freight depot until it was torn down in 1971.

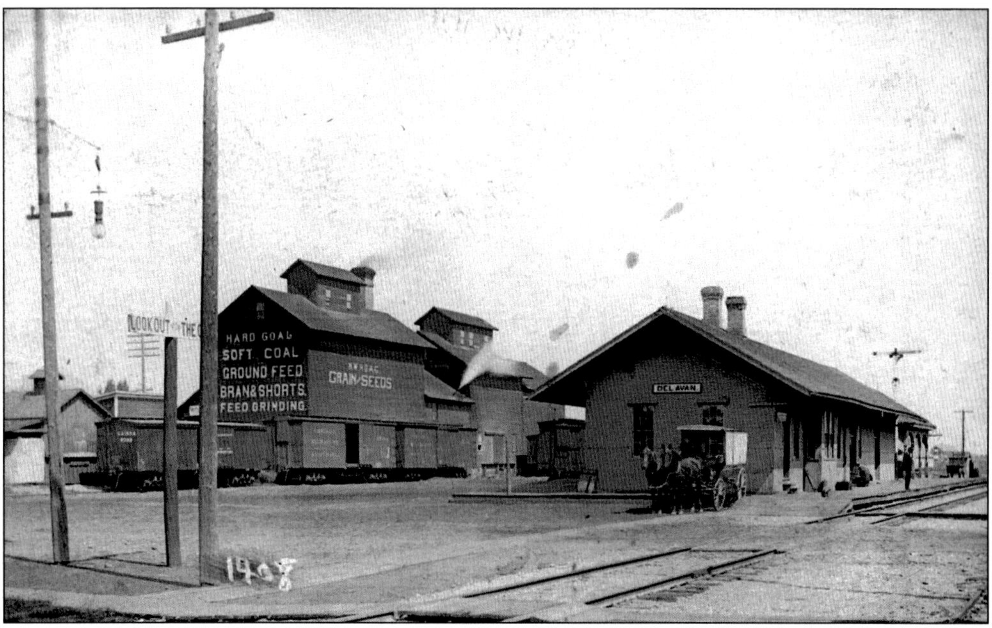

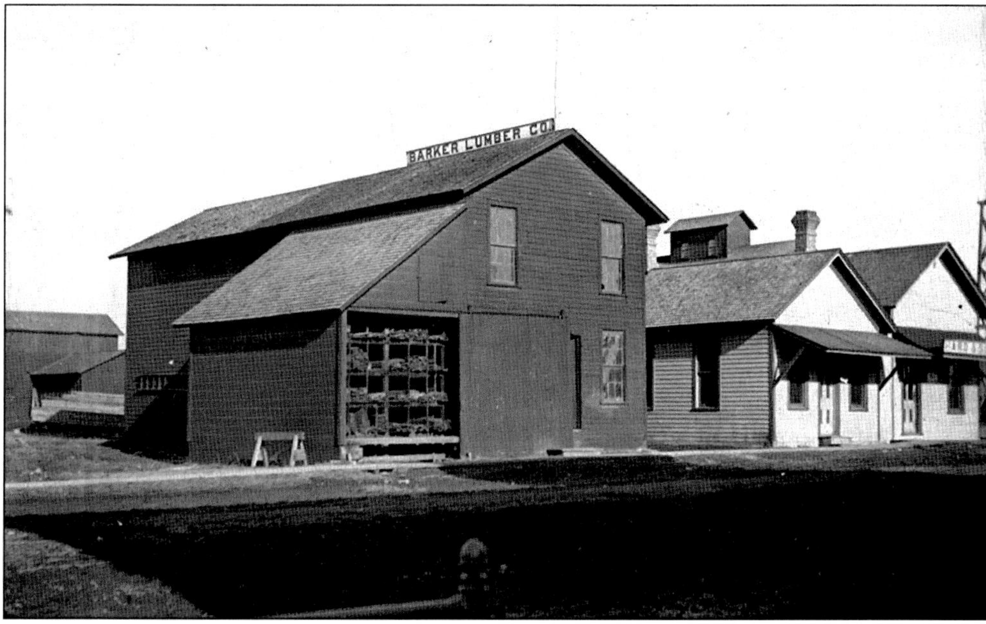

In 1881, Barker Lumber Company bought out a preexisting lumber company in Delavan, 10 years after opening a building supply company in Elkhorn. The company soon had its main office in Delavan. The lumber yard was located on South Seventh Street on the north side of the railroad tracks. The photograph above shows Barker Lumber Company in Delavan in its early years. In about 1917, Barker sold the lumber yard to Doyne-Rayne, shown here in 1936. The main office for Barker remained in Delavan. In the early 1960s, Barker Lumber Company bought Mawhinney Lumber at 327 South Seventh Street, and they were back in business in Delavan again, this time on the south side of the railroad tracks.

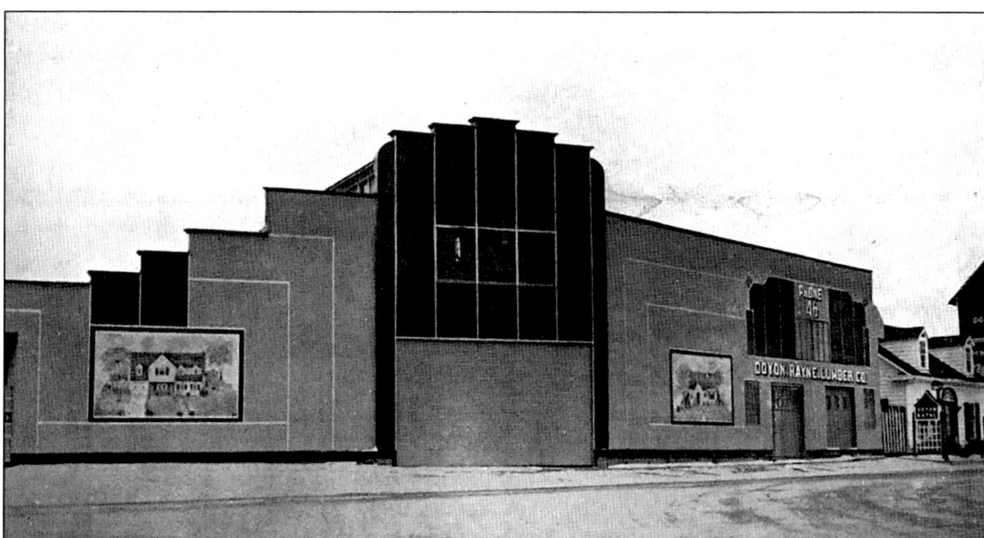

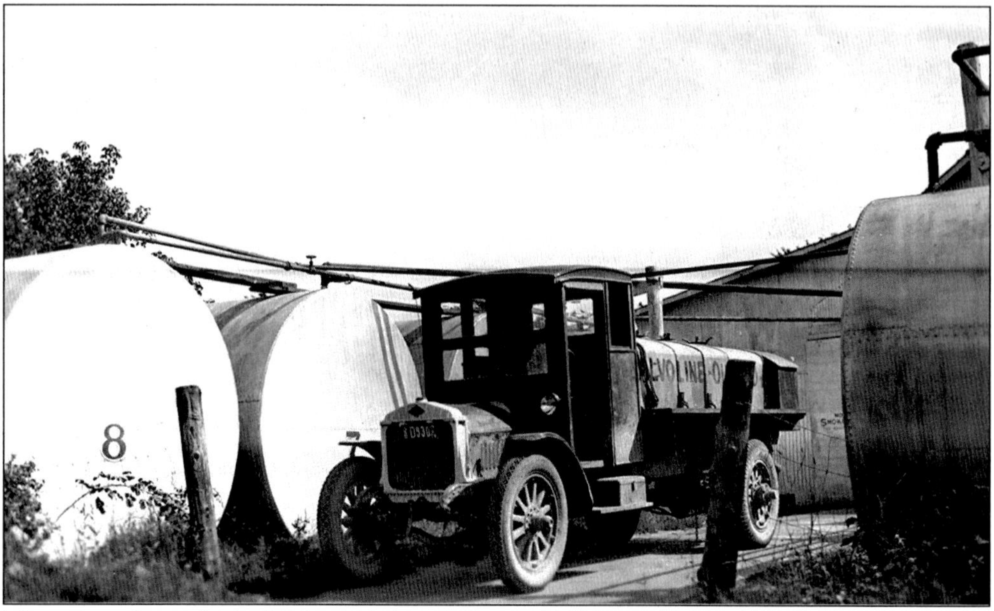

This image shows the bulk plant on Ann Street, owned by Fernie Batchelet and E.D. Fiske in 1924. Bulk plants were where wholesale gas and oil dealers held their fuel. For transportation and delivery purposes, the bulk plants were located by the railroad tracks on Ann Street, but later moved to other sites closer to the edge of the city.

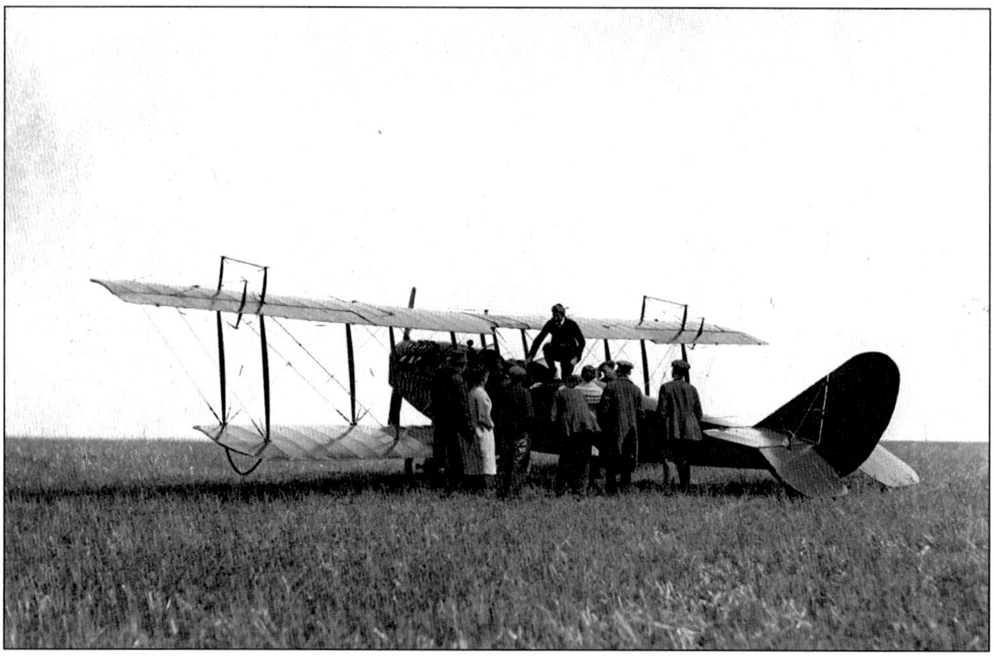

Don Campbell shows off his Curtis Jenny airplane in 1919. This photograph was taken at the "old airfield," located at the northeast corner of Highway 50 and Wright Street. An abandoned K-Mart is in this location now. After World War I, many Curtis Jenny planes were sold on the civilian market, and in the 1920s this style was a popular barnstormer.

Three

EDUCATION & RELIGION

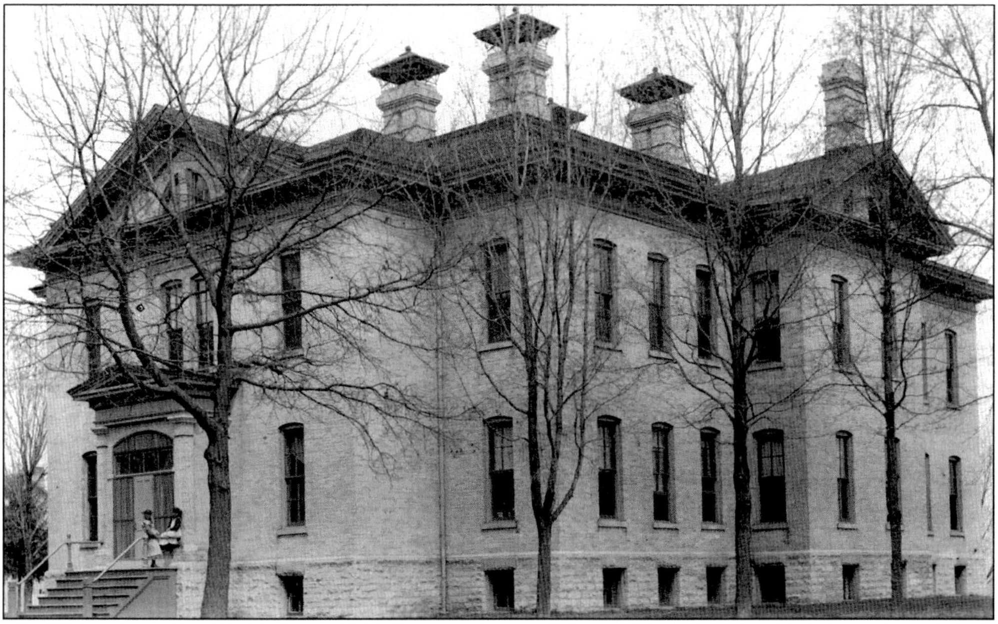

When Ebeneezer Cheseboro came to Delavan from New York in the late 1830s, he brought his family, which included his daughter Ariadna, who was deaf and a former student of the New York Institute for the Deaf and Dumb. Delavan had no such facility, but the Cheseboros still wanted their daughter educated. Fortunately for them, a former New York Institute graduate was living nearby and he was hired to school their daughter and a neighbor boy who was also deaf. Over a few years, the student base for this deaf class grew to eight students, but the Cheseboros were having a difficult time funding the education of all of these students. In 1852, with the help of family and friends, they petitioned the state legislature to establish a school for the deaf. Franklin Phoenix, a family friend and son of Samuel Phoenix, offered to donate land to the state for the school. They were successful and on April 19, 1852, the governor signed the law appropriating the funds for the Wisconsin School for the Deaf. Thousands of students have graduated from the Wisconsin School for the Deaf, which has continued to uphold a high standard of education for over 150 years. The school pictured here was built in 1854 and destroyed by fire in 1879.

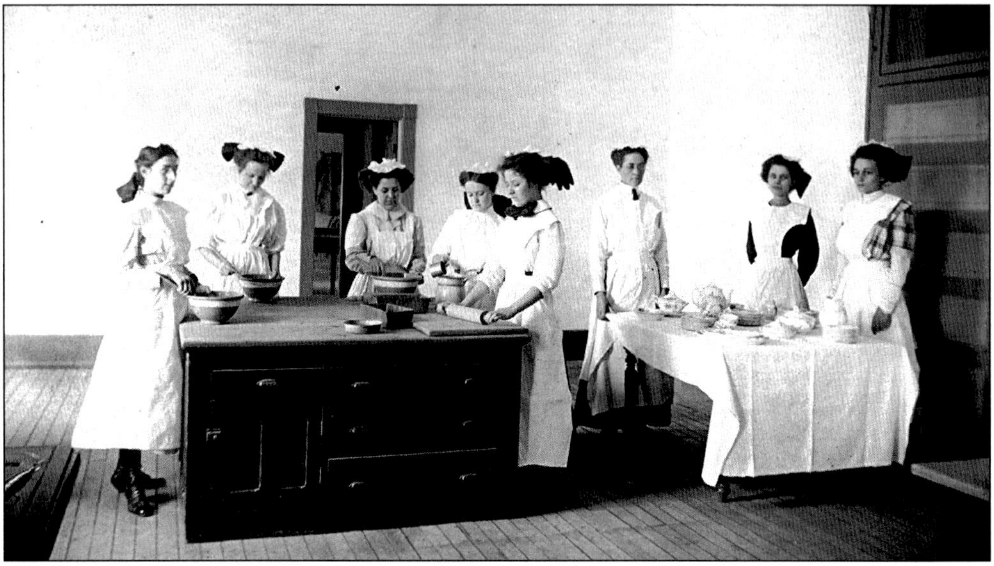

Students who lived at the Wisconsin School for the deaf not only attended standard educational classes, they were also taught skills that would have normally been learned at home from their parents. Each student had chores they were responsible for. Pictured here in the kitchen, these students not only learned to cook, but provided meals for the teachers and students.

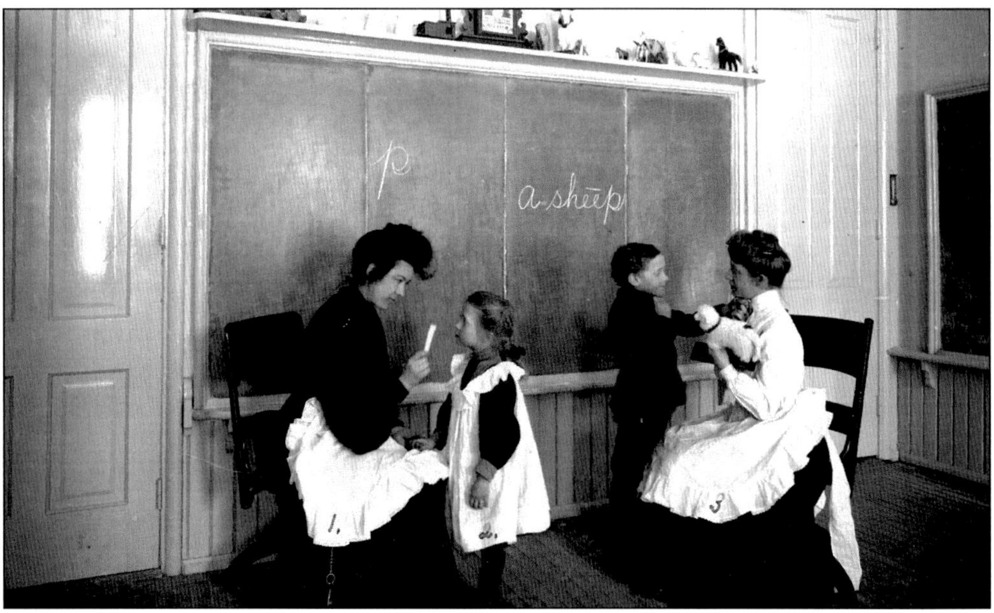

At the Wisconsin School for the Deaf, teachers still tried to teach an auditory class to its students. This photograph was taken around the turn of the century in a classroom at the school. Pictured from left to right are Miss Katherine Williams, Sibyl Smith Kalinberger, Mrs. Dora Hendrickson Lowe, and Christian Hirte.

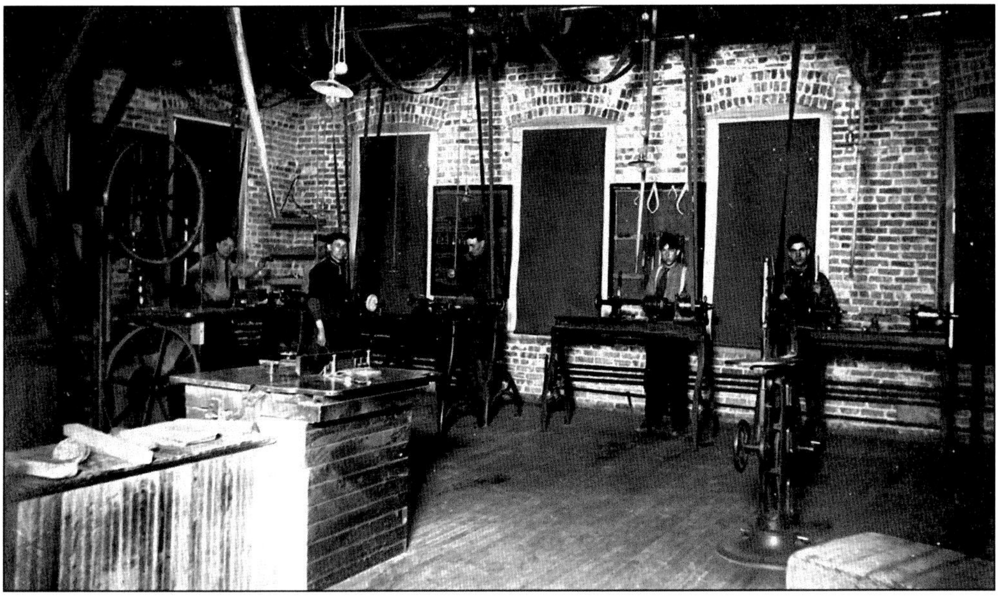

The boys at the Wisconsin School for the Deaf had shop classes in which they learned a trade and also made furniture for the school to utilize. Pictured here are two different wood shops. In the museum located at the Wisconsin School for the Deaf there are some wonderful furniture pieces created by students in the early 1900s. In addition to wood shops, the school also had a cobbler shop where students would learn to make and repair shoes. The school was organized so well that it functioned like a small city.

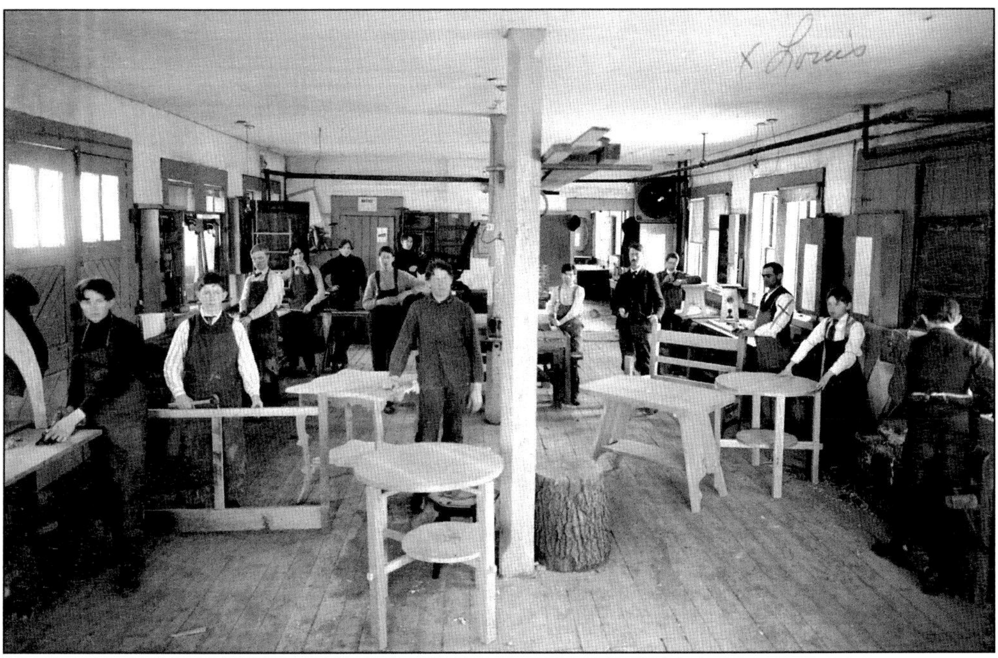

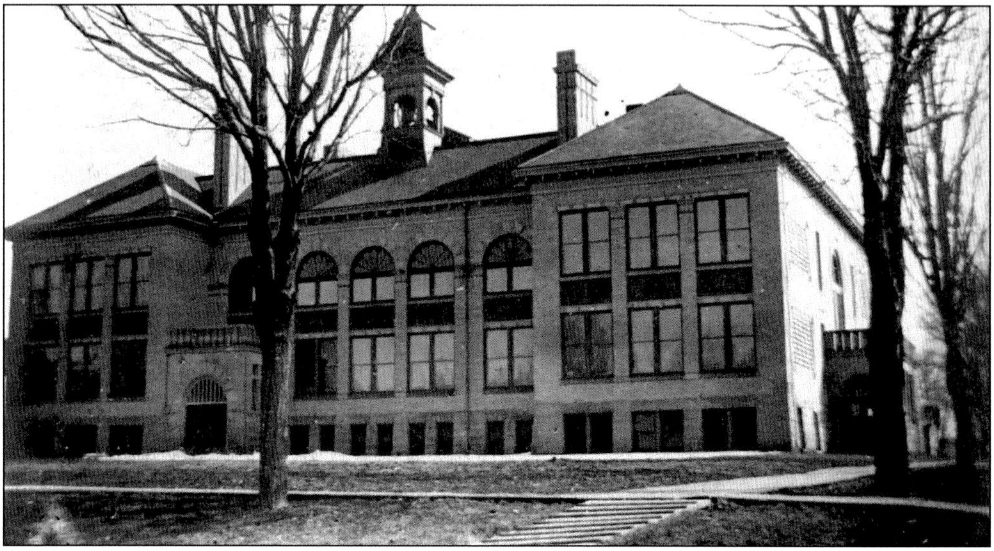

The Delavan Public School, pictured above, was built in 1894 at the cost of $35,000. It was located on the south end of Phoenix Park on the corner of Wisconsin and South Main. The building would serve the children of Delavan for only 10 years before it was destroyed by fire on October 17, 1904. School children were displaced to makeshift classrooms in churches and other buildings around town.

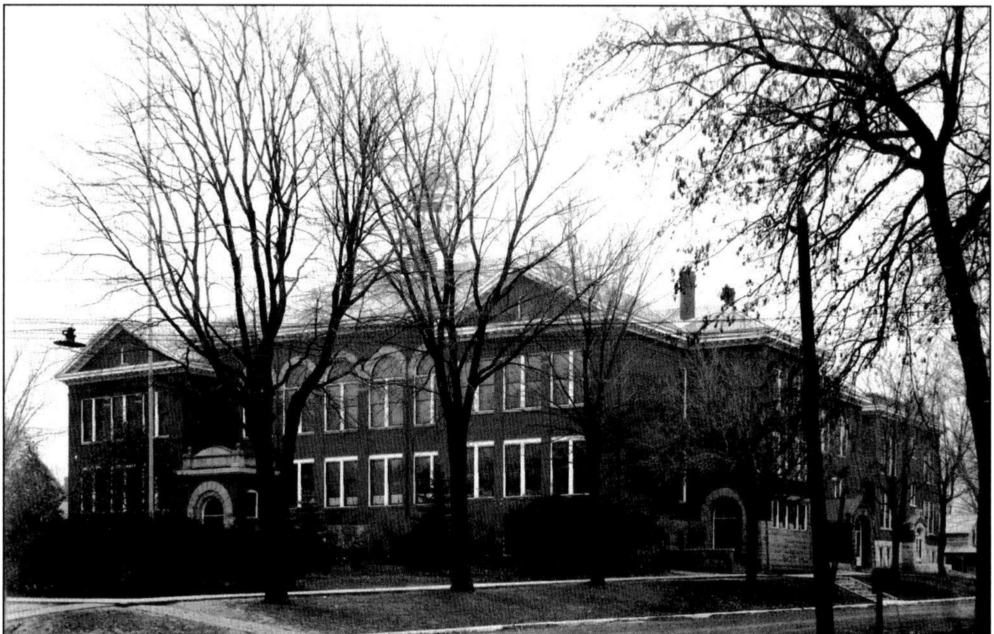

This was the "new school," completed in 1906. This view from the north shows the high school addition that expanded the building in 1924. After the new, separate high school was erected in 1957, the school remained this way until 1967 when the north section of the high school was razed. In 1995, the building was torn down and a senior apartment building replaced it.

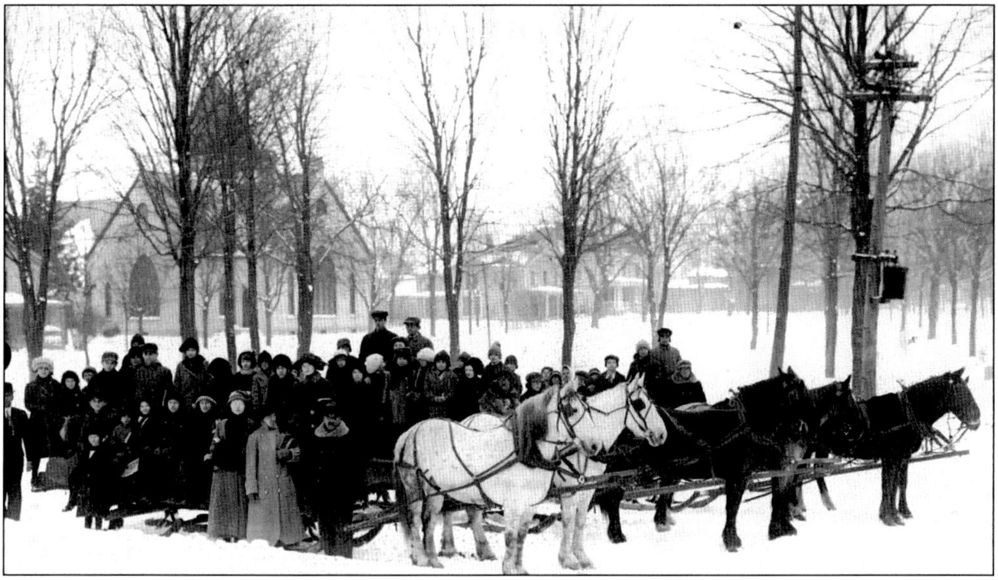

This photograph was taken at Phoenix Park from the public school. The Baptist Church can be seen in the background. It's four o'clock on February 29, 1913, and the buses are ready to take everyone home. Until motorized school buses came into use about 1926, this is how the children got to school.

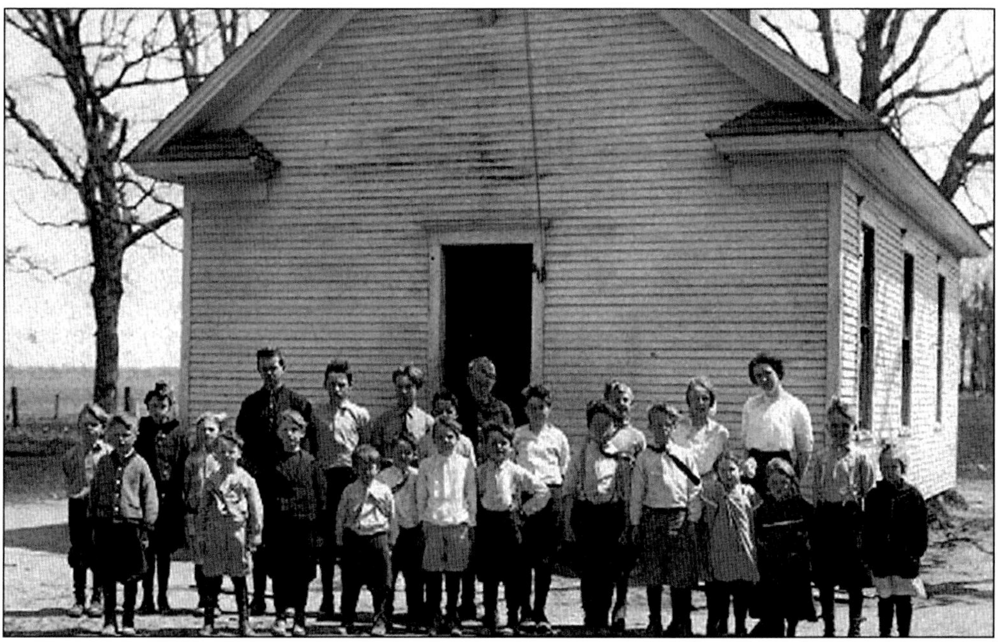

Bailey School was first built in 1852 on South County Trunk F, on land donated by the father of Phoebe Bailey. The original school was moved to North County Trunk F, where it functions today as part of a house. A new school made of brick was built to replace the old. Bailey School held its last classes during the 1975–76 school year. It was later sold to the Delavan Lake Sanitary District.

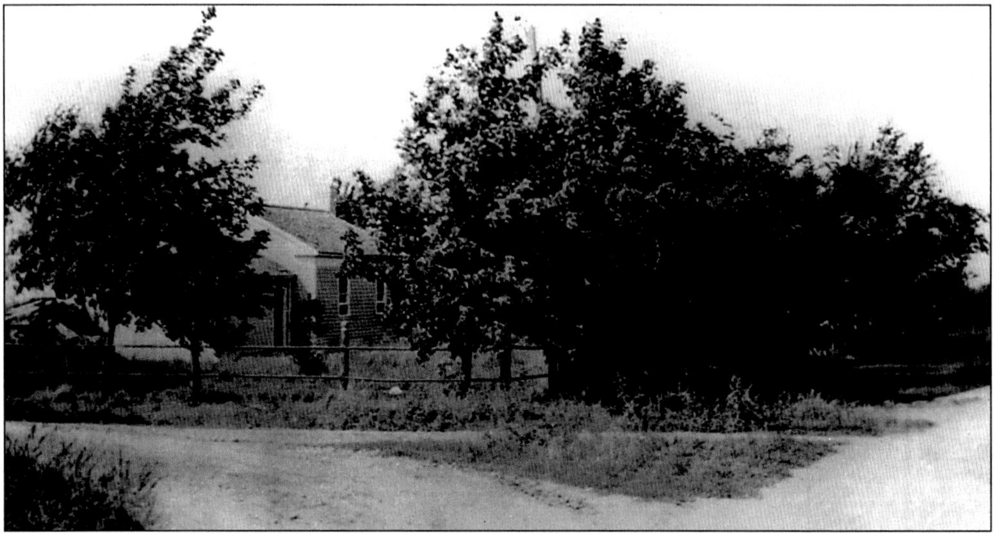

Shadowlawn School was originally called Bangs School and was built as early as 1879. Located on County Trunk F South and Mound Road, it was built on property donated by the Bangs family. This is Shadowlawn School as it looked in 1900. The school underwent several additions over the years until it was closed in 1976 due to decreasing enrollment.

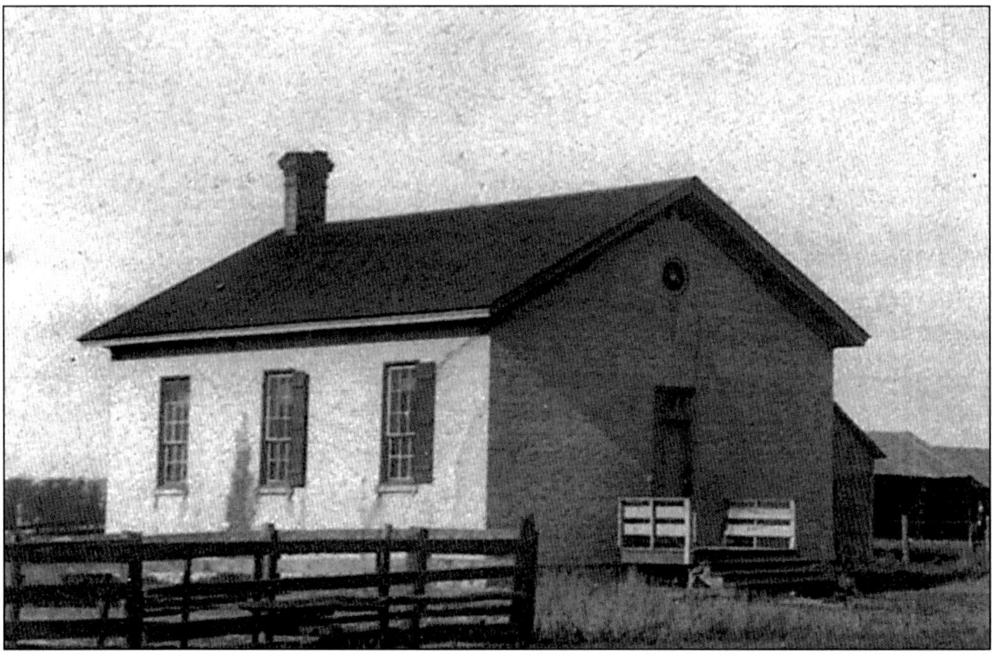

East Delavan School was located at Theater Road near the East Delavan Baptist Church in Delavan Township. The first log schoolhouse was built in 1845 on land donated by the Woodford family, who owned a blacksmith shop and farm nearby. The log school was used until 1870, when it was replaced by a frame building and later, the brick building pictured here.

The present-day Wagon Wheel restaurant was built in 1862 and functioned as a schoolhouse for many years. Pictured above as it looked in 1967, it was called the "Branch School," and located south of the Village of Delavan on the corner of North Shore Drive and County Trunk O. The Branch School served the rural school children from 1862 until 1926. It was later operated as a refreshment stand and filling station, and after Prohibition it became a tavern. It was owned and operated for many years by the Applegate family. Many additions have been added through the years, as seen in the 1935 image below.

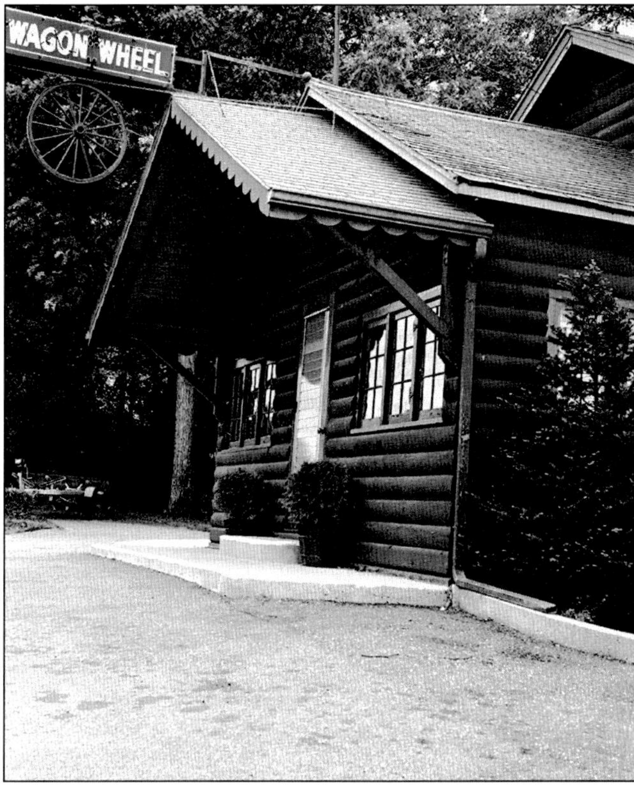

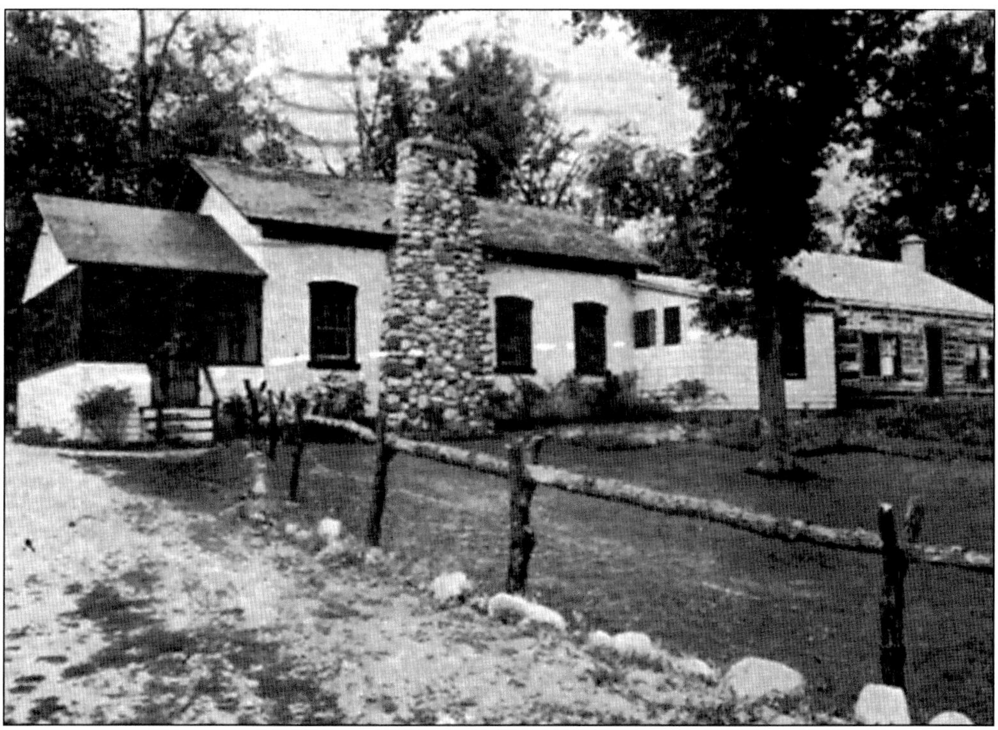

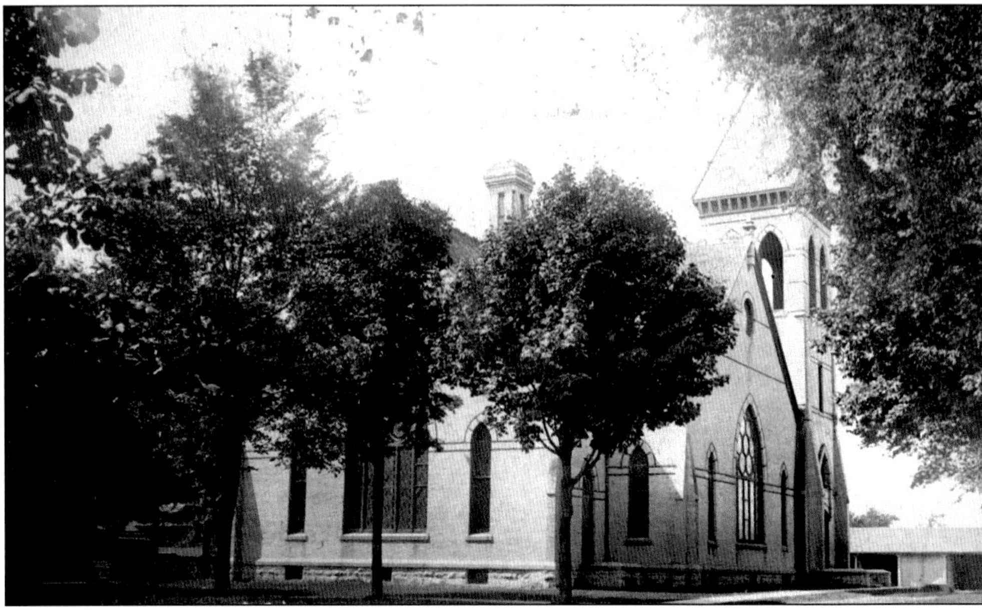

Delavan received its first house of worship when the Baptist Church was built in 1841. It was at this church that the Territory of Wisconsin's first anti-slavery meeting was held in 1842. The church was replaced in 1855 and then again in 1880. The 1880 structure is still standing and is utilized as part of the present-day church pictured here in 1909.

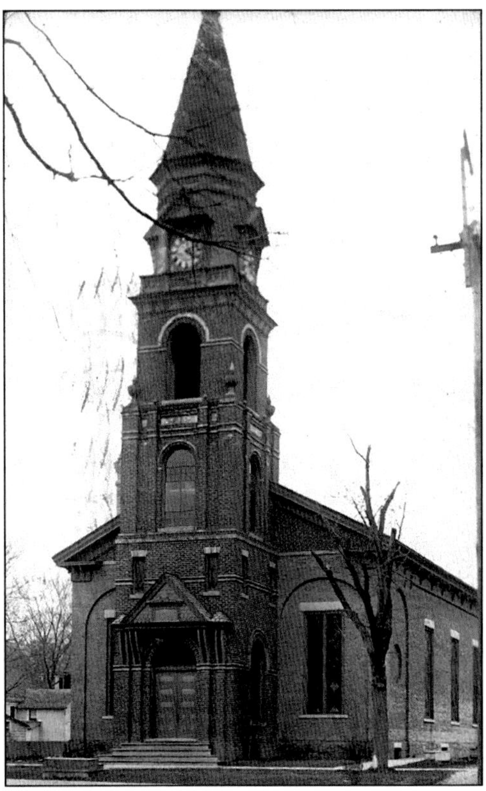

The Congregational Church was organized in 1841, but not until 1844, when its membership rose to 60, did they act on the necessity to erect a church. The location of the original church was slightly west of its present site. In 1856, the new church was dedicated on land purchased from the Phoenix family. Although it has undergone some remodeling over the years, the structure built in 1856 still stands today.

Episcopal services began in Delavan as early as 1843, but it wasn't until 1848 that the group received church status. They built their first church on the south side of Phoenix Park on Wisconsin Street. In 1879, they built their Gothic-style church at 503 East Walworth Avenue. In 1920, the church lost its tall steeple when it was destroyed by fire. The building has undergone several modifications over the years.

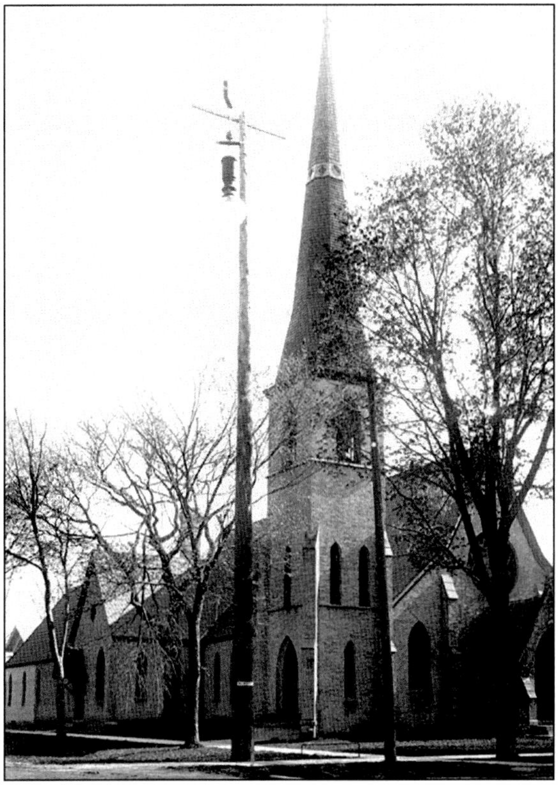

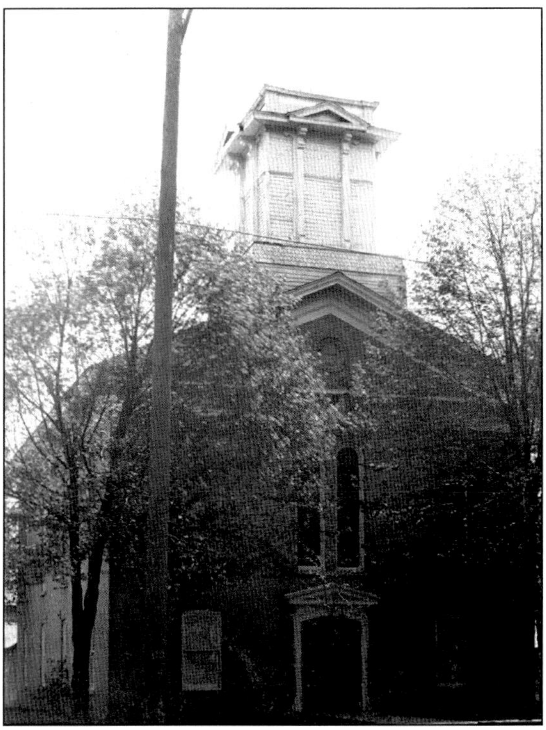

The first Methodist Episcopal Church in Delavan was organized in 1853. In 1854, the trustees of the church received the deed to their current church site as a gift from the estate of Henry Phoenix. After a five-year building campaign, the church was completed in 1864 and located at 213 South Second Street. Additions have been incorporated into the original structure over the years.

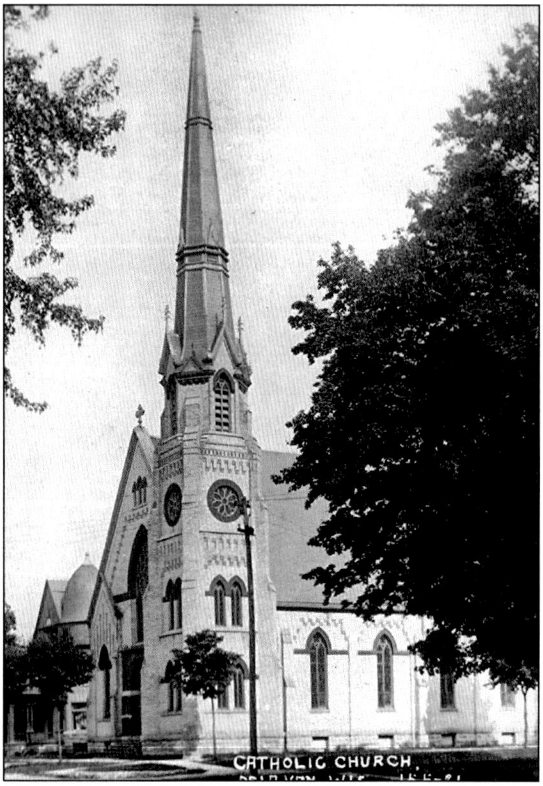

The first Catholic masses in Delavan were not held until 1851. In 1856, a small church was erected at South Fourth and Matthew Street. It was remodeled in 1867, but increasing membership created the necessity for a much bigger church. The first mass at the new brick church was held in the basement in 1895, and the church was dedicated in 1899. The old church was moved out to the Assembly Grounds and used as a residence by Mrs. Adele Barnes.

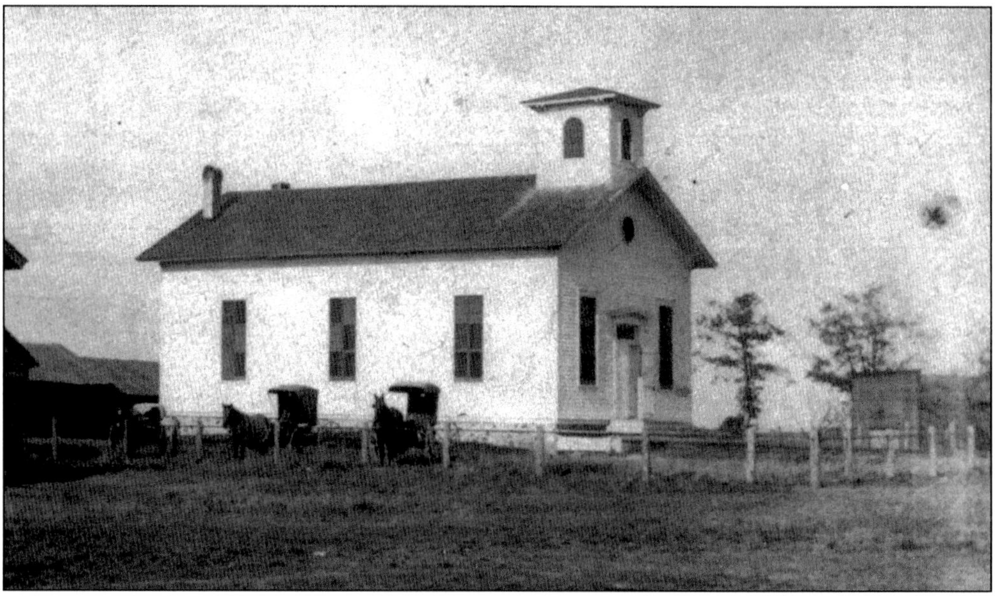

The Delavan and Geneva Baptist Church was organized in 1845 in East Delavan. The first church building in 1848 was built adjacent to where the present church stands today. In 1858, the name of the church was changed to East Delavan Baptist church. By 1868, the church was deteriorating and the need for a new church was apparent. Within a year, a new church was completed. The 1869 structure in this photograph was replaced by the present church in 1972.

Four

"19TH CENTURY CIRCUS CAPITAL OF THE NATION"

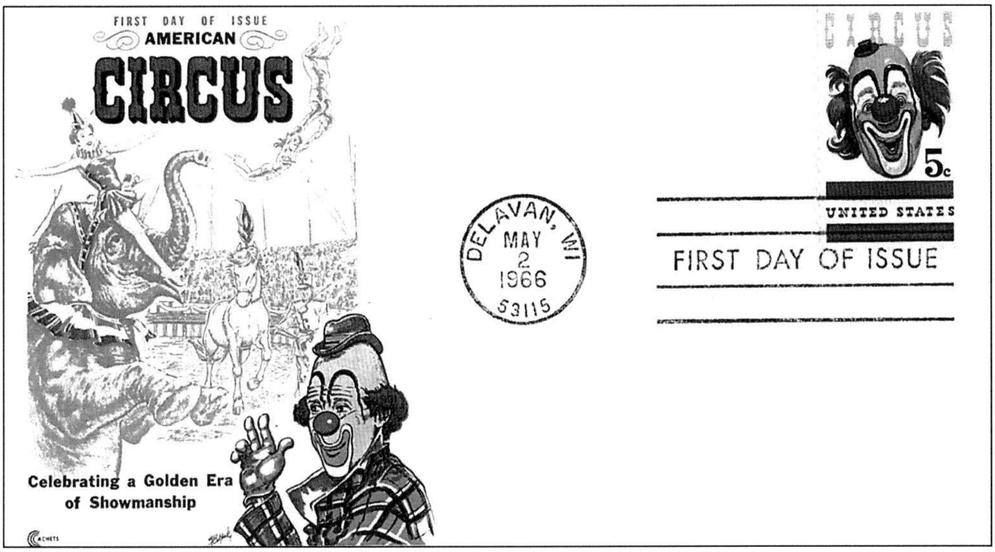

When Jeremiah and Edmund Mabie, owners of the Mabie Brothers U.S. Olympic Circus, saw the beautiful banks of Delavan Lake, lush in its primitive state, they knew immediately that their circus animals would thrive well here throughout the winter. And when it came time to travel, instead of traveling "out west" from New York, they would already be centralized by having winter quarters in Delavan. Other circuses soon followed.

Although Somers, New York, is considered by some to be the birthplace of the American circus, 28 circuses called Delavan home between 1847 and 1894. In 1966, these two towns would battle over who was entitled to issue the first day cancellation for the American Circus Commemorative Stamp. That battle was eventually settled when Somers, the earlier birthplace, won the privilege of unveiling the stamp and also re-canceled covers flown in from Delavan, the official site. Delavan would come to be known as the "19th Century Circus Capitol of the Nation."

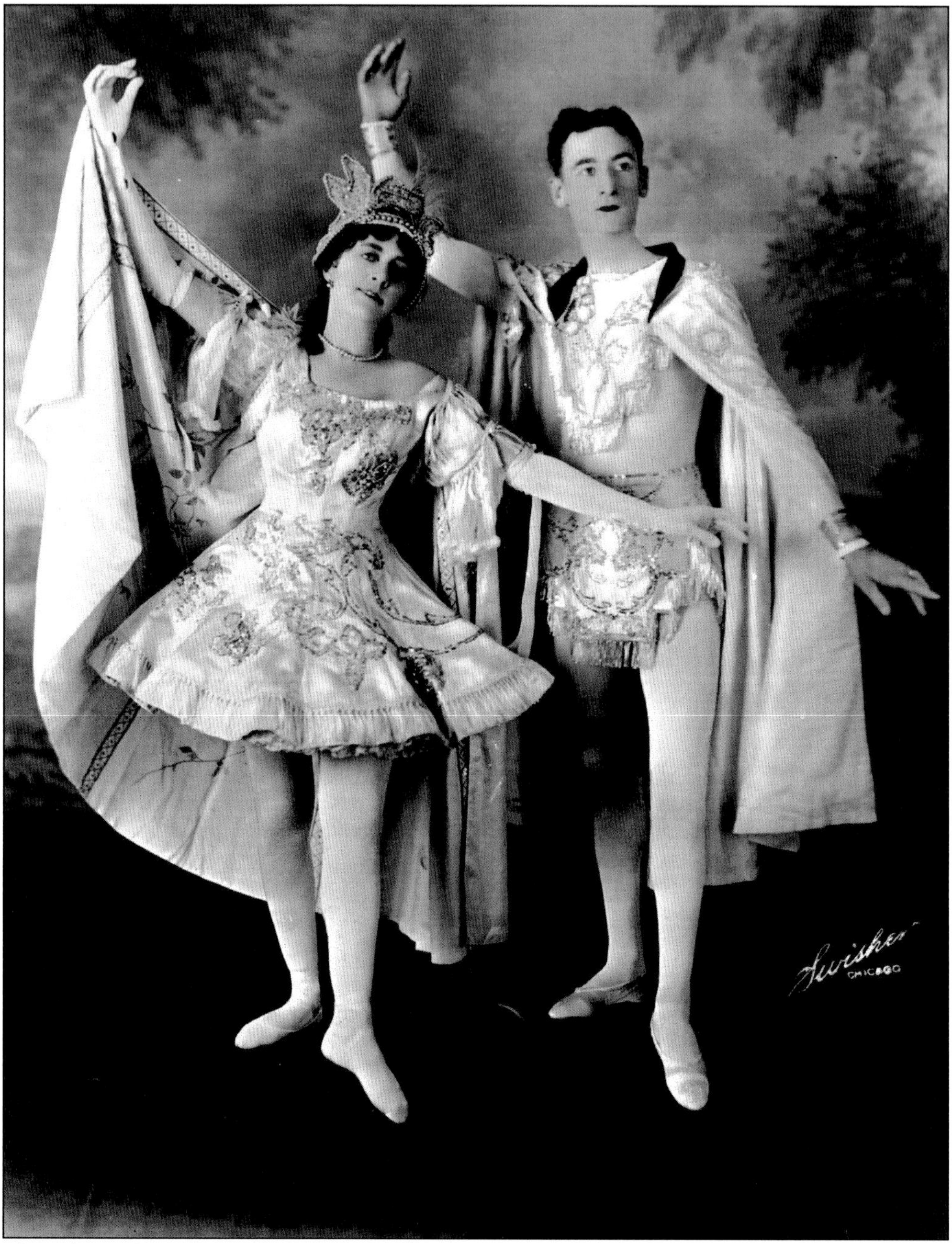

The John and Honora Holland family came to town with the Mabie Brothers Circus, but made Delavan their home for a few generations. The grandson of John and Honora Holland, George E. and his wife, Rose Dockrill Holland, were noted equestrians whose long careers lasted over 40 years, and who called Delavan their home during their off-season. The Holland family circus reign would last 109 years and span three generations. The Holland family was inducted into the International Circus Hall of Fame in 1980. This is a 1912 publicity photo of Rose Dockrill and her husband George E. Holland.

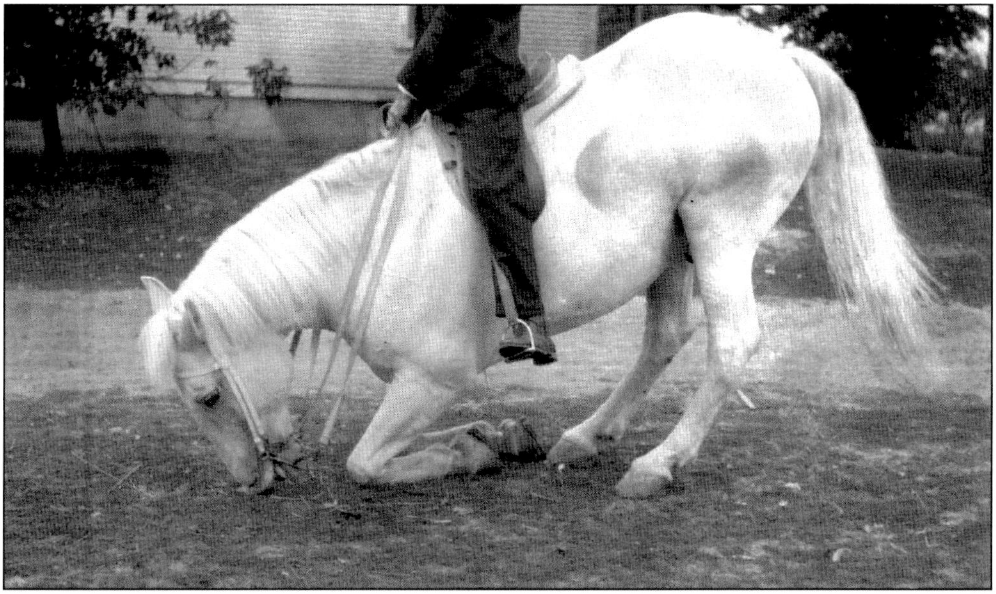

The Holland's trick horse Dolly was part of the equestrian act in the Holland Family's circus. Not only was she an important part of the equestrian show, she was also a movie star. Dolly had a part in the 1932 movie *Polly of the Circus*, which starred Marion Davies and Clark Gable.

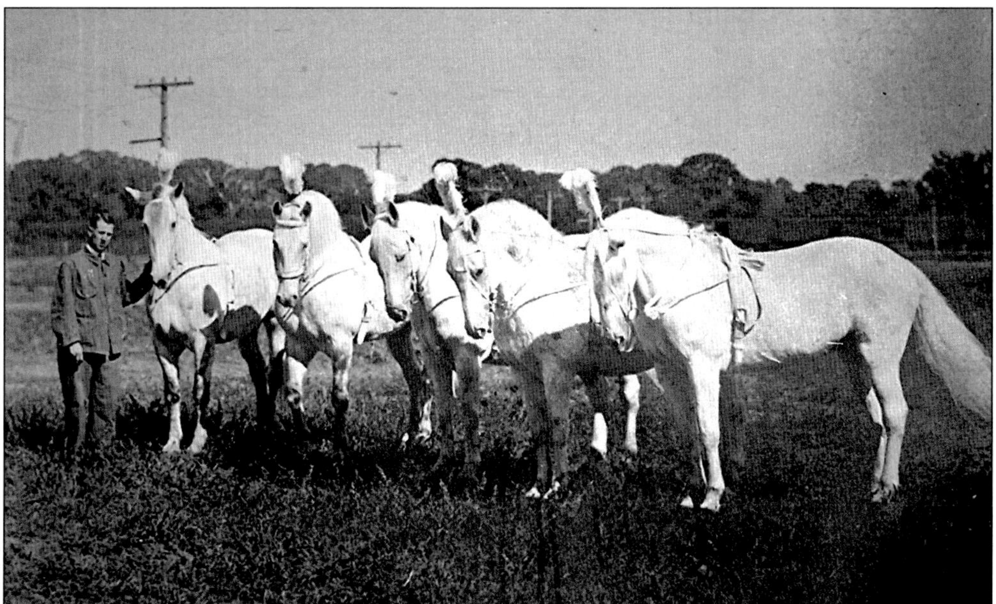

Shown here are the Holland Horses in 1918. These horses were utilized in George and Rose Dockrill Holland's exciting equestrian act. The Hollands raised and trained their horses on their farm on the north shore of Delavan Lake, and then later at North Terrace Street, just outside the city limits.

The GREAT VAN AMBURGH SHOW.

Sturtevant, Holland & Co., Proprs.

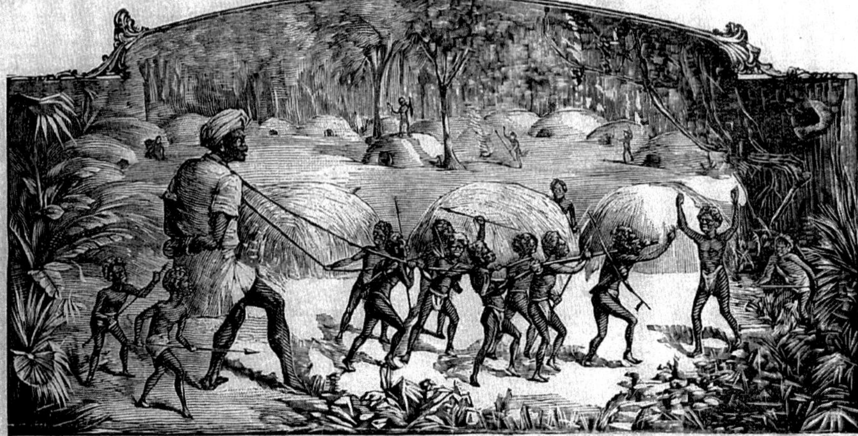

Circus, Museum, Menagerie and Congress of Wonders

The only African Pigmies in America. The curious historical Wambuti Dwarfs, the strange people now exciting the wonder of the civilized world.

Golden Menagerie of Savage Beasts. A school of education for the masses. Birds of Beautiful Tropical Plumage. Monkies, Apes, etc., Man's Only Imitators.

The World's Greatest Equestrienne, Miss Julia Lowande.

W. C. Rollins, Daring Hurdle Rider. Edward C. Shipp, Bounding Jockey and 6-Horse Rider.

TRIPLE CIRCUS. ELEVATED STAGES.

The Adair Family, Jugglers, Aerialists, Equilibrists, Rope Walkers.

The Jenier Family, French Trapeze, Bar, Perch and Wire Performers.

The Two Graces—Without an Equal—Premier Contortionists.

A. C. Gilmore, J. W. Dempsey, Gracie Dempsey, Lena Grace, C. R. Ollin, Watson Bros.. John Mix, Ada Brown, Capt. Innery, Albert Jenier, Clara Adair and others.

25 EMINENT MUSICIANS, 25. 20 TUMBLERS, 20.

18 EDUCATED ANIMALS, 18. 5 FUNNY CLOWNS, 5.

A Vast Amusement Aggregation for the Masses. The People's Greatest Educators. The Distinction of Honesty and Morality Maintained. No Games of Chance. Patrons Protected.

Grand Free Street Parade at Noon.

After which the Free Outside Show will be given. Will exhibit at

Delavan, Saturday May 9th

Delavan native James B. Sturtevant became partners with E.G. Holland in the 1891 Sturtevant and Holland's Van Amburgh Circus. Prior to this, Sturtevant was the treasurer with the Holland, Bowman, and McLaughlin's United Circus. He was from a prominent Delavan family, owned a local grocery store for several years, and served a year on the city council. Edward Holland was born into circus life in Delavan Township in 1853. His parents were performers in the Mabie Bros. Circus. His circus career would span 67 years as a performer, manager, and agent. This 1891 advertisement shows the attraction of the "Great Van Amburgh Show, Sturtevant, Holland & Co., Proprietors," which the Delavan Republican gave rave reviews to, claiming "Delavan still holds its own as Circus Town of the West." This was one of the many circuses that had its winter quarters in Delavan.

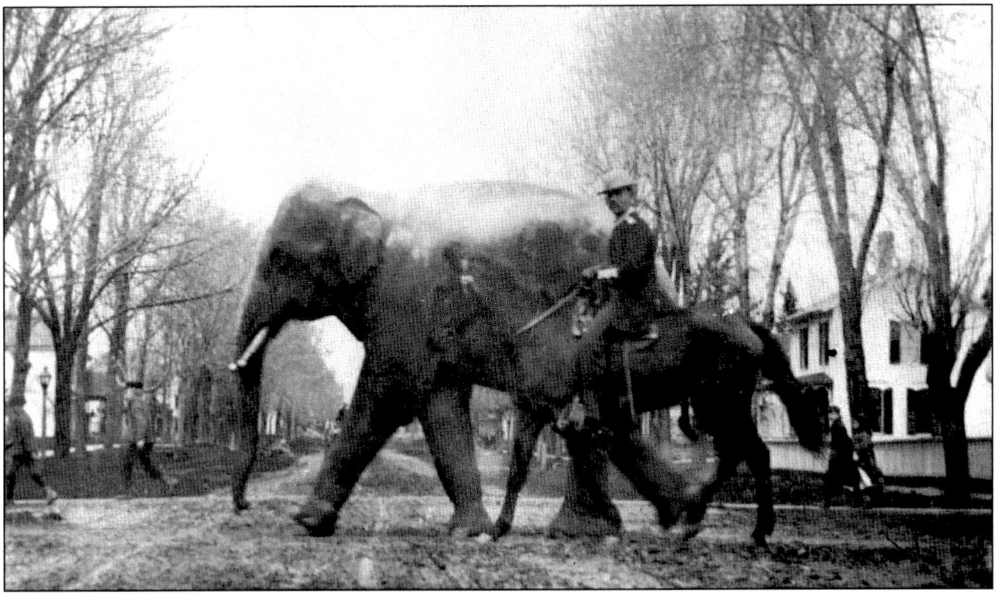

In the 1890s, it was not uncommon to see elephants and other circus animals strolling down the street. When the circus people filled the town, Delavan was referred to as a wild place, and was occasionally a temporary home some unsavory characters. Pictured here is Albert, a performing elephant with the Holland-Gormley Circus, taking a walk through Delavan under the close supervision of his trainer in 1899.

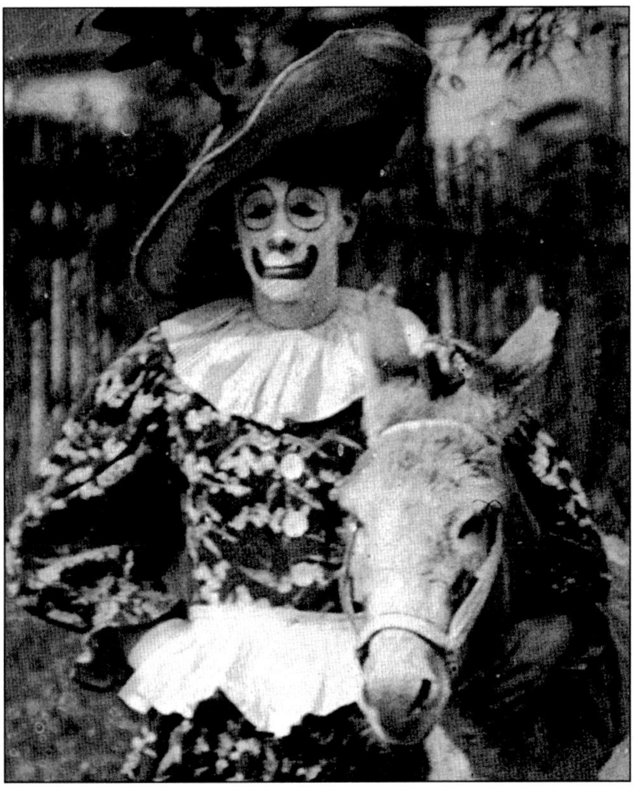

Gil Holland was from the third generation of the famed Holland circus family. He was the son of George F. and Kate Holloway Holland. As Gil and his brothers started getting older, their parents decided to put together a family show and tour. Gil was about 19 when he retired from the circus. He later took a job with the city of Biloxi, Mississippi. Gil is photographed here about 1909 in his clown attire.

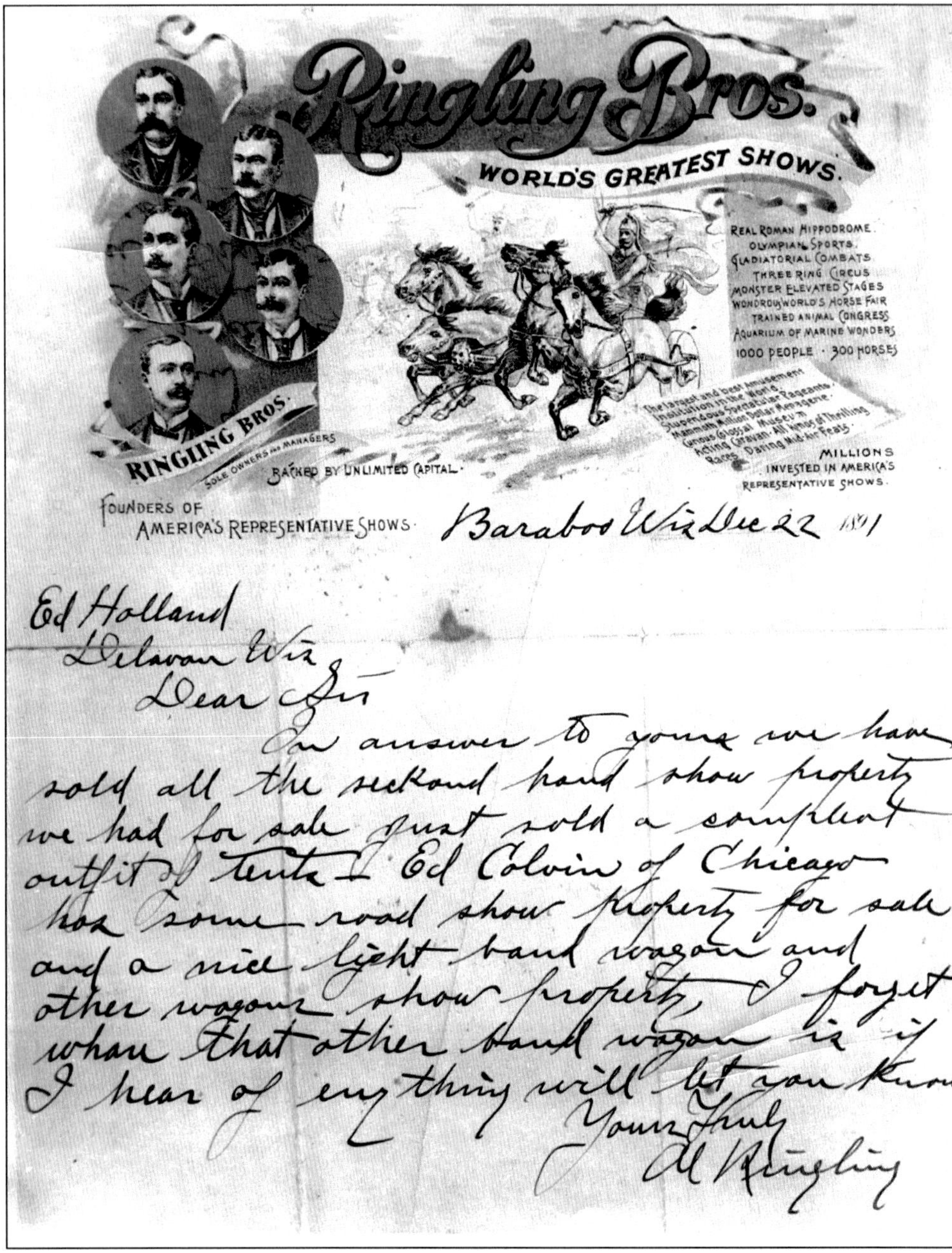
Ringling Bros.
WORLD'S GREATEST SHOWS.
REAL ROMAN HIPPODROME. OLYMPIAN SPORTS. GLADIATORIAL COMBATS. THREE RING CIRCUS. MONSTER ELEVATED STAGES. WONDROUS WORLD'S HORSE FAIR. TRAINED ANIMAL CONGRESS. AQUARIUM OF MARINE WONDERS. 1000 PEOPLE · 300 HORSES
RINGLING BROS. SOLE OWNERS AND MANAGERS
BACKED BY UNLIMITED CAPITAL.
MILLIONS INVESTED IN AMERICA'S REPRESENTATIVE SHOWS.
FOUNDERS OF AMERICA'S REPRESENTATIVE SHOWS.

Baraboo Wiz Dec 22 1891

Ed Holland
Delavan Wiz
Dear Sir
In answer to yours we have sold all the seckond hand show property we had for sale just sold a compleat outfit of tents Ed Colvin of Chicago has some road show property for sale and a nice light band wagon and other wagons show property I forget whare that other band wagon is if I hear of enything will let you know
Yours Truly
Al Ringling

This letter is from Al Ringling of Ringling Bros. Circus in response to a letter he received from Ed Holland. Dated December 22, 1891, from Baraboo, Wisconsin, the winter quarters of the Ringling Circus, Ringling explains that he has no spare second-hand show property for sale. Ringling further encourages him to contact Ed Colvin in Chicago, who has some items to sell. Edward Holland made his circus debut in 1857 with his parents John and Honora Holland at the age of four. He performed as an acrobat rider for 28 years before organizing the Holland-MacMahon Circus in Delavan. He would remain active in the circus until he retired in 1924. Prior to his retirement, he took a short break of about 12 years to help his brother George build the Hollandale Hotel, and hold a position in law enforcement in the village of Delavan.

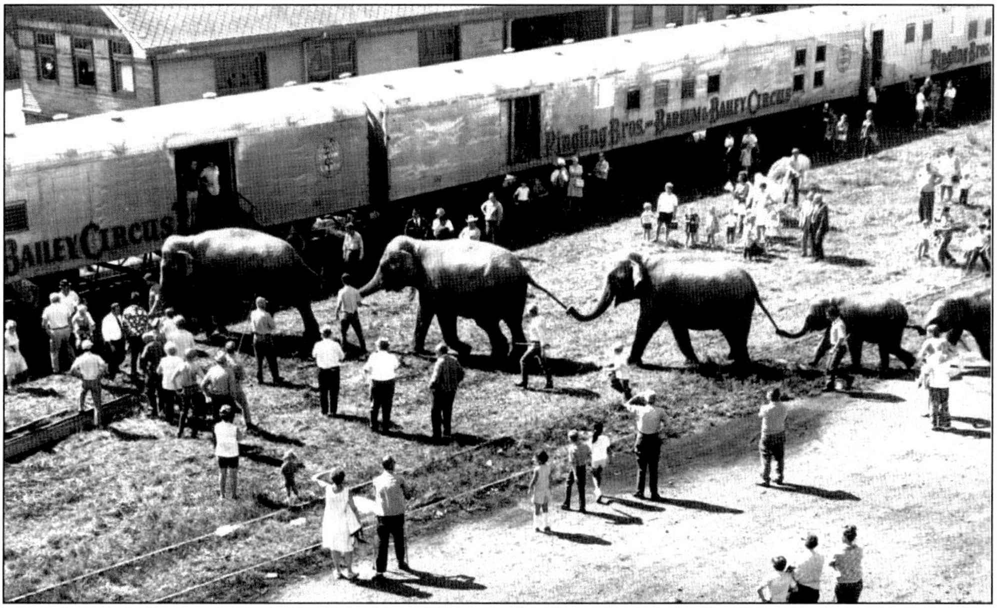

On September 8, 1970, the Ringling Bros. Barnum & Bailey Circus stopped in Delavan as part of its centennial tour. A small crowd begins to gather to watch the elephants load back onto the circus train. It was 100 years ago that the P.T. Barnum Circus was conceived and organized in Delavan by William Coup and Dan Castello. In 1871, the P.T. Barnum Circus left from the same depot for Brooklyn, New York, where it would perform its first show. This historical marker is located in the municipal parking lot at the corner of Seventh and Wisconsin, erected in 2000 to commemorate this event.

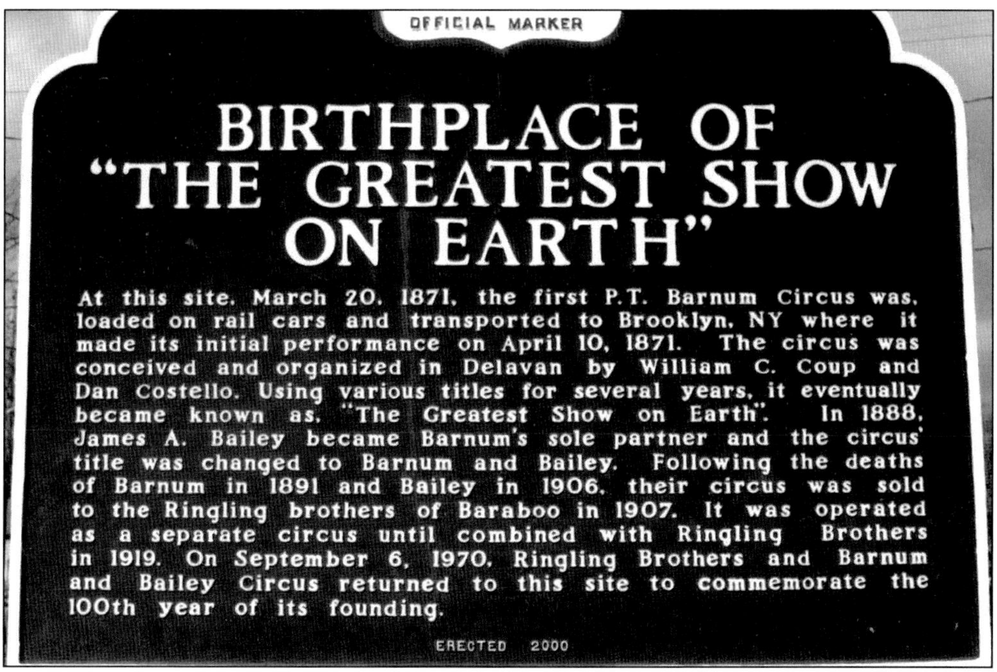

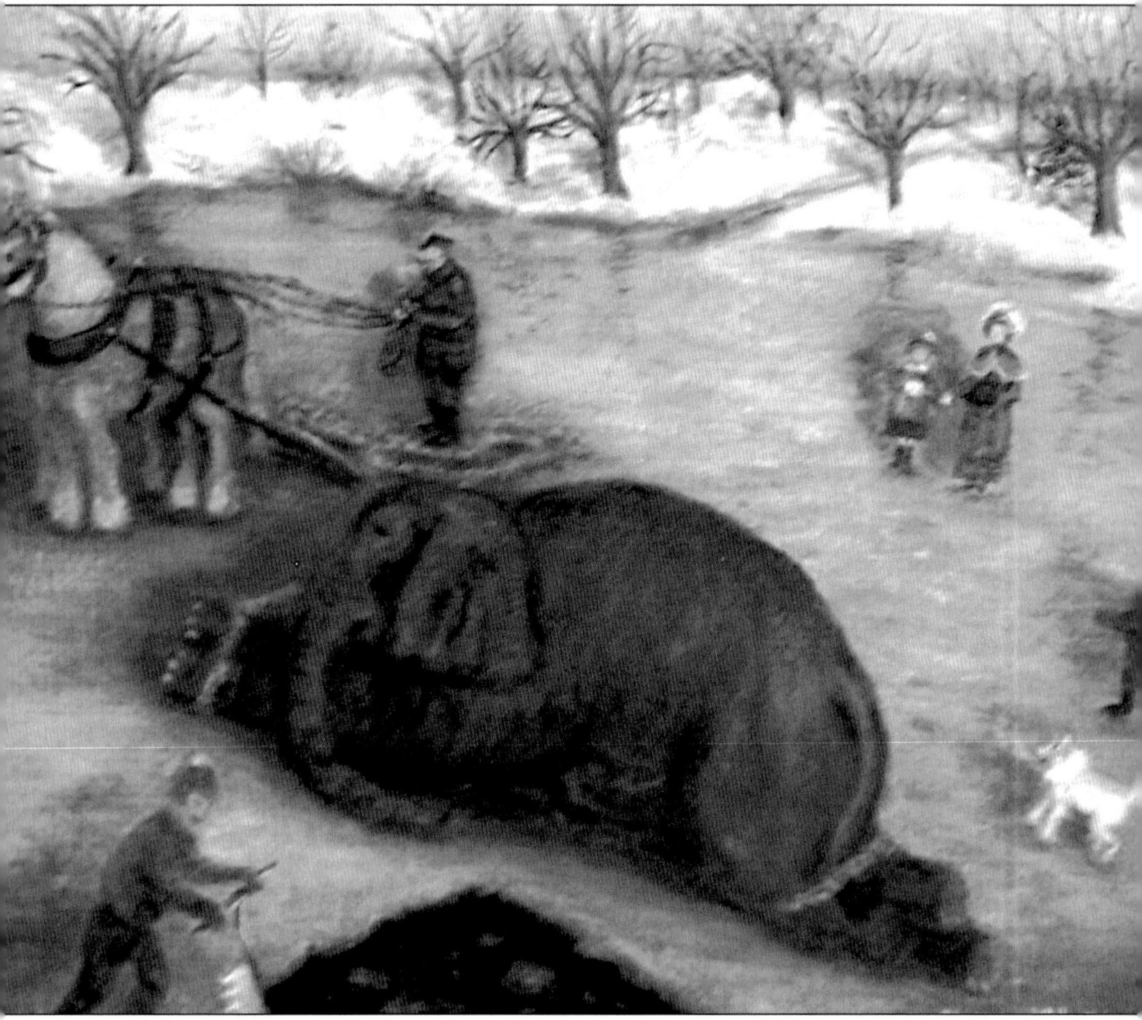

Depicted here in a painting by local artist Eleanor Williams is the burial of Juliet. Juliet, a very docile elephant, was brought over from Ceylon in 1854 and pulled a bandwagon in the Mabie Bros. Street parade, as well as performed in the ring. It was 1863 when she became ill. She developed a bowel obstruction and nothing could be done to save poor Juliet. She expired in February of 1864 at the Mabie Bros. Winter Circus headquarters in Delavan. The ground was frozen solid, so a traditional burial was not an option. Instead, a hole was cut into the ice, and Juliet's lifeless form was weighted down and deposited into the dark cold waters of Delavan Lake, making this her final resting place.

In 1948, Delavan was the site of the Wisconsin Circus Centennial featuring the Cole Bros. Circus. During this celebration, the Cole Bros. Circus gave two performances and a captivating street parade. This celebration drew over 25,000 people to Delavan, including the governor of Wisconsin, Oscar Rennebohm. A commemorative ceremony was held at W.C. Coup's gravesite, in which a wreath was laid on Coup's grave by the Cole Bros. Circus. The Cole Bros. steam calliope wagon, America, is pictured here during the July 21, 1948 festivities.

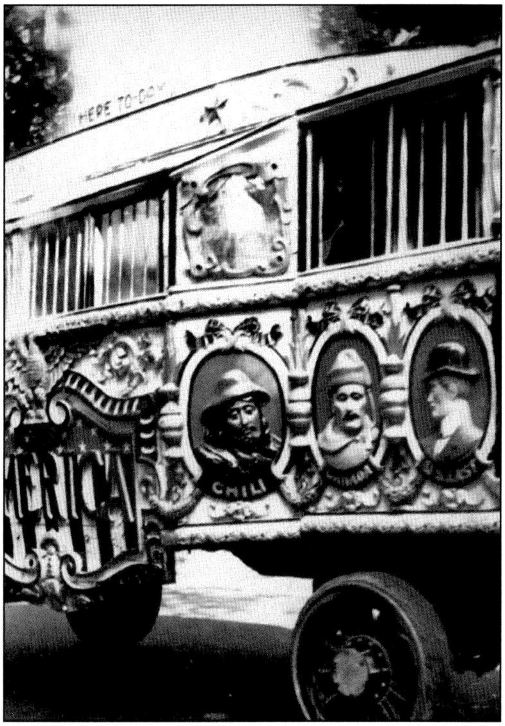

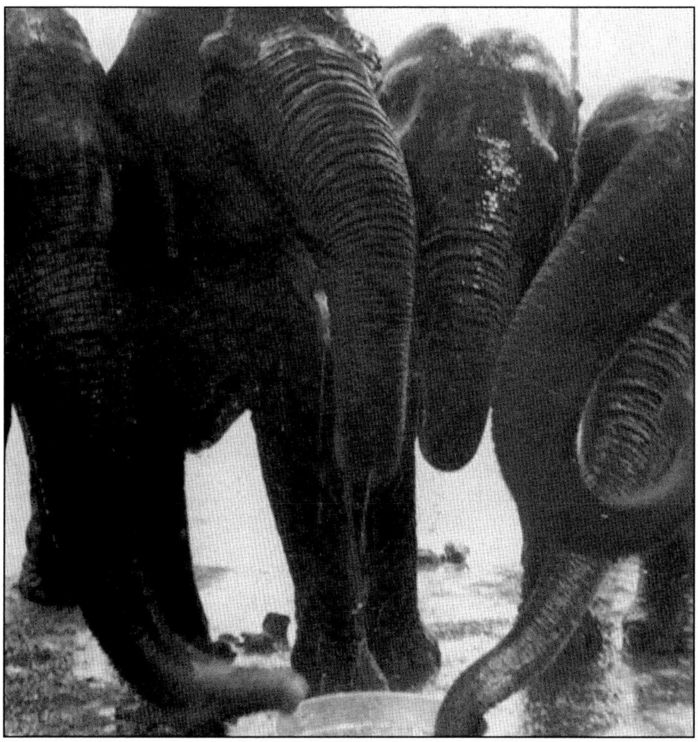

These Cole Brothers Circus elephants prepare to entertain children by taking water into their trunks and spraying it into the air during a 1948 performance in Delavan. The job of the elephant in the circus has always been one of entertainer and laborer. Audiences watch the elephant perform tricks in the ring, but they are also used to pull wagons and set-up tents, feats that would take many men to accomplish.

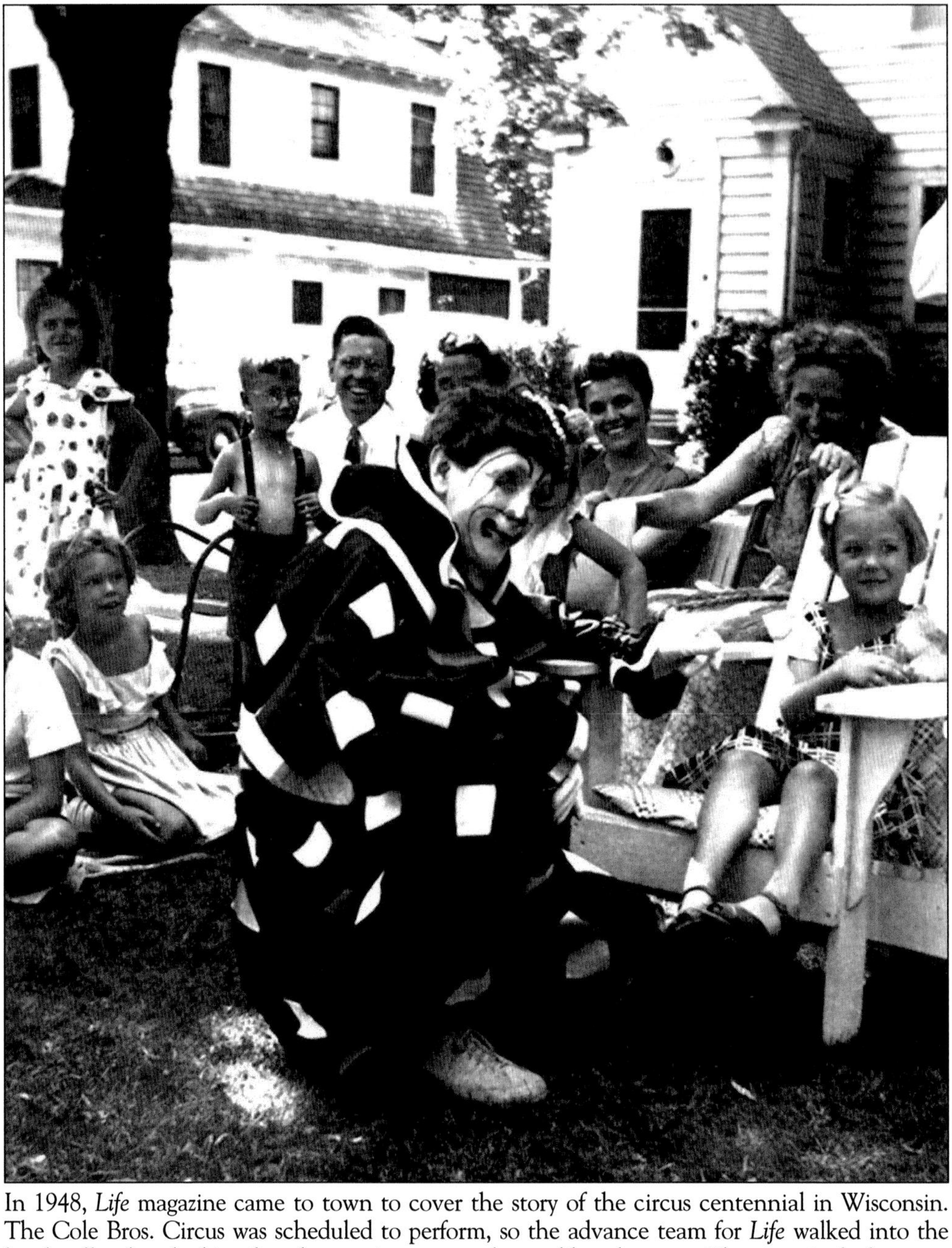

In 1948, *Life* magazine came to town to cover the story of the circus centennial in Wisconsin. The Cole Bros. Circus was scheduled to perform, so the advance team for *Life* walked into the local coffee shop looking for a human interest angle to add to the story. They inquired of patrons if there were any sick children in town and someone said the little Patterson girl had rheumatic fever. This was the kind of story they were searching for. But their hopes were dashed when Dr. Werbel said Linda Patterson was too sick to ride in the circus and be queen for the day. The Cole Bros. Circus heard about Linda, and on there way to the circus site, the procession stopped in front of her house on Racine Street and held a private performance. Pictured here with the Patterson family and friends are Linda Patterson, seated, and the Cole Brothers Circus clown "Bozo."

Five

Delavan's Art Culture

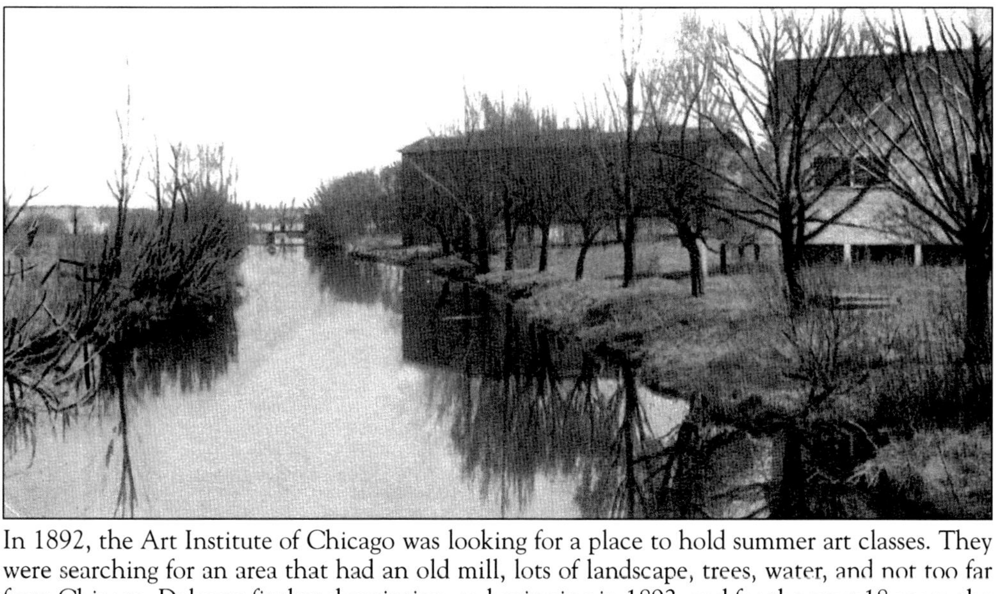

In 1892, the Art Institute of Chicago was looking for a place to hold summer art classes. They were searching for an area that had an old mill, lots of landscape, trees, water, and not too far from Chicago. Delavan fit that description, so beginning in 1892, and for the next 18 years, the Art Institute of Chicago held summer classes in Delavan each July. The artists with their easels set up, busily painting on their canvases was a lovely sight. So lovely in fact, the sight of the artists began to draw visitors to Delavan to watch the painters create their masterpieces. The village council quickly realized the summer art school was impacting Delavan's economy, and appropriated funds for an art studio to be built on the channel between the Mill Pond and Lake Comus. Several prominent artists also had studios here, including Adolph Robert Shulz, Ada Walter Shulz, William Thorne, Frank Dudley, and Frank Phoenix.

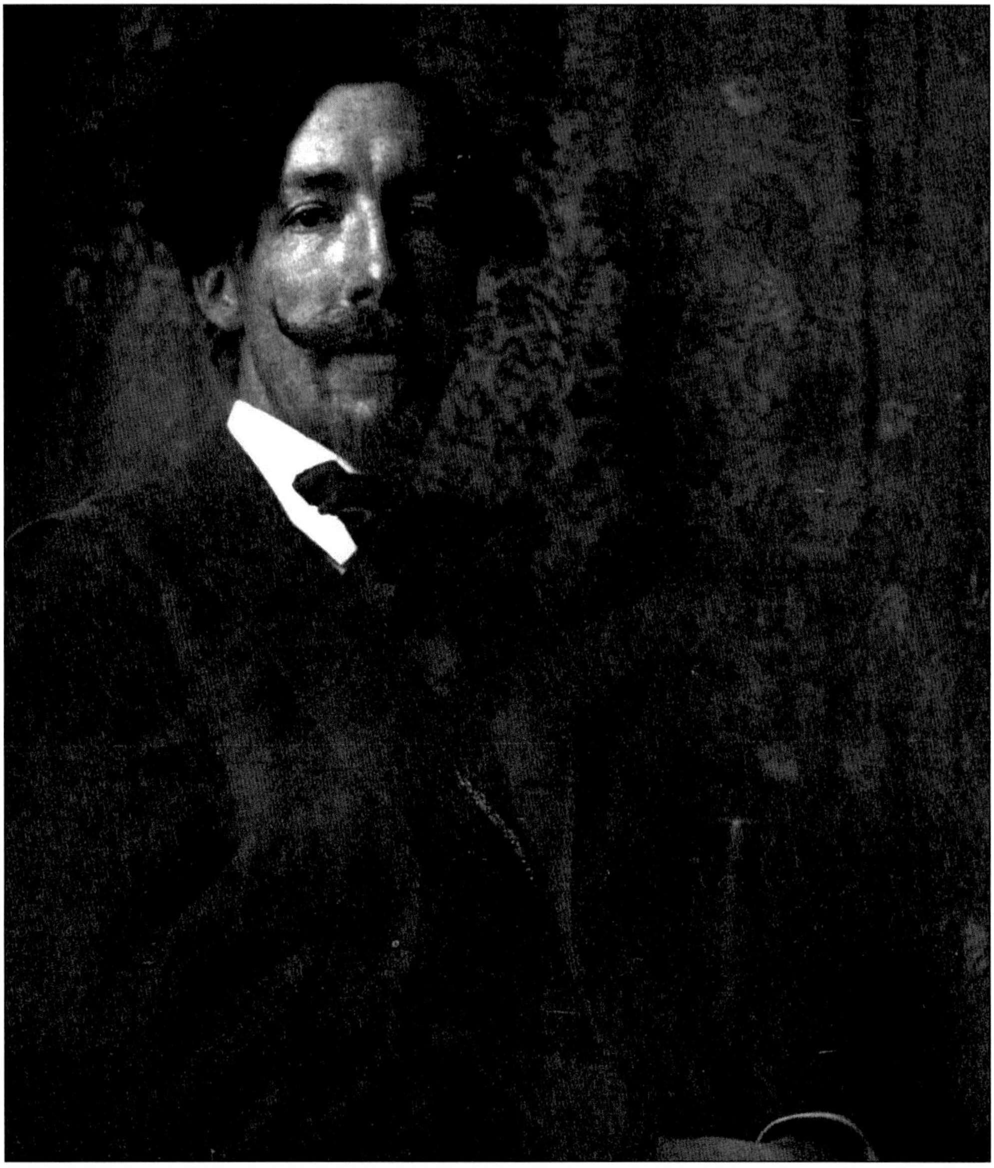

Adolph Robert Shulz (1869–1963) was born in Delavan and took art lessons with Albert McCoy, a local art teacher, who suggested he further his studies at the Art Institute of Chicago. He studied in Chicago for two years, followed by one year at the New York Art League, three years in Paris, and then Munich. Shulz married Ada Walter in 1894, an artist whom he'd met while she attended the summer art classes in Delavan. The couple set up a home and studio in Delavan at 58 East Walworth Avenue. Shulz was primarily a landscape painter, but did some portraiture. In 1900, he discovered the unspoiled beauty of Brown County, Indiana, and started spending summers there, painting. Shulz was very disappointed with cows in Delavan invading landscape he was trying to paint. He and Ada would move to Indiana permanently after the death of their only child in 1918. They divorced in 1927 and Shulz married another artist, Alberta Rehm. Shulz is largely responsible for Nashville, Brown County, Indiana's, establishment as an art colony.

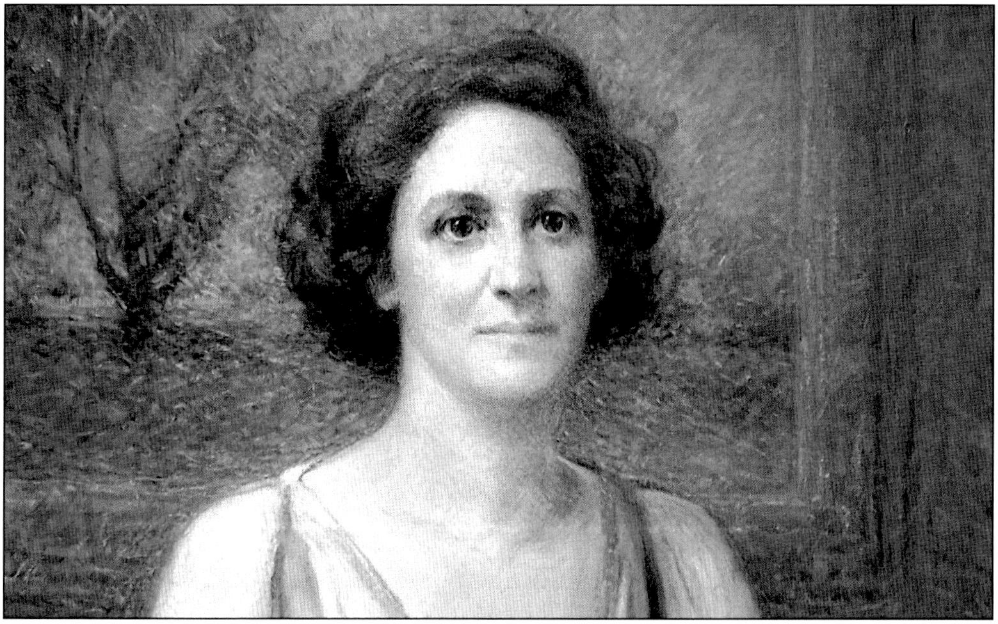

Above is a portrait by Adolph Shulz of his second wife, Alberta Rehm Shulz. Although he was better known for his landscape, on occasion he would do a portrait. He received many awards for his paintings and today they command a good price. In later years, Shulz and his wife Alberta wintered in Sarasota, Florida, still relatively undiscovered in its lush vegetative state and very appealing for this landscape artist. He continued to paint and stayed in touch with several friends in Delavan until his death in 1963. This portrait is in the permanent collection of the Aram Public Library. The Shulz landscape is in a private collection.

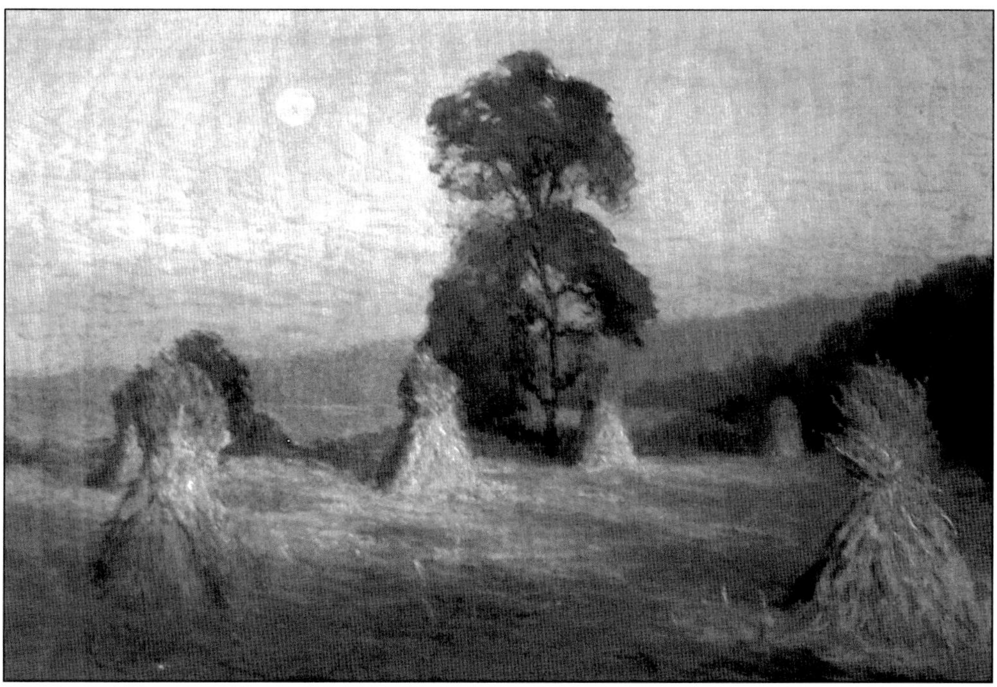

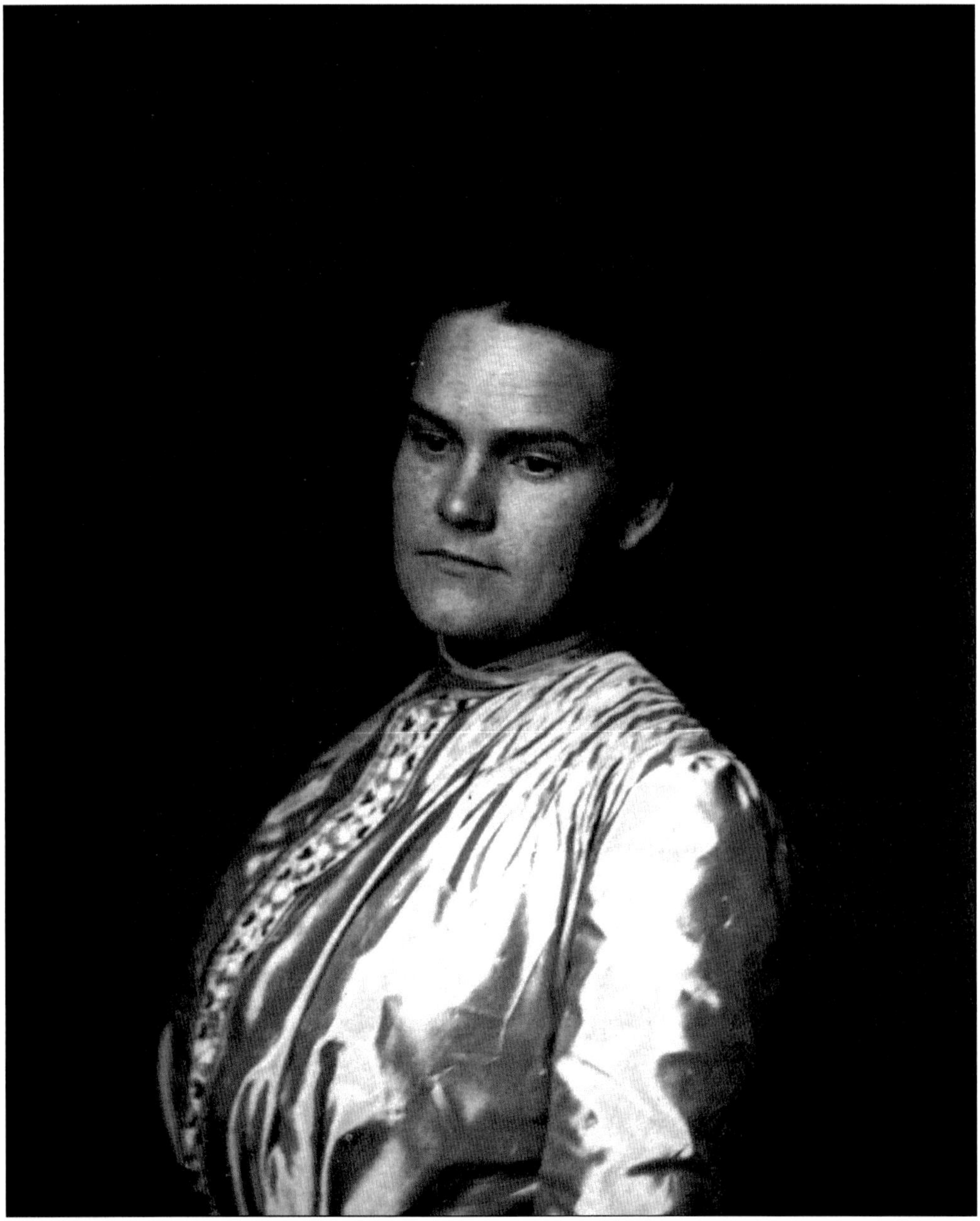

Ada Walter Shulz (1870–1928) was born in Terre Haute, Indiana. She studied at the Art Institute of Chicago, where she met her future husband, Adolph Shulz, while taking summer classes in Delavan. After the two married, they studied together in Paris and Munich before returning to their home in Delavan. Ada's paintings focused on mothers, children, and animals, and assorted combinations of the three. While living in Delavan, Ada gave birth to a son, Walter, and while raising him didn't do much painting. As he grew older she began painting again. Her son would enlist in the military and fight in World War I, but sadly die of diphtheria during the occupation. The death of their son put a strain on the marriage, and they divorced in1927. One week after the divorce, Ada was diagnosed with cancer and died six weeks later. Her remains were brought back to Delavan and buried next to her son at Spring Grove Cemetery.

Ada Walter Shulz won numerous awards for her paintings and some were featured on magazine covers such as *Women's Home Companion and Literary Digest*. Her "Mother and Child" won the 1917 Chicago Municipal Art League Prize. The selling price of Ada's paintings continue to increase very well. This is a beautiful example of her work. This painting is part of the permanent collection of the Aram Public Library.

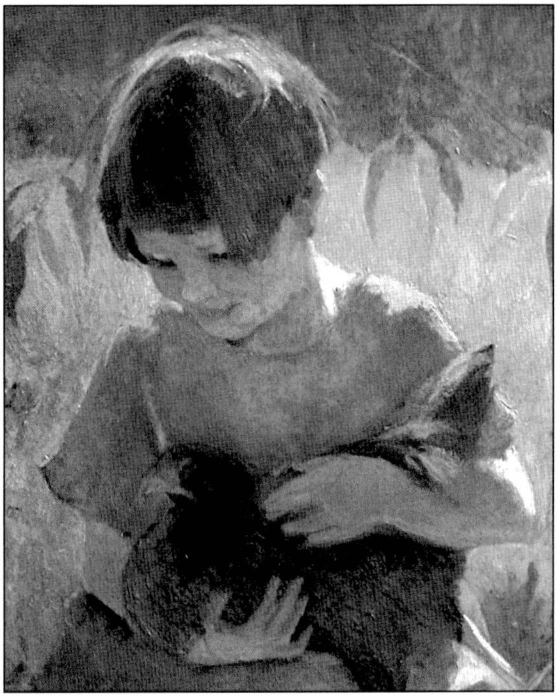

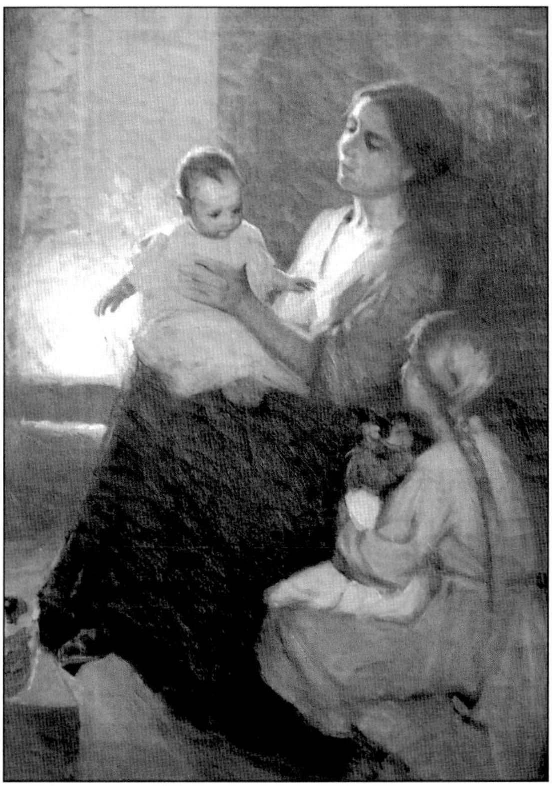

Ada was well-loved in her community while living in Nashville, Indiana. Where all the other Brown County artists were interested only in landscapes, Ada was more interested in people. She is remembered as a gentle lady who loved children. If she saw a child she wanted to paint, she would follow them home and ask their parent's permission. This painting is in the permanent collection of the Aram Public Library.

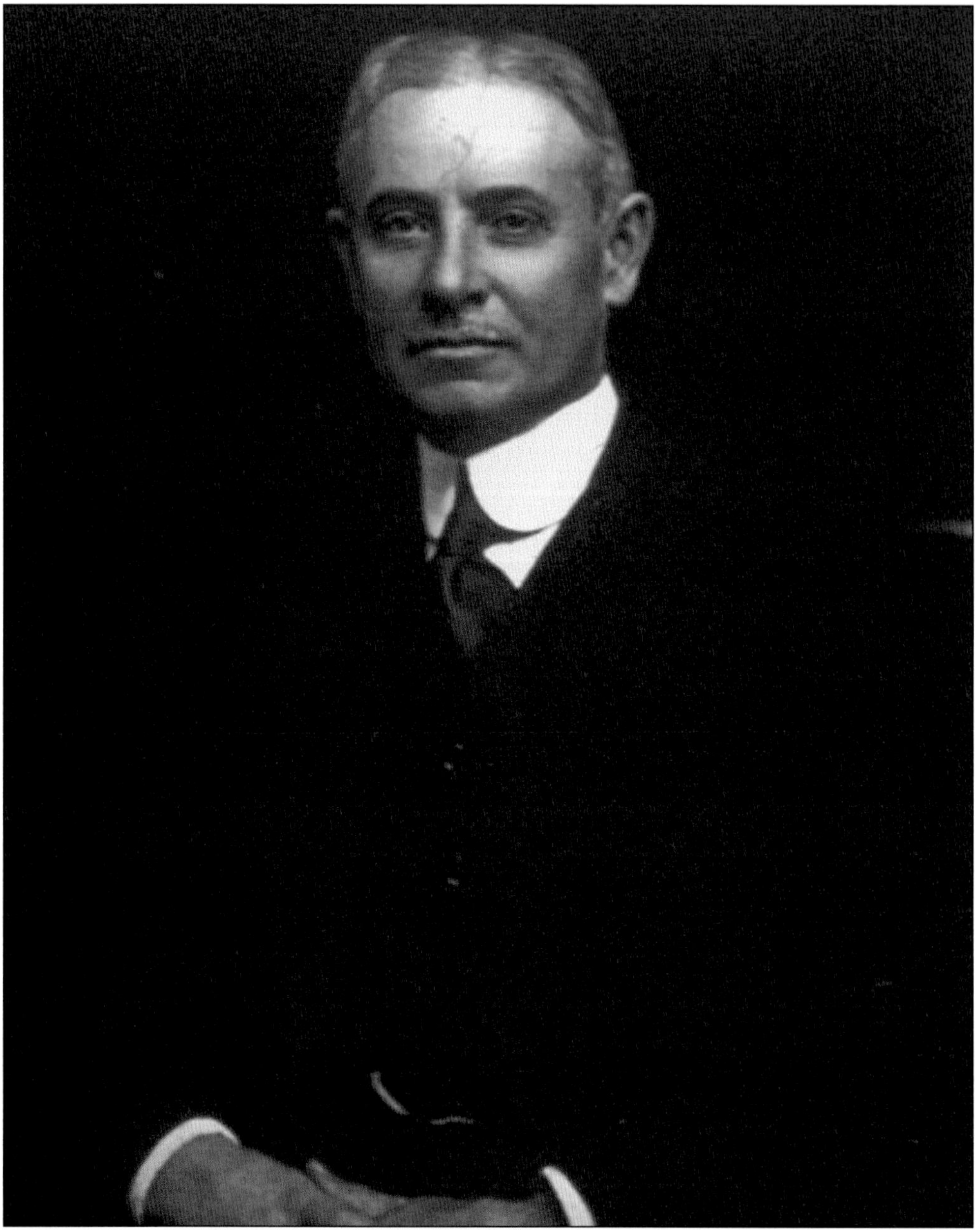

William Thorne (1863–1956) was bon in Delavan. He took lessons with Albert McCoy, a local art teacher, and he was the first of McCoy's students to attend the Art Institute of Chicago. He studied for two years in Chicago, followed by a year at the New York Academy of Design. In 1887, Thorne was off to Paris to study at the celebrated Julien Academy for three years. An extremely talented portrait painter, his 1891 "Song Without Words" won an award at the Paris Salon from the Societes Des Artists Francais. After returning from Paris, he operated a studio in Carnegie Hall in New York until 1926. While in New York, he befriended another portrait artist, John Singer Sargent, and they painted each other's portrait. Thorne married Delavan native Margaret Lowe and kept a studio in his home on North Fourth Street. William Thorne is considered the dean of Wisconsin portrait artists.

William Thorne was commissioned to paint some very prominent people while in New York, including the Gould, Carnegie, Finch, and Mellen families, as well as some British dukes and duchesses. In 1893, he was commissioned to paint Mary Gordon Landon Pratt, then wife of successful New York dry goods merchant, Charles Griswold Landon. This painting is in the permanent collection of the Aram Public Library.

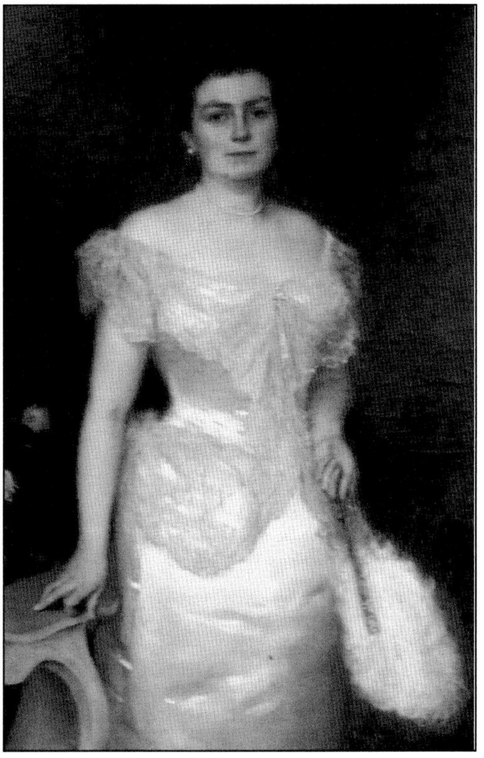

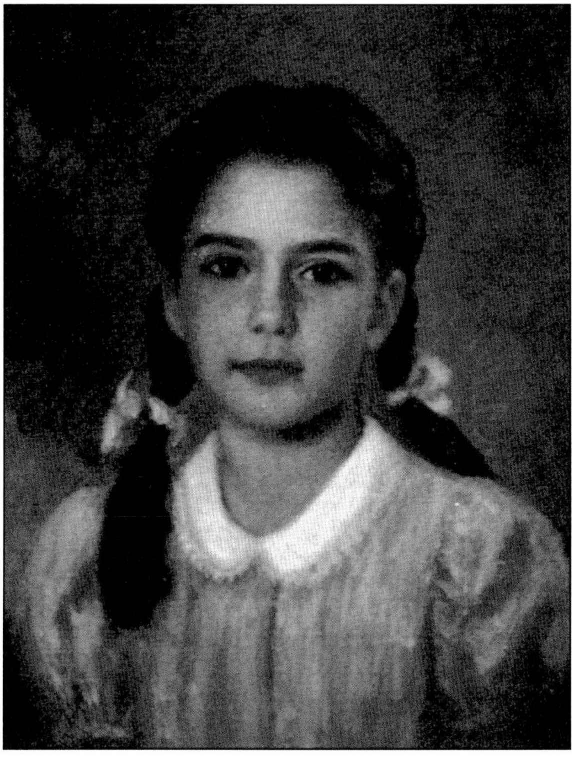

Thorne continued to paint until he was in his late 80s, after which his health would not allow him to continue. His granddaughter Margaret Ann Hollister was his last portrait subject in 1948. He won many awards with his talented realistic style. One of the very few artists who spent their lives in Delavan, William Thorne died at age 93 and is buried at Spring Grove Cemetery. This painting is in a private collection.

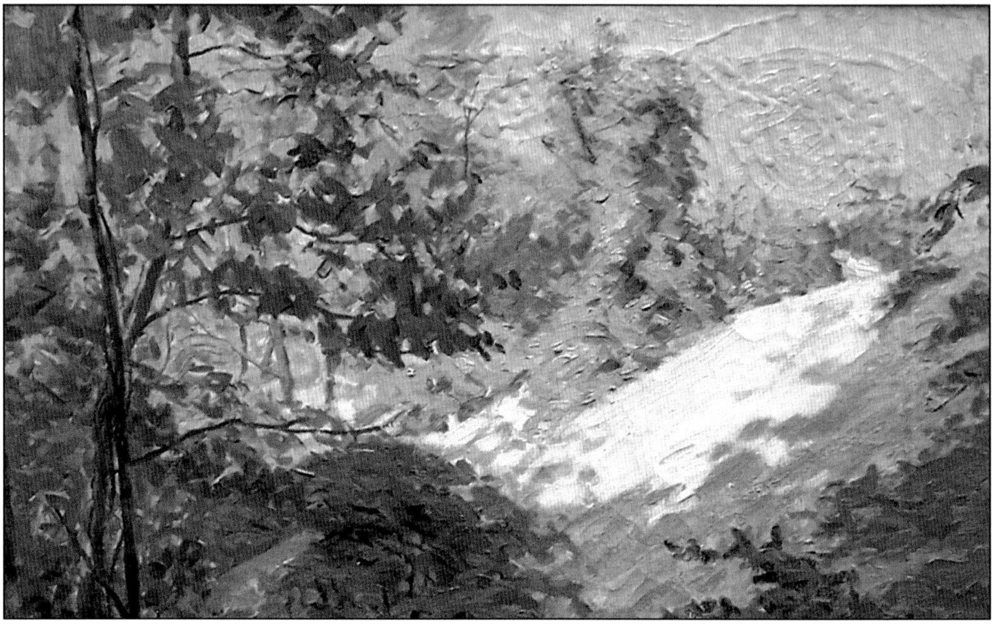

Frank Dudley (1868–1957) whose work is shown here, was born in Delavan to deaf parents. Dudley studied at the Art Institute of Chicago. He later became frustrated when he found himself unable to make a living selling his art. Eventually, he found his niche in the art world when he began painting the Indiana Dunes. Dudley's awards spanned his 50-year career. Frank Dudley is buried at Spring Grove cemetery. This painting is in the permanent collection of the Aram Public Library.

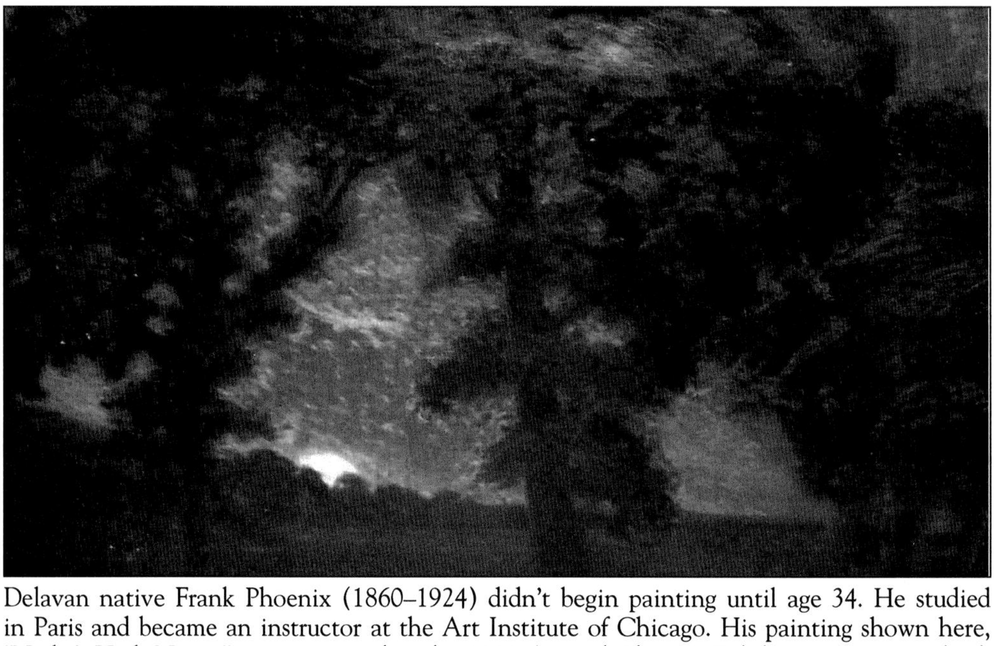

Delavan native Frank Phoenix (1860–1924) didn't begin painting until age 34. He studied in Paris and became an instructor at the Art Institute of Chicago. His painting shown here, "Night's High Noon," won an award at the 1909 Annual Chicago Exhibition. He came back to Delavan for a short time before moving to Brown County, Indiana, and later to Des Moines, Iowa. This painting is in the permanent collection of the Aram Public Library.

Six

Delavan Lake Resort and Ballroom Era

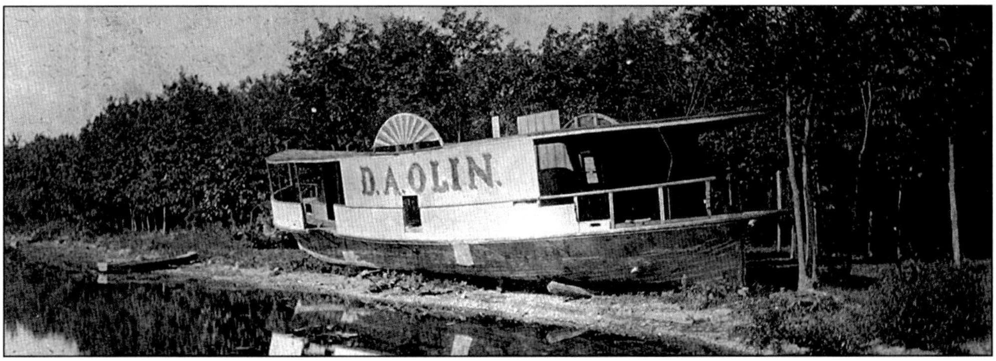

As Delavan Lake became more popular, camp grounds, picnic areas, hotels, and resorts started popping up on the shoreline. By 1890, there were lots of options for where to find a night's accommodations on the lake. When vacationers arrived by train, the hotel or resort where they were staying would send a carriage or wagon to pick up their guests and deliver them to the property. Independent "bus lines" would service the establishments who didn't have their own transportation. Once at the lake, the fastest and most fun mode of transportation was the streamer or excursion boat. The first steamer was launched in 1878, and owned by Dr. F.L. Von Suessemilch, who also had the first permanent residence on Delavan Lake. The *D.A. Olin* was large, but a little too large for Delavan Lake. So in 1883, the upper deck was removed and the pilot house lowered, giving the steamer a sleek new profile. During the 1880s and 1890s, many more faster, more efficient steamers would be added to the lake. They had scheduled stops at the different resorts, hotels, and piers. The *D.A. Olin* is shown "resting" here on the shore of Lake Lawn property.

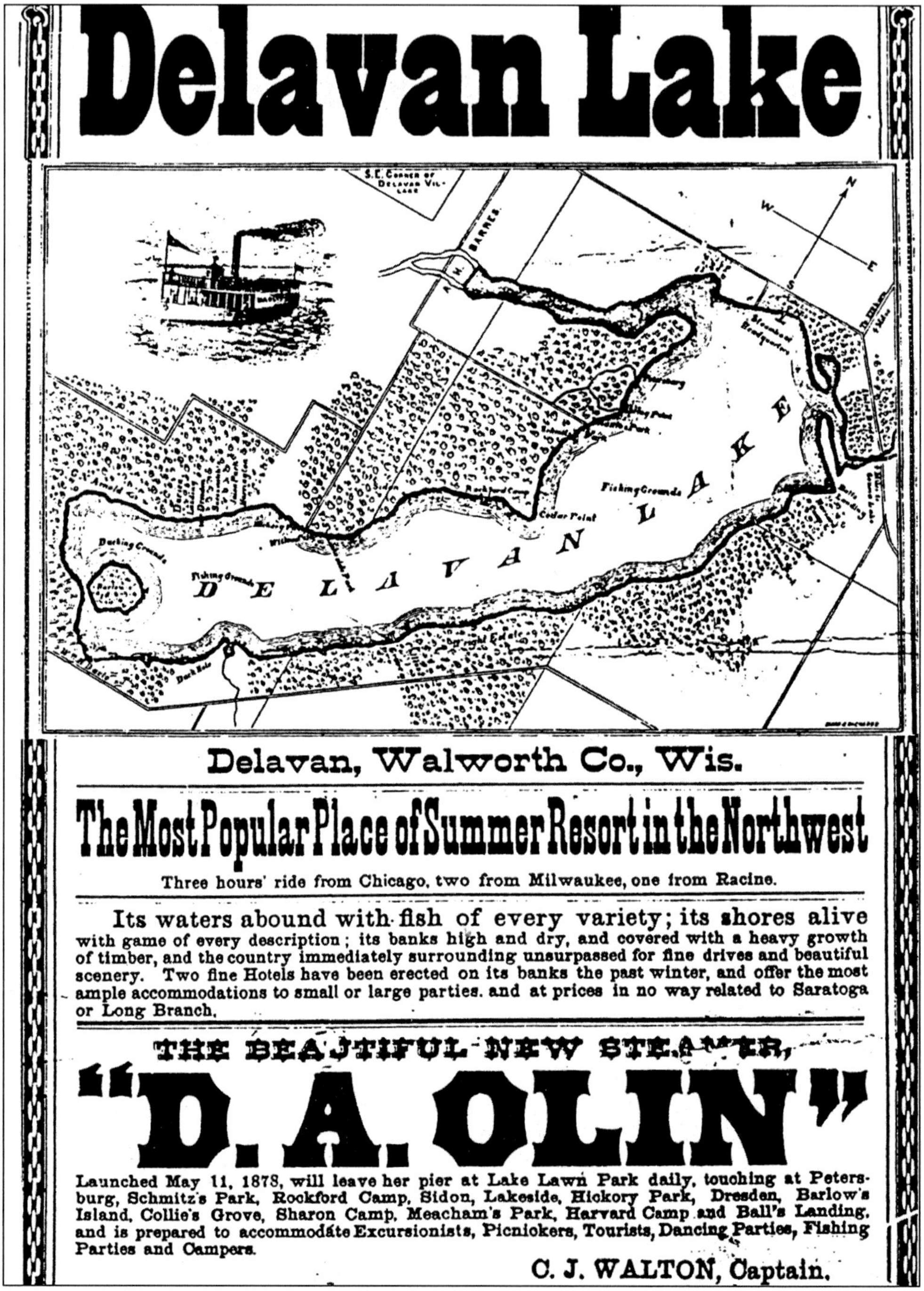

The *D.A. Olin*'s appearance on Delavan Lake was big news. It was the first pleasure steamer launched, on May 11, 1878. The *D.A. Olin* was captained by C.J. Walton and made various stops at the hotels and campgrounds along the lake. Captain Walton would assist people in making fishing arrangements or lodging accommodations for no charge, as seen in this 1878 advertisement. The *D.A. Olin* was later sold to the Phillips Brothers, proprietors of the Lake Lawn Hotel.

This Lake Lawn Hotel brochure from 1891 advertises the wonderful features of the property. In the late 1800s, the hotels around the lake would open in April or May and be closed for the fall and winter months. Usually there were caretakers who would live on the property during that time to ensure the safety of the building and make improvements.

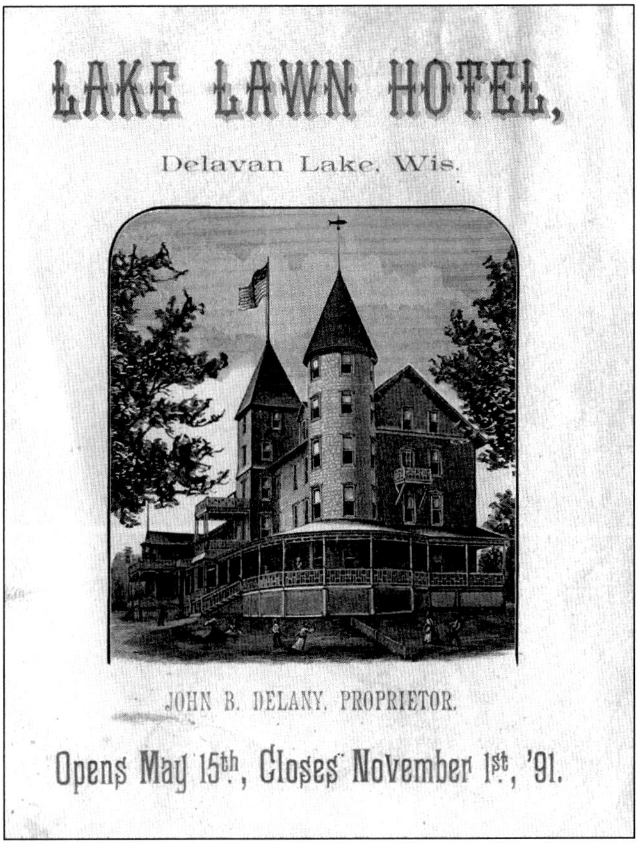

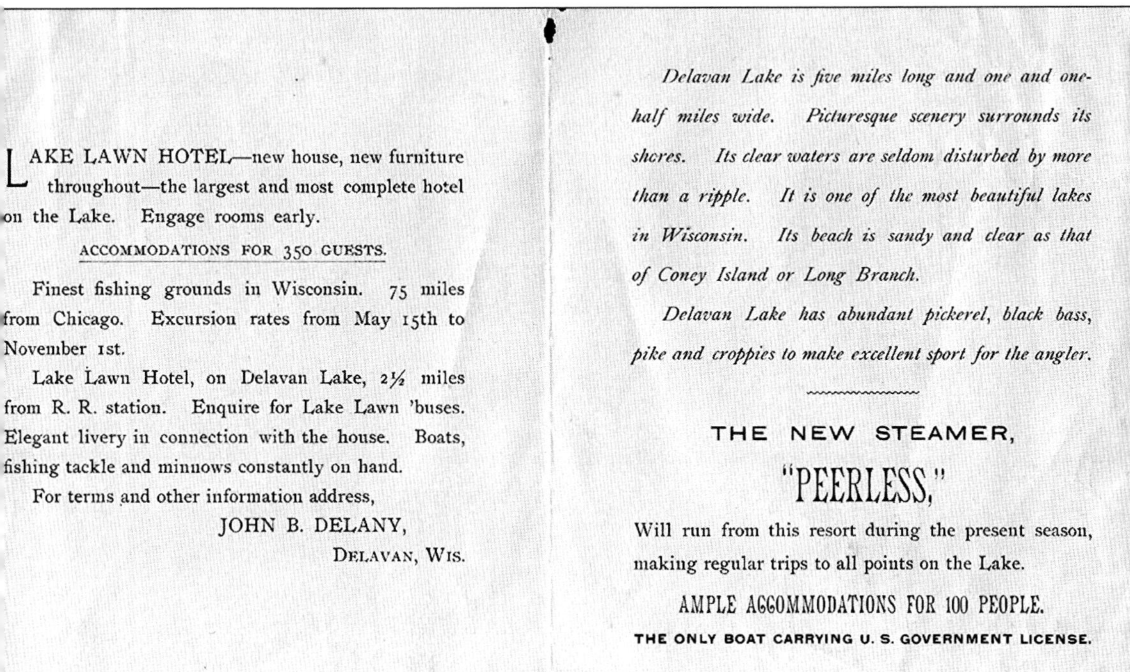

LAKE LAWN HOTEL—new house, new furniture throughout—the largest and most complete hotel on the Lake. Engage rooms early.

ACCOMMODATIONS FOR 350 GUESTS.

Finest fishing grounds in Wisconsin. 75 miles from Chicago. Excursion rates from May 15th to November 1st.

Lake Lawn Hotel, on Delavan Lake, 2½ miles from R. R. station. Enquire for Lake Lawn 'buses. Elegant livery in connection with the house. Boats, fishing tackle and minnows constantly on hand.

For terms and other information address,

JOHN B. DELANY,
DELAVAN, WIS.

Delavan Lake is five miles long and one and one-half miles wide. Picturesque scenery surrounds its shores. Its clear waters are seldom disturbed by more than a ripple. It is one of the most beautiful lakes in Wisconsin. Its beach is sandy and clear as that of Coney Island or Long Branch.

Delavan Lake has abundant pickerel, black bass, pike and croppies to make excellent sport for the angler.

THE NEW STEAMER,

"PEERLESS,"

Will run from this resort during the present season, making regular trips to all points on the Lake.

AMPLE ACCOMMODATIONS FOR 100 PEOPLE.

THE ONLY BOAT CARRYING U. S. GOVERNMENT LICENSE.

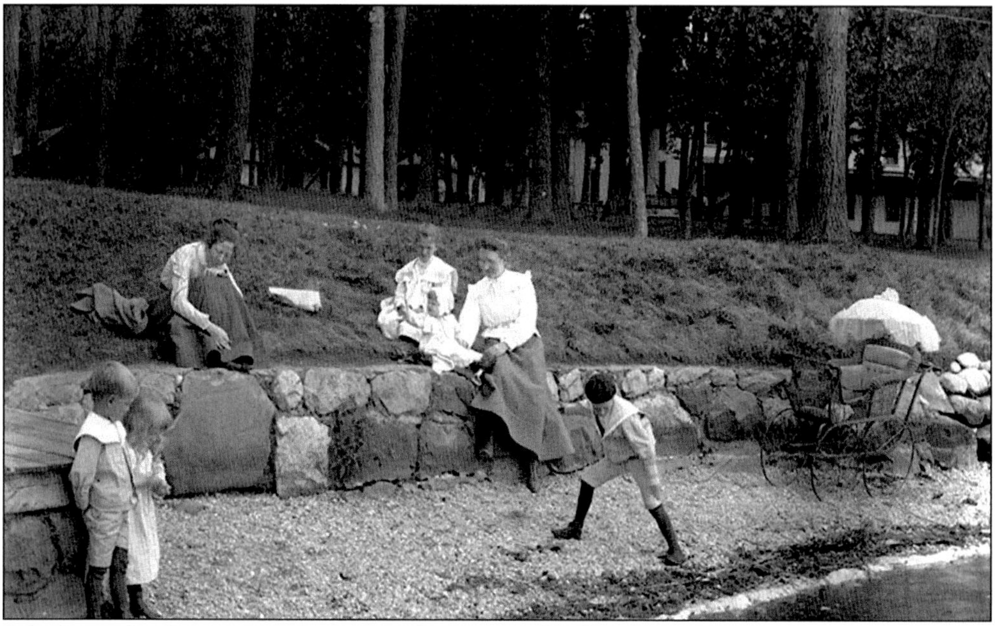

Lake Lawn has been a popular tourist destination for decades. Families would arrive by train or automobile to spend memorable summers at Delavan Lake. Pictured here is a family from Chicago enjoying the relaxing grounds of the Lake Lawn Hotel, *c.* 1898. Lake Lawn has always been one of the largest resorts on the lake.

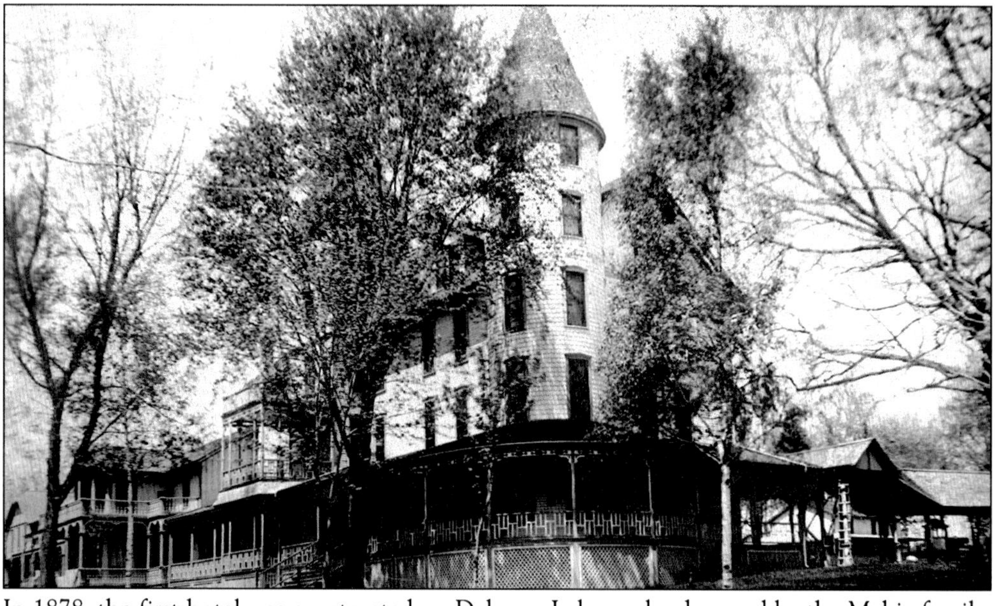

In 1878, the first hotel was constructed on Delavan Lake on land owned by the Mabie family. This structure remained the same until 1898, when a new section was added due to increased business. At the time, the grounds were densely wooded around Lake Lawn, but by 1900 a majority of the trees were cleared, giving the hotel a commanding view on the northeast shore of the lake.

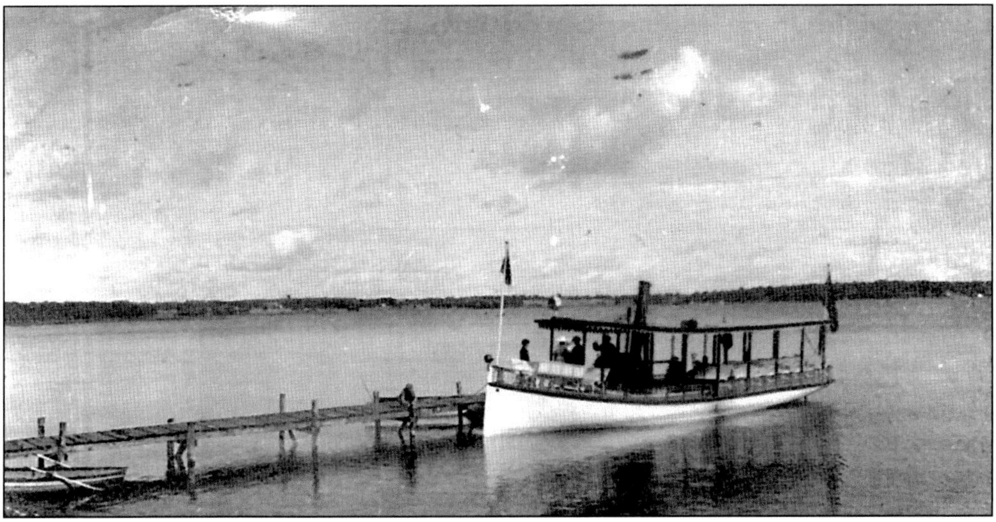

When the steamer *D.A. Olin* started making rounds on the lake, it was operated from the pier at Lake Lawn Hotel. By the 1890s, Lake Lawn was promoting the steamer called *Peerless*, which operated from their pier. In 1894, twin engines were added and in 1897 it was purchased by Chester and Ernest Phillips and christened *Lake Lawn*. The steamer *Lake Lawn* is pictured here in 1912.

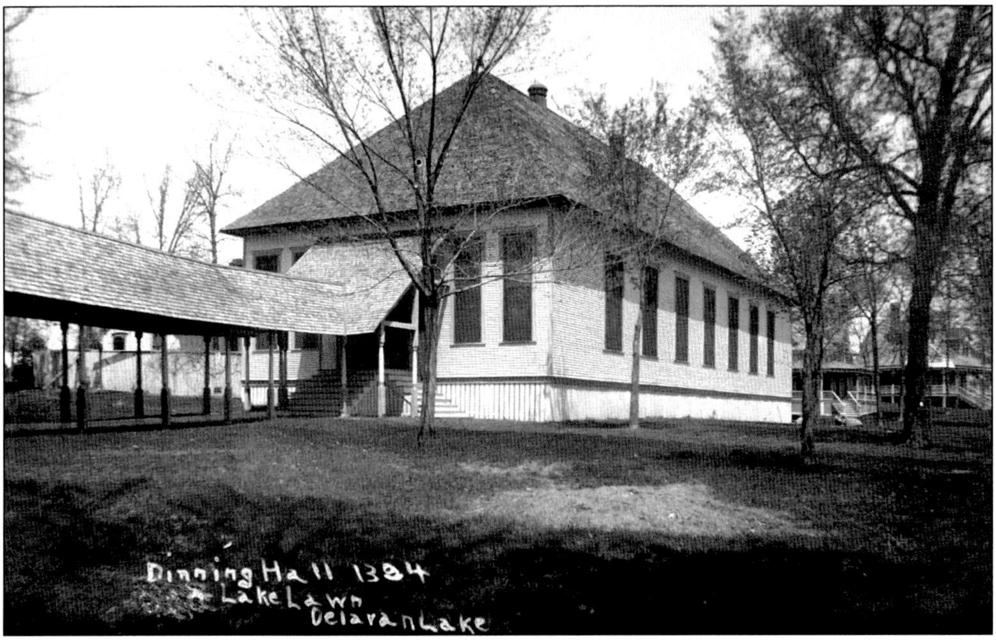

The dining hall shown here was erected specifically to use as a summer dining hall when occupation was high and the need for a larger dining facility was crucial. The regular or "winter" dining room was located in the main building. A coffee shop was later added to the left side of the building. It was torn down in the early 1950s to make room for the new dining room.

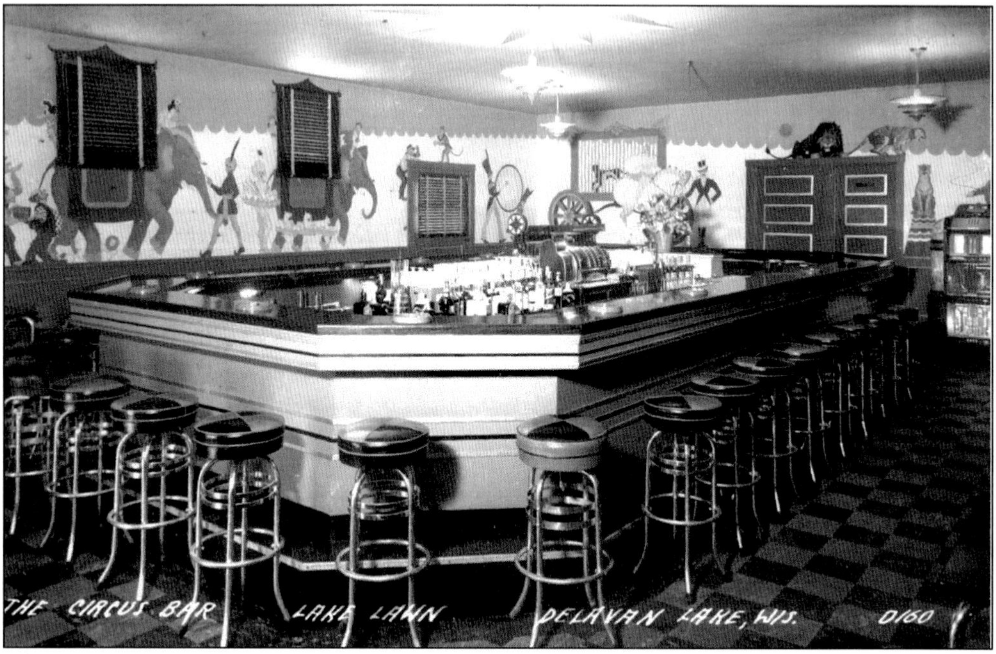

The Circus Bar at Lake Lawn was built in the mid 1940s and accommodated patrons visiting the resort and ballroom. It was attached to the annex. Not long after this image was taken, the motif was changed—it was said the decor made patrons act a little wild.

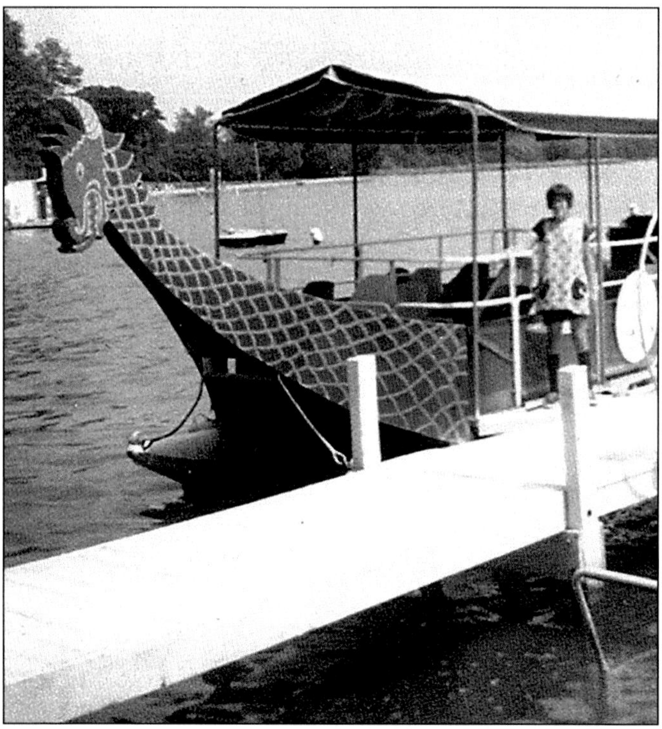

Cecil the Sea Dragon was a common site around the late from the late 1960s to the mid-1970s. *Cecil* was used as an excursion boat when the Johnson's managed the marina at Lake Lawn Lodge. *Cecil the Sea Dragon* is seen here making a stop at the Assembly Park pier, waiting to take on passengers.

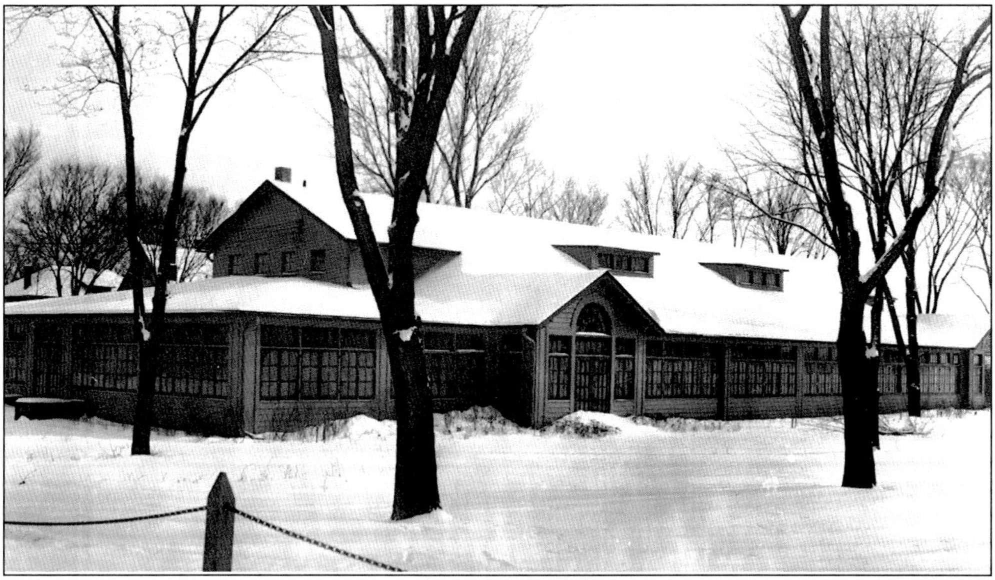

The Lake Lawn Ballroom was erected in 1929, just before the stock market crashed. The Jungle Bar was added in the 1940s. Many well-known bands graced the stage and entertained crowds in the well-attended ballroom, including a young Lawrence Welk in 1941. Shown in the picture below is a 1944 dance in the renamed Victory Ballroom, formerly called the Oriental Ballroom. Music was provided by Tiny Hill as war weary patrons enjoyed a pleasant diversion. The ballroom era at Delavan Lake was ending by the time Lake Lawn hired its last expensive band in 1955. This was the last ballroom standing when it was removed in 1978, despite a last ditch effort to preserve it by the Delavan Historic Preservation Society.

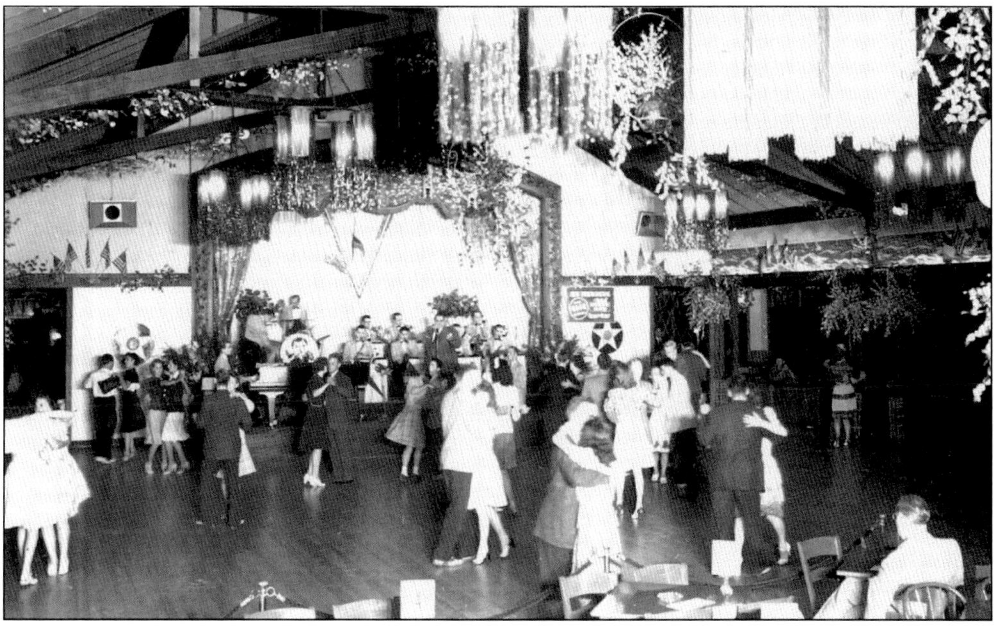

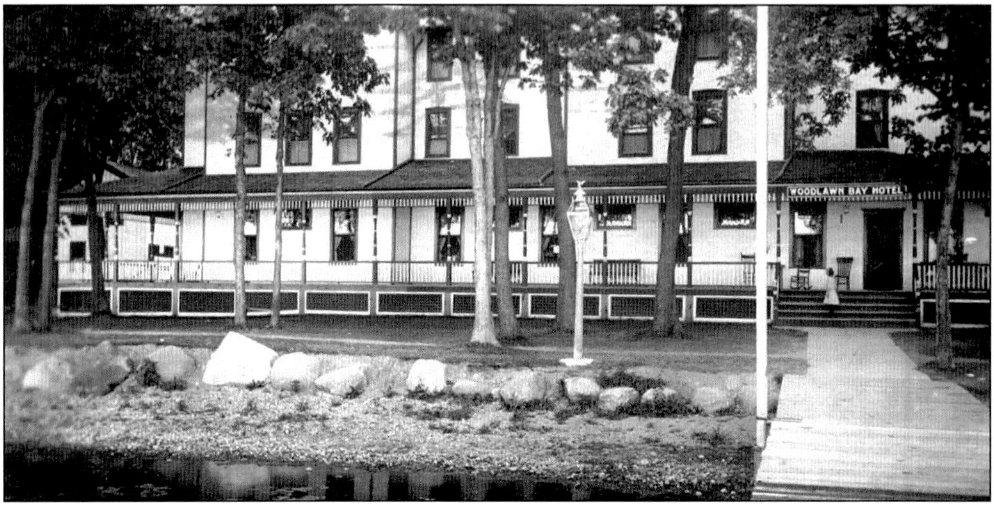

The Woodlawn Bay Hotel, pictured here about 1911, was located on the north shore of the lake. The hotel began in 1898 as Strow's Park and was subsequently purchased by August Melges. The property was christened Woodlawn around 1891 and underwent many changes through the years. It was under the management of Melges' son Bill that the new elaborate ballroom was constructed in 1927. The hotel built in 1898 was torn down in 1939. The ballroom was destroyed by fire in 1944.

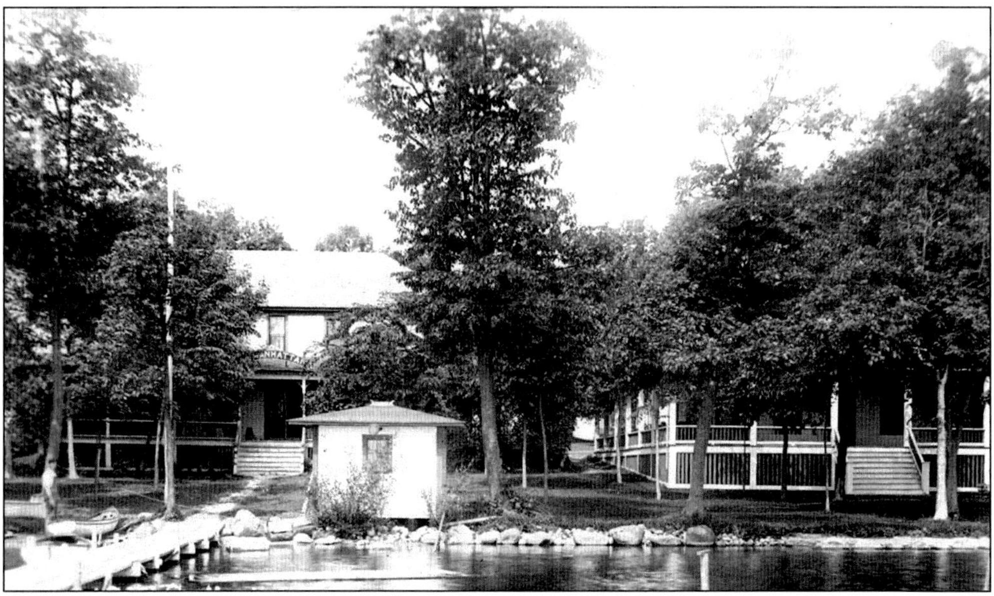

Before the Manhattan was built in 1905, the Hollandale stood in its place. It was located where the Inn Between now stands. The Hollandale was built by George Holland of circus fame, in 1894, and destroyed by fire in 1901. The hotel was rebuilt and renamed the Manhattan. The Manhattan was moved to site just off North Shore Drive in about 1925 and was utilized as a ballroom named Delavan Gardens.

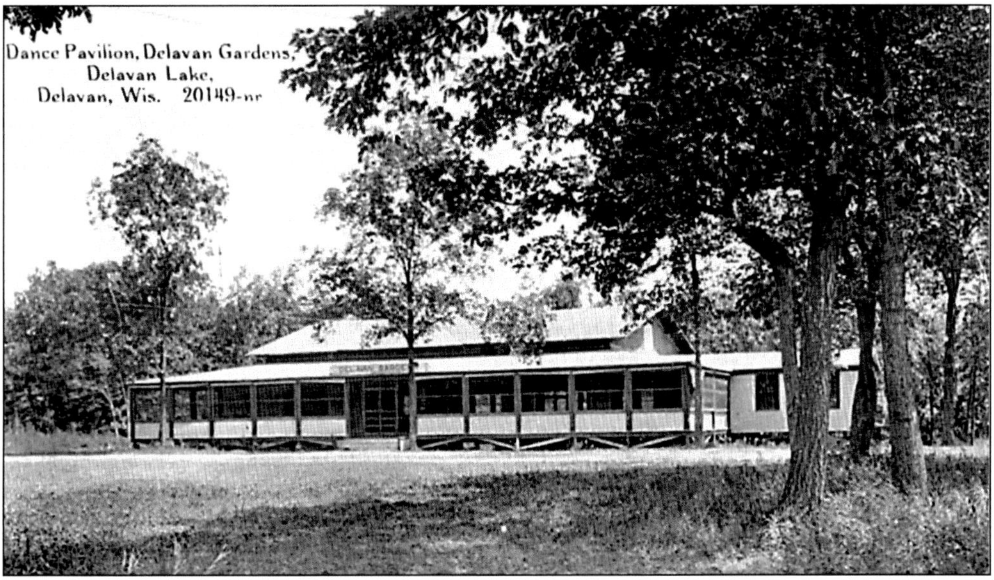

The Delavan Gardens ballroom, once located between just off North Shore Drive near Woodlawn Lane, enjoyed 32 years at the top. It was formerly the Manhattan ballroom and was moved uphill about 500 feet and a little west, making it closer to North Shore Drive. This original ballroom was destroyed by fire in April 1939 and within 60 days a new one was built and ready in time for opening season. The new structure hosted many famous acts, including Louis B. Armstrong and Frankie Yankovic. The popular Delavan gardens reign at the top came to an end when faulty wiring caused a gas explosion in 1957. The ballroom was not rebuilt, but was for several years a go-kart track, prior to the Delavan Gardens condominiums construction.

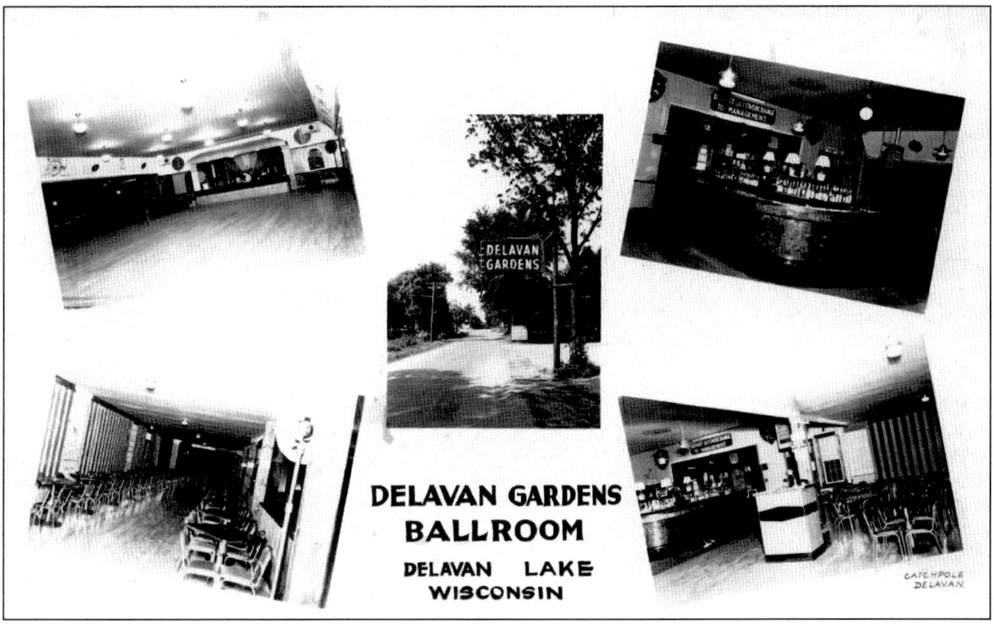

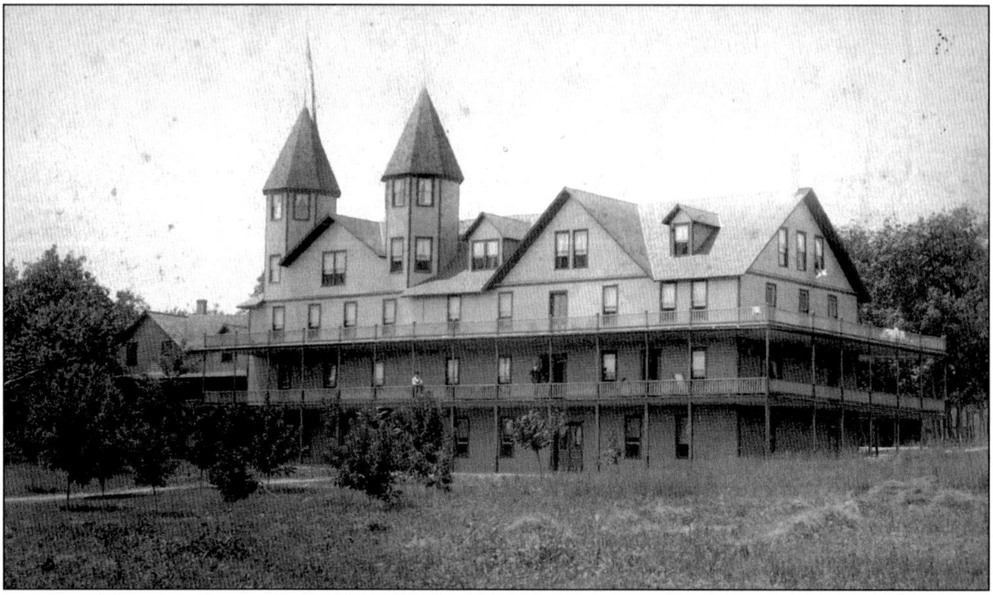

The Highland Hotel was built in 1893 and located between Cedar Point and the Rockford Colony on the north shore. Owned by the Sage family for over 50 years, the Highland was one of the very few resorts that operated on temperance principles. Fred and Belle Sage Goodrich help to run the hotel for about 10 years before selling their share to Charles Sage in 1905. It was the first resort on the lake to have electrical refrigeration, cement tennis courts, and a modern sewer system. During its heyday, the large hotel included a lower-level ballroom and adjacent dining hall, a nine-hole golf course, billiard hall, soda fountain dug store, ice house, and many cottages. The hotel and other buildings were torn down in 1941.

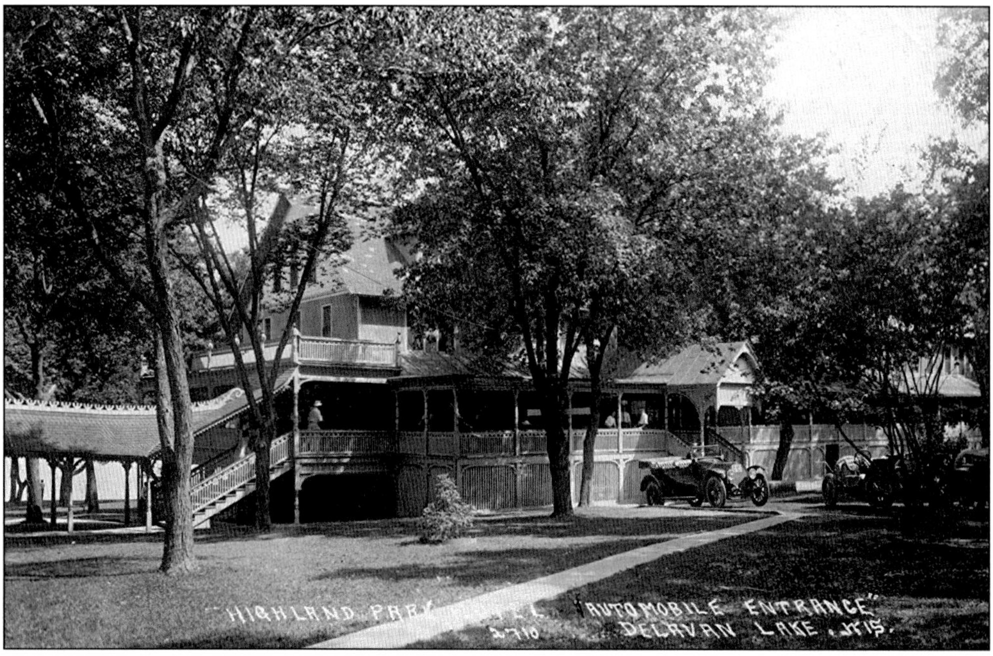

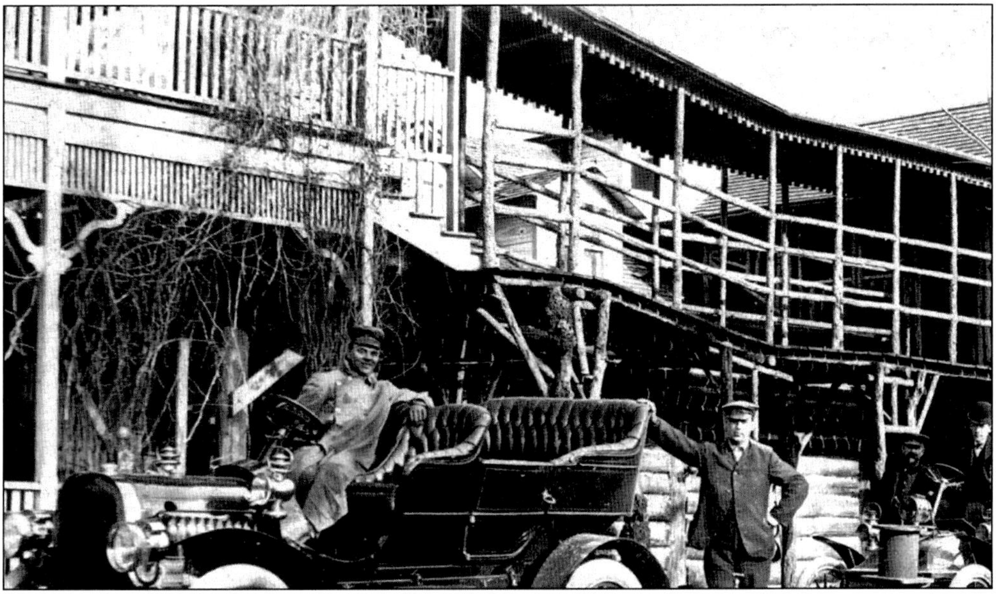

The Log Cabin Resort was located on Willow Point on the north shore of the lake. It was developed by Eugene Hollister in about 1880 and consisted of a small hotel, several cottages, dining hall, barroom, and adjacent dance hall. The Van Velzer Orchestra provided music at the Log Cabin for several seasons. In 1914, Hollister announced the property would be purchased by investors planning to build a Frank Lloyd Wright Hotel there. The deal never materialized and the property was sold to be developed into homes. The bar from the Log Cabin was removed to Fleming's Tavern, where it remained for over 50 years.

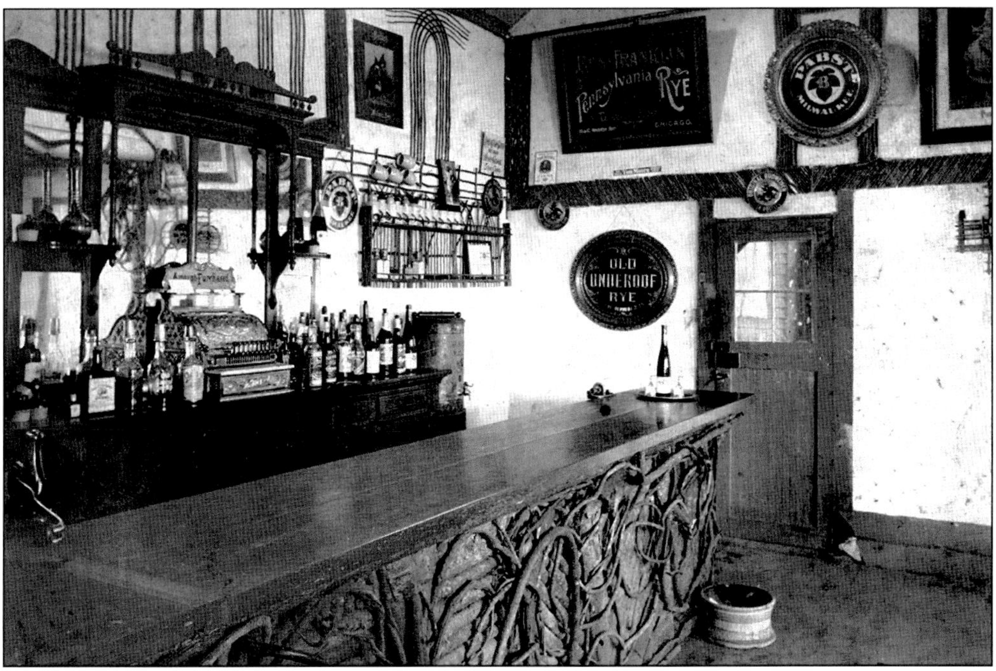

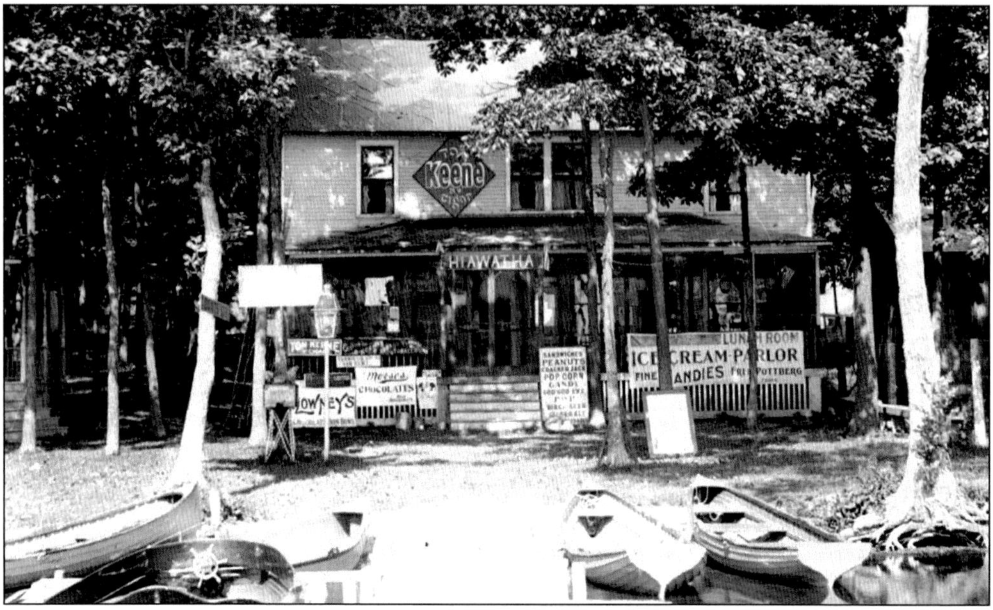

The Hiawatha resort was located on the north shore at the end of Hiawatha Drive. Built in 1903 by the Smiley brothers of Beloit, the Hiawatha had a dance hall and refreshment stand on the main floor and offered rooms to let on the second. The resort also offered fishing and boating to its visitors. It was owned and operated for several years by Jim and Margaret Moore. The Hiawatha would later be known as the See Level Tavern and was claimed by fire in 1981.

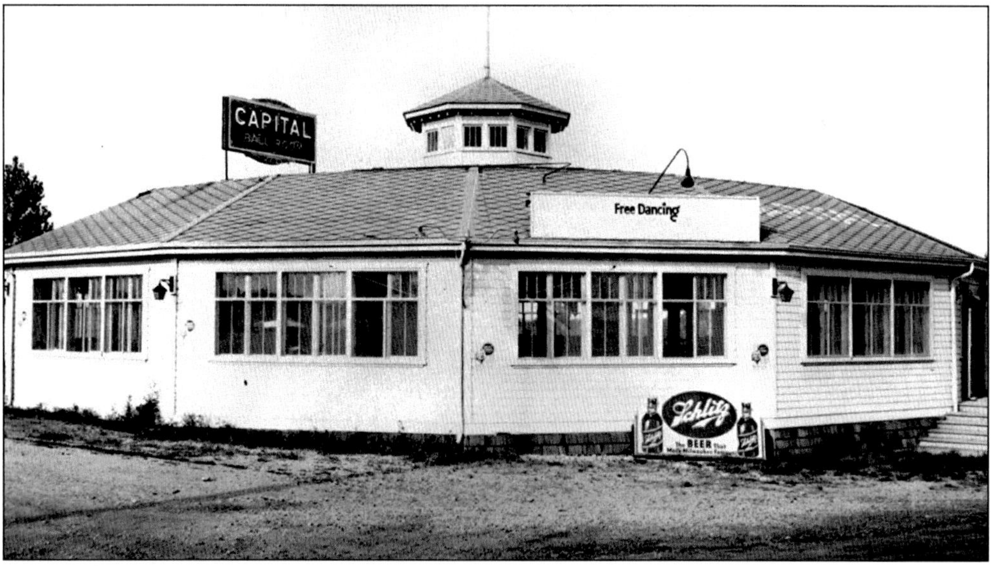

Designed as a miniature state capitol, the Capitol Ballroom was built in 1929 by Otto and Awald Sturmer. The Capitol Ballroom struggled through the Depression with major competition from the other ballrooms in the area. Located on the northeast corner of South Shore Drive and County Trunk O, across from what is now Millie's Pancake House, it was torn down by Otto Sturmer for lumber salvage during the war. A house now sits in its place.

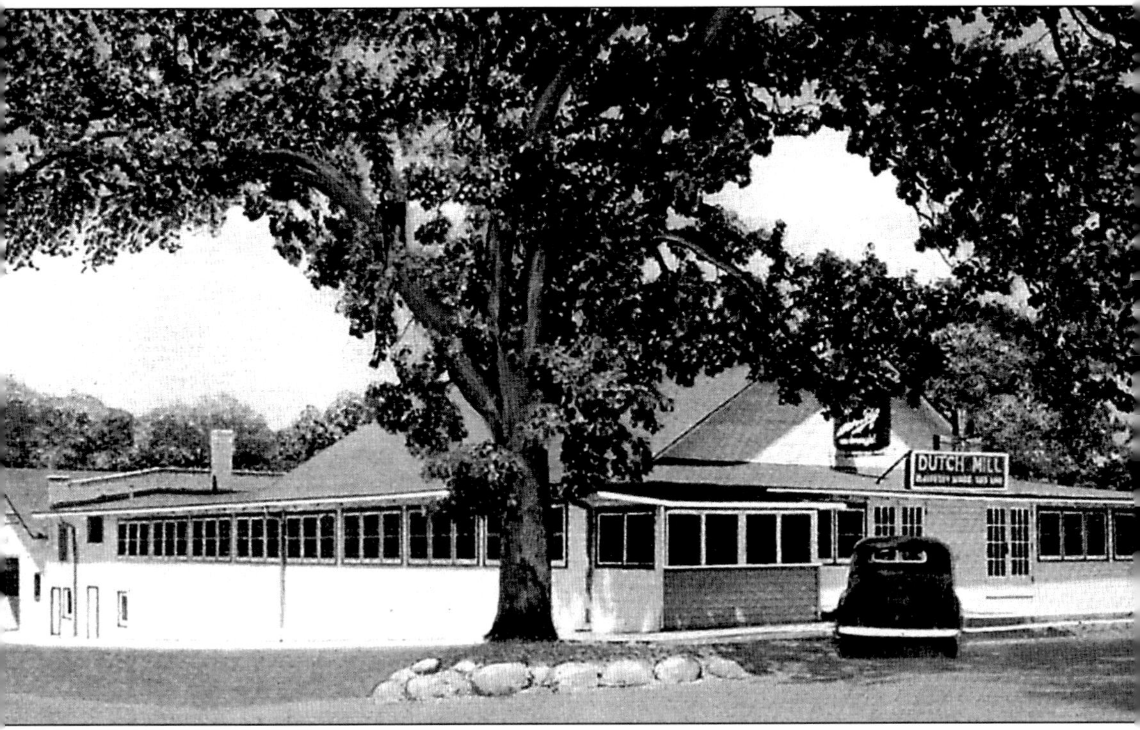

The Dutch Mill Ballroom was built in 1919 by Jack Potter, owner of the Potter House, which was adjacent to the ballroom. During Prohibition, the newspapers reported that liquor was found during raids. In 1934, the Dutch Mill was sold to Tony Rinella, who had a strong musical background and also introduced slot machines to the Dutch Mill. Who had "control" over these slot machines was to be struggled with by out-of-state syndicates and because of this, the Dutch Mill suffered a bombing in June 1941. In November of the same year, arson was suspected in a fire that would burn the building to ashes. It was replaced by a brick structure in 1942. As World War II continued on, the ballroom enjoyed great success and the nation's top bands entertained crowds, including Tommy and Jimmy Dorsey, Duke Ellington, Les Elgart, and Billy May, to name a few. Its popularity continued into the 1950s, but as the 60s approached, a decline in patronage was apparent and the ballroom era around Delavan Lake was coming to an end. The last dance at the popular establishment was on September 8, 1962, as fire would once again claim the Dutch Mill on April 22, 1963, leaving Lake Lawn as the last remaining ballroom.

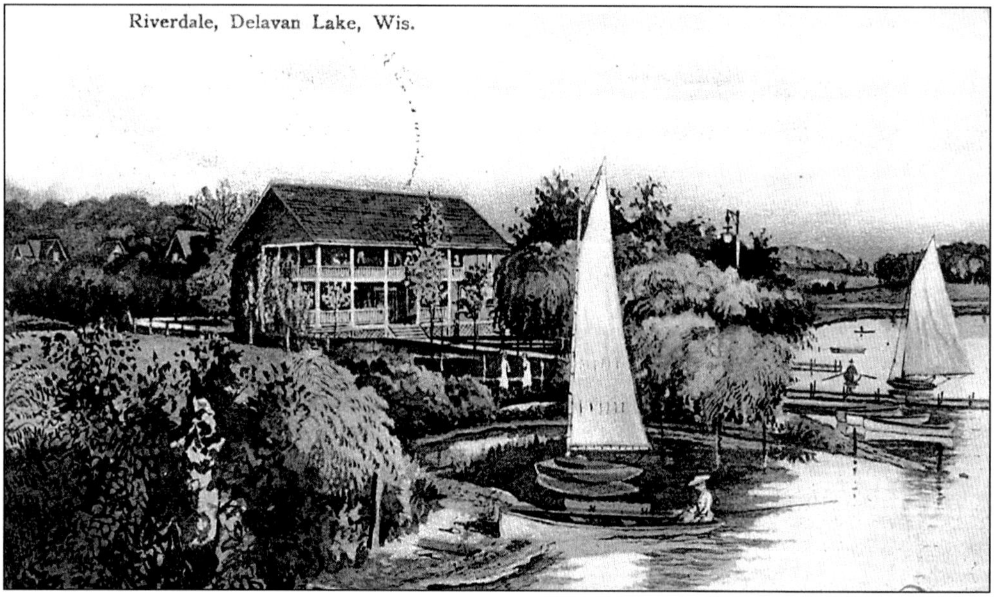

Riverdale got its name from owner John P. Rivers. Rivers and his wife started a business in 1897 that they called Camp Pleasant. Camp Pleasant offered swimming, fishing, and picnicking. In 1900, they constructed a large two-story frame building, thus turning the site into a resort. They renamed their new resort Riverdale, which was complete with hotel and ballroom. Rivers sold the business in 1912 and it changed hands again in 1915 when William Flynn purchased it and changed its name to Flynn's Inn. The Red Diamond would also operate on this site before it was razed in the early 1950s.

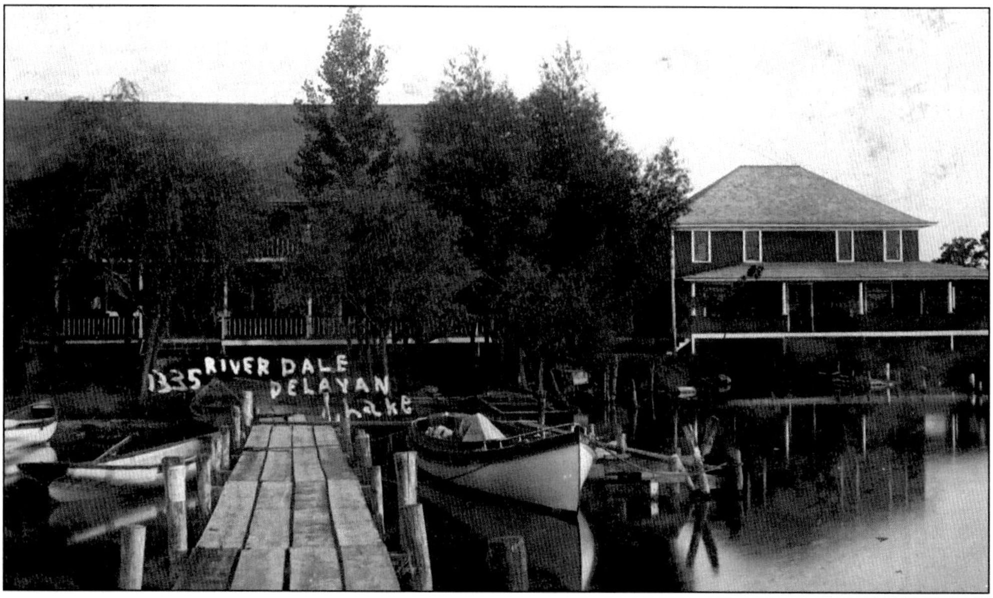

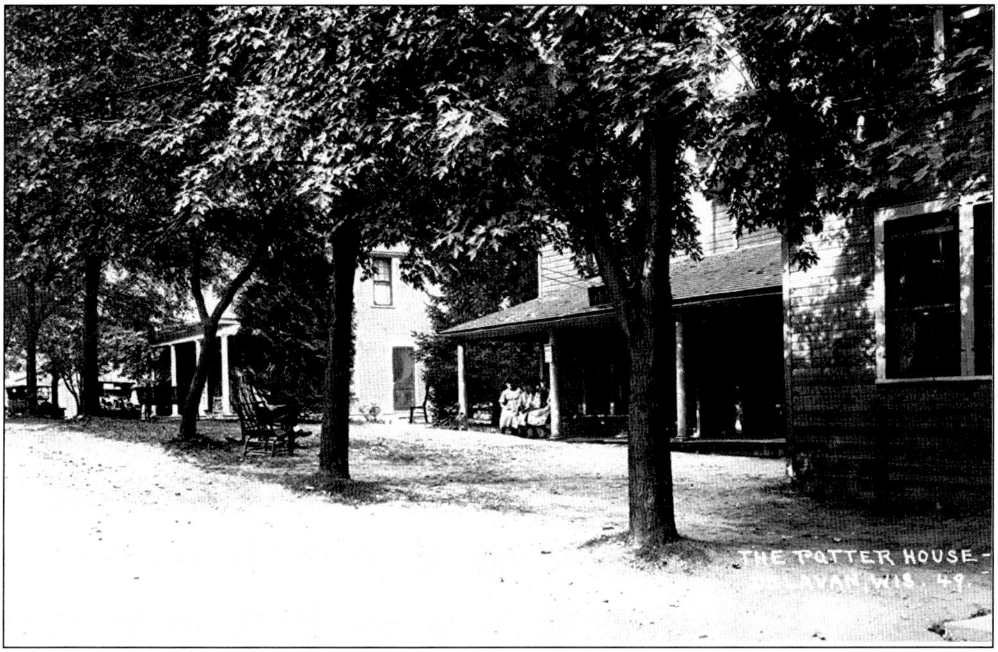

The Potter House got its start as the Spring Lawn Resort. It was located on Blue Gill Road on the south shore of the lake. It consisted of two main buildings, the Spring Lawn Hotel and the Spring Lawn Log Cabin. Jack Potter bought the property in 1918 and renamed it Potter House; he later owned the property to the west where the Dutch Mill was located. The Potter House met its end by fire in 1963.

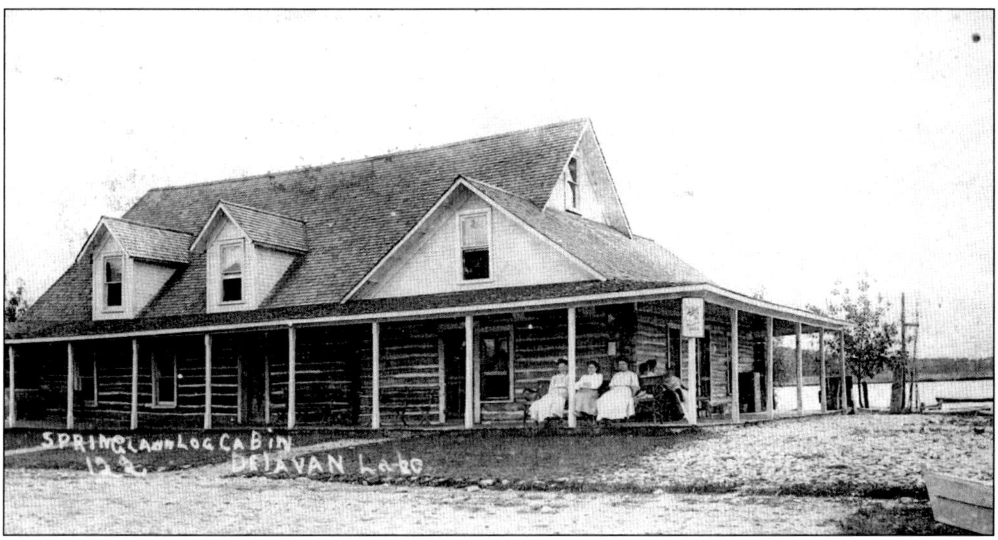

The Spring Lawn Log Cabin later became know as the Log Cabin and had several different owners. Although not as large as other dance halls, in the 1920s music was introduced and it was enjoying good attendance. In the 1960s, musical bookings changed from dance and big band to rock and go-go girls, and the Log Cabin remained a hotspot. The exciting Log Cabin was silenced by fire in 1974.

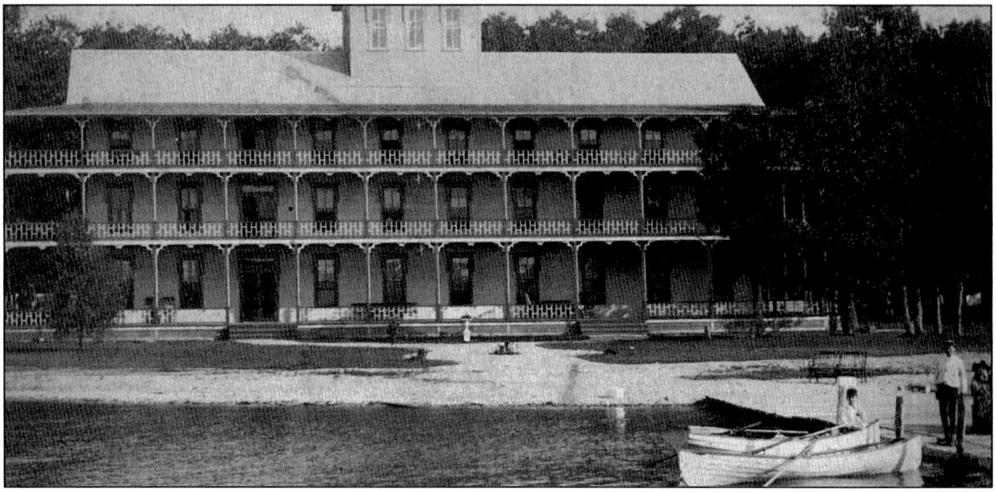

Mettowie was built in 1892 by James Weed. His son Henry assisted in management for three years, after which it was leased out. It was located on the south shore just west of the present-day Del-Mar subdivision. Mettowie featured a dinging room, ballroom, and 60 guest rooms. The resort had many cottages, a billiard hall, bowling alley, and could accommodate 250 guest, but sadly burned in 1900.

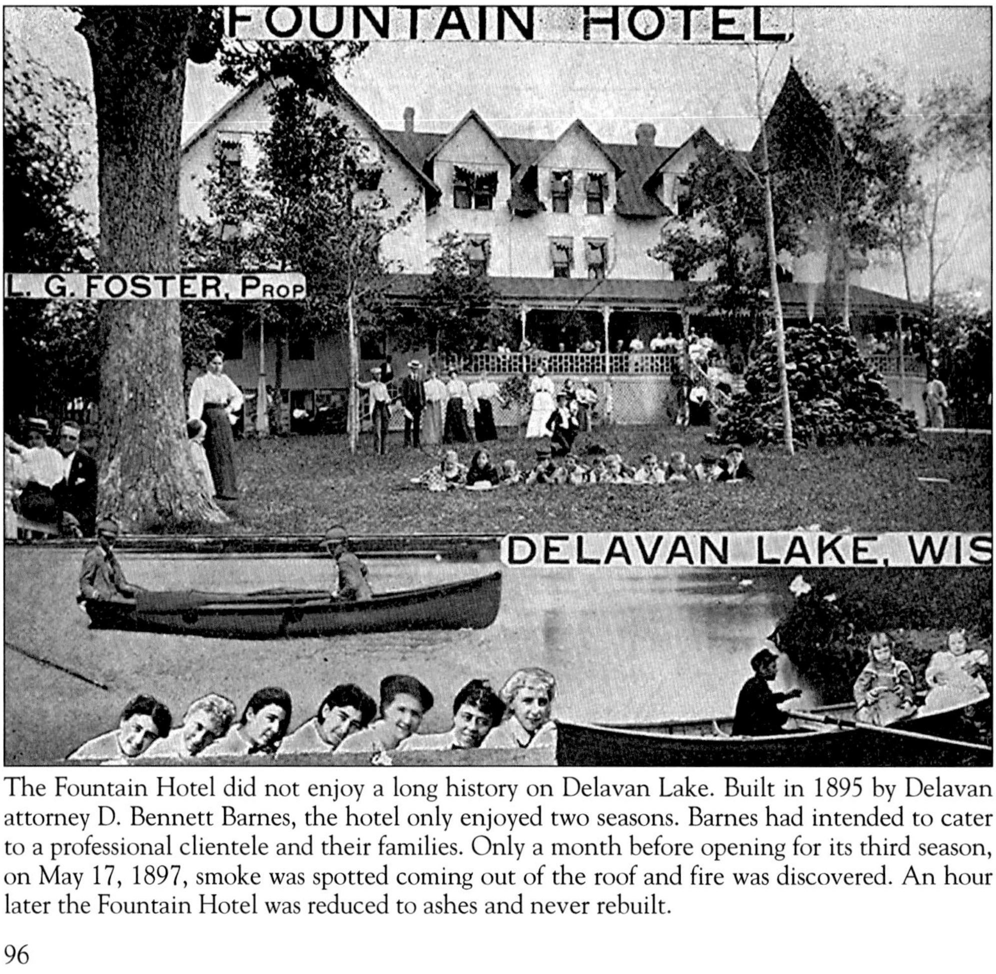

The Fountain Hotel did not enjoy a long history on Delavan Lake. Built in 1895 by Delavan attorney D. Bennett Barnes, the hotel only enjoyed two seasons. Barnes had intended to cater to a professional clientele and their families. Only a month before opening for its third season, on May 17, 1897, smoke was spotted coming out of the roof and fire was discovered. An hour later the Fountain Hotel was reduced to ashes and never rebuilt.

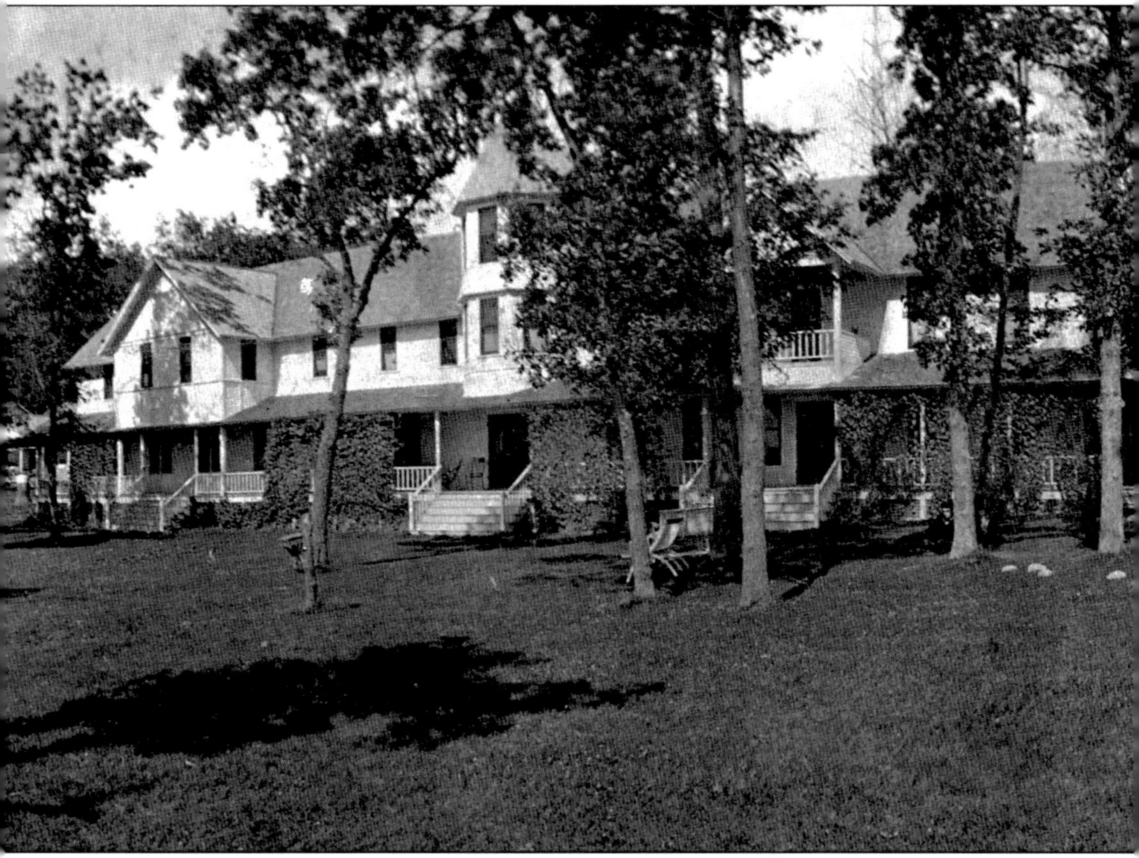

The Kennilworth Inn was built by Charles Meacham in 1893 on the south shore about a quarter mile down from the present-day Village Supper Club. Able to accommodate 125 guests between the hotel and cottages, the Kennilworth provided its visitors with the finest in boating and fishing facilities. A laundry building and ice house were also available on the grounds. On October 27, 1901, a fire broke out on the second floor and high winds encouraged the blaze to engulf the hotel. Because of the high winds, the safety of the nearby Halls Park Resort was a concern, but not harmed. The Kennilworth was not rebuilt.

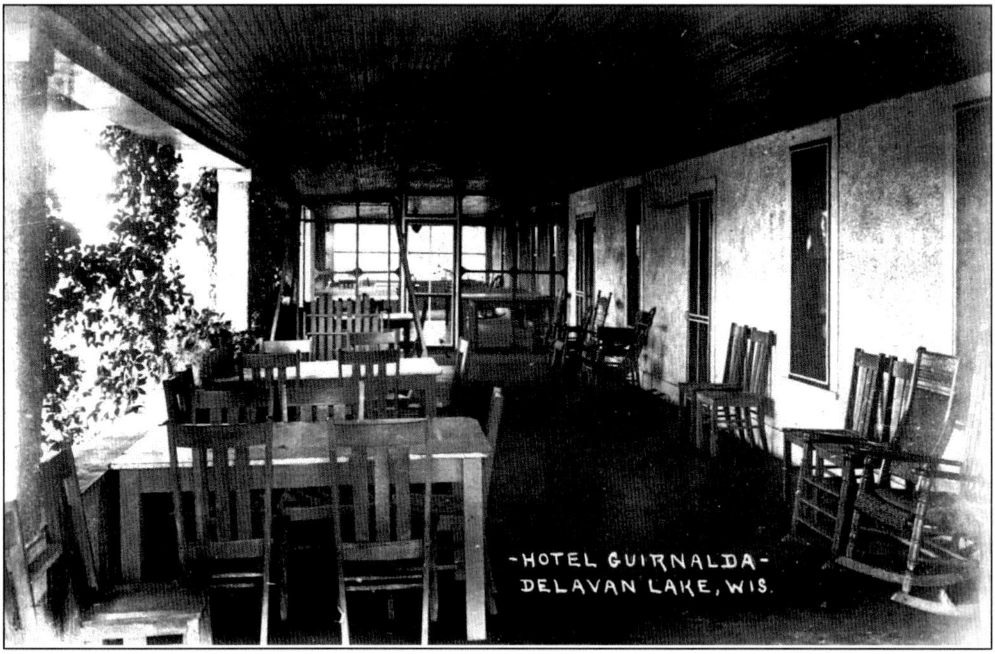

The Hotel Guirnalda, at one time known as the Broadview Hotel, was one of the lesser known hotels on Delavan Lake. It was built in 1916 by B.F. Hoag, east of South Shore Manor on the south shore of the lake. The Guiranlda was said to have possessed a fine dance pavilion, dining room, and 20 guest rooms. The porch of the hotel was 134 feet long and faced the lake. As good as a dance floor it was storied to have been, the business slowly failed and in 1937 it was demolished. During the demolition one man was killed when the tractor he was operating tipped backward, crushing him.

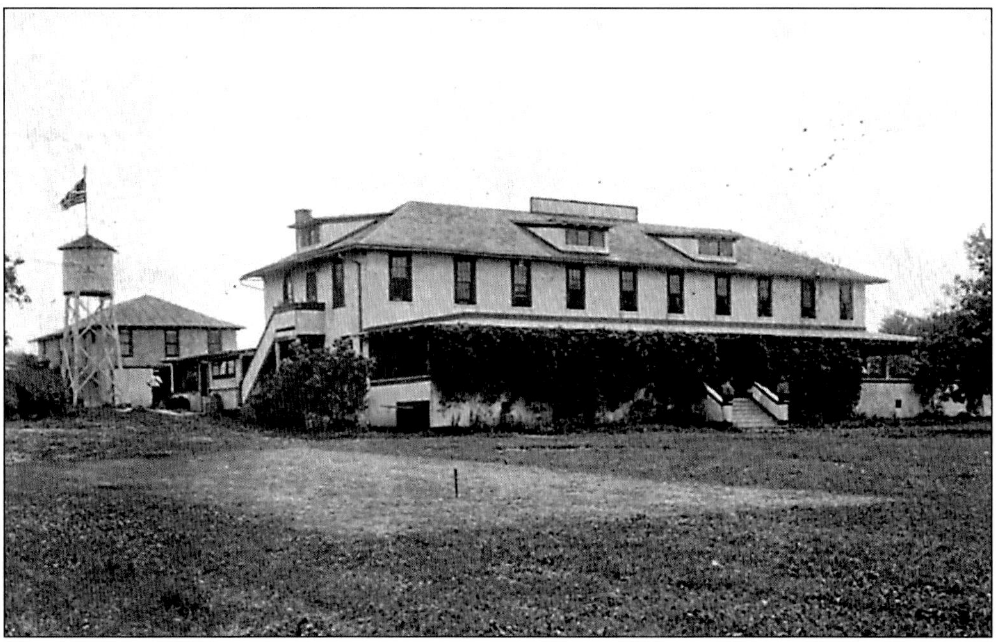

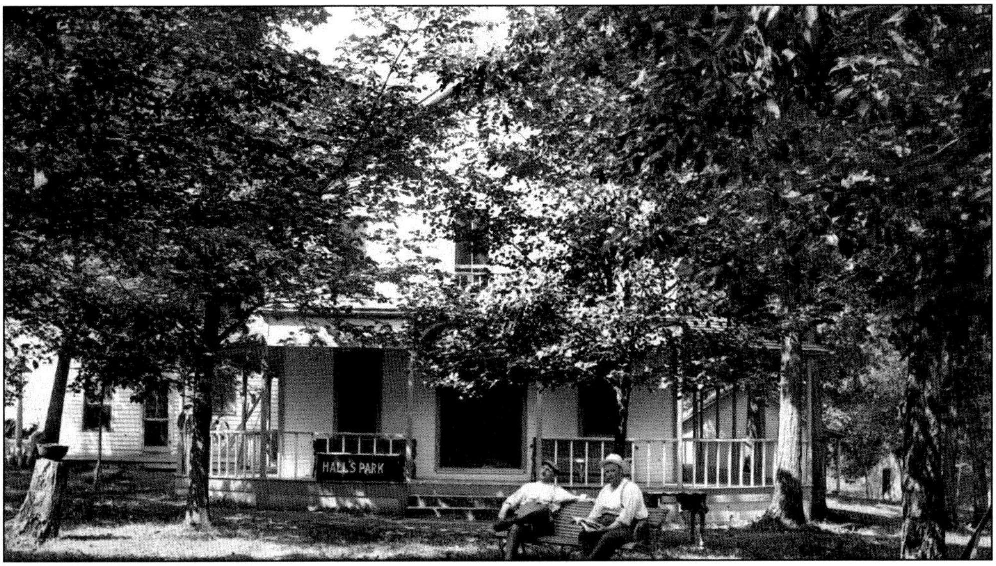

Park Resort was developed on the south shore of the lake on the farm owned by Civil War veteran John W. Hall. Hall moved his family to their farm in 1882, where they built a dwelling and began to take in boarders. Their enterprise became so successful that within a few years they erected a hotel on their property and began renting out boats. For 45 years, Hall's Park, under the proprietorship of the Hall family was a popular boating, fishing, and swimming resort. After the death of Mr. Hall in 1917, his wife continued to run the resort with her son-in-law and daughter, Herbert and Clarabelle Hall Welsher, until it was sold after the 1929 death of Mrs. Hall.

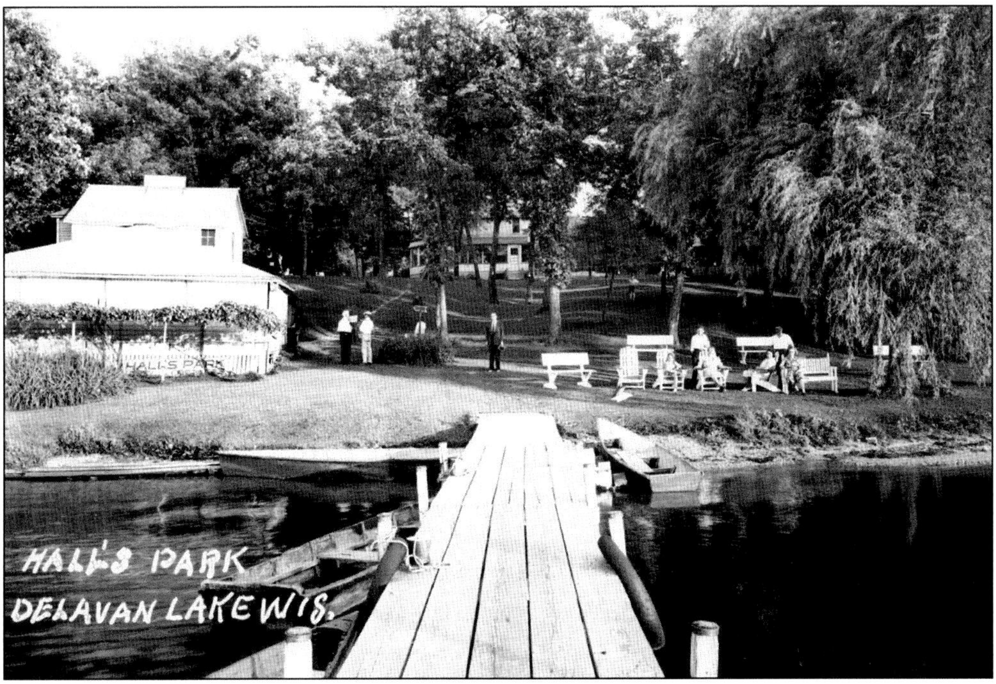

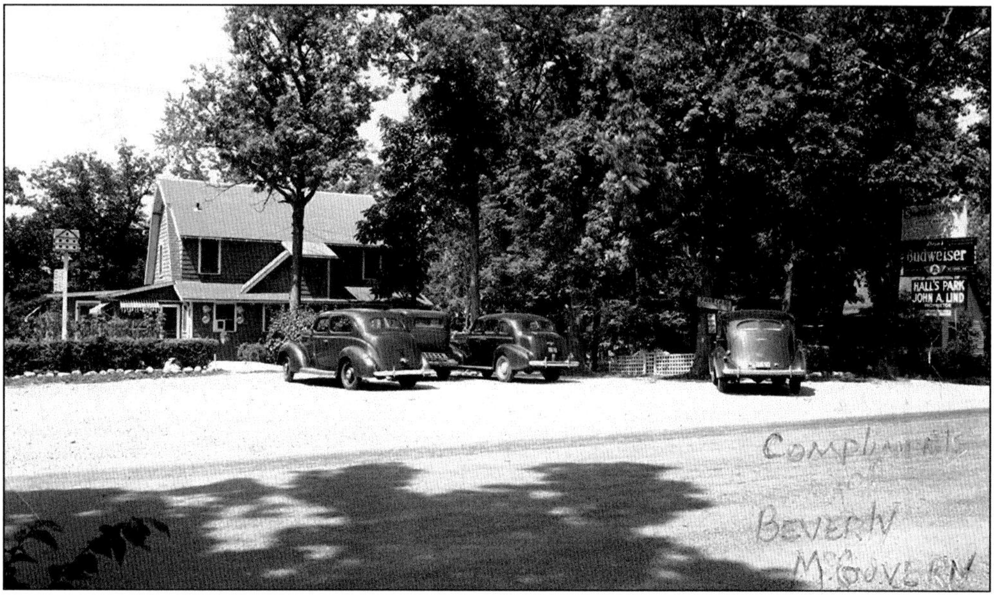

Hall's Park was purchased in 1930 by Frank and Charles Baumeister. The resort suffered a fire in 1934, which destroyed the hotel and a cottage. The property was sold to John Lind in the late 1930s, who rebuilt the main building as a restaurant and tavern with rooms above, and added several cottages. He continued to rent out cottages under the name Hall's Park, and his successful restaurant was named the Swedish Village. The Swedish Village offered a smorgasbord, which remained the fare through the next few owners—Stanley Nelson, Charles Stronghart, and Orv Gunderson. It was purchased in 1966 by Nick and Doris Marsicano and Clarence and Betty Iverson in 1966. A few years later the Marsicanos bought out the Iversons and renamed it the Village Supper Club—it is still operated by the Marsicano family today.

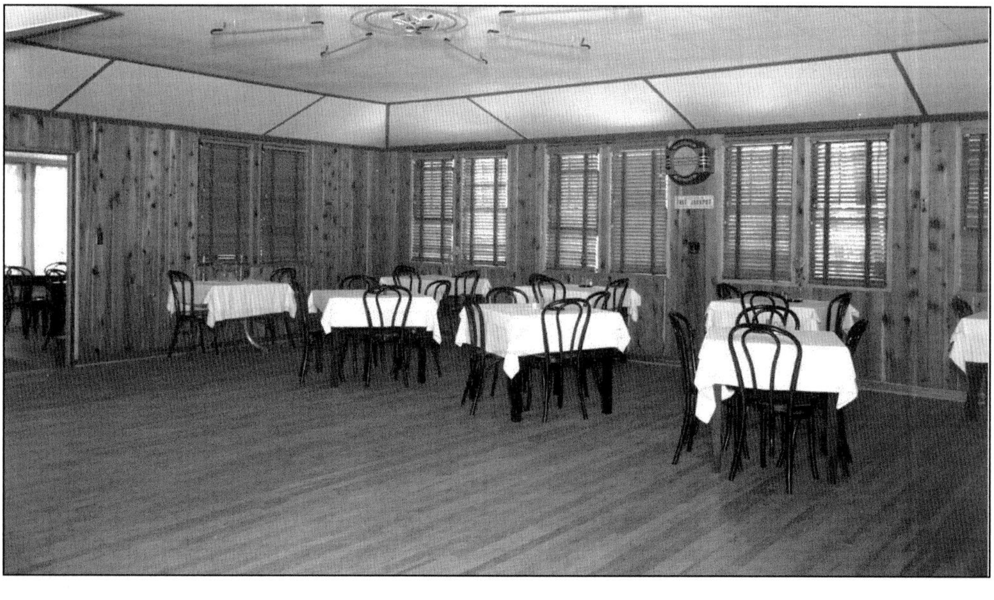

Seven

AROUND DELAVAN LAKE

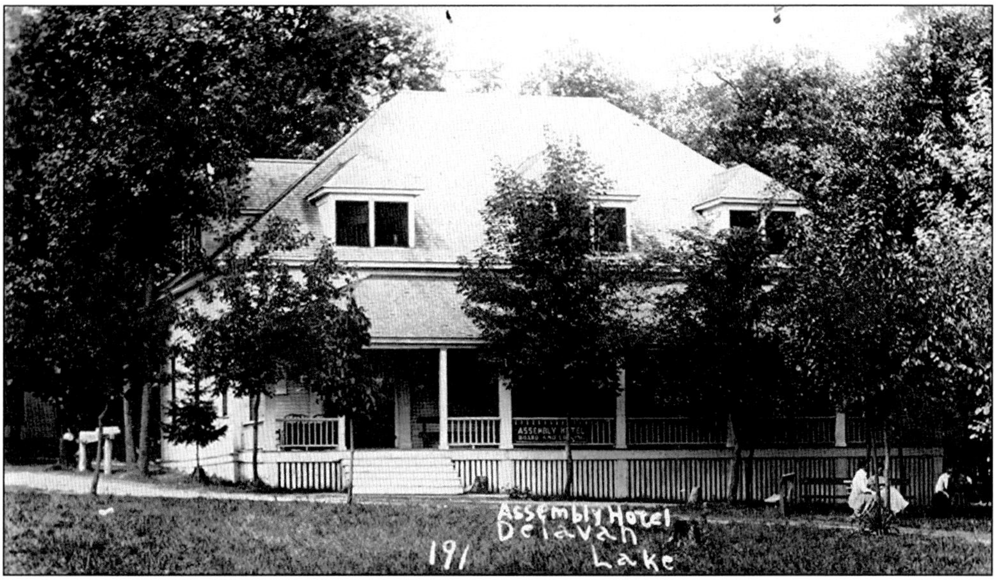

Pictured here in 1909, the Assembly Hotel, located on the Assembly Grounds, served as a dining hall for a period of time during the Chautauqua assemblies, after which it was remodeled and used as a hotel. In the 1930s, it was known as the Georgann Inn, which advertised rooms for rent and housed a grocery store. The hospitable proprietors of the Georgann Inn were George and Ann Hatch. Later, images of the building show a gas pump by the side of the building, and tables and chairs on the porch. The hotel was razed by fire in 1947 and was replaced by a Quonset hut that served as a grocery store and meeting place for years. Prior to World War II, Assembly Park was known as Assembly Grounds and in early days was restricted to gentiles only.

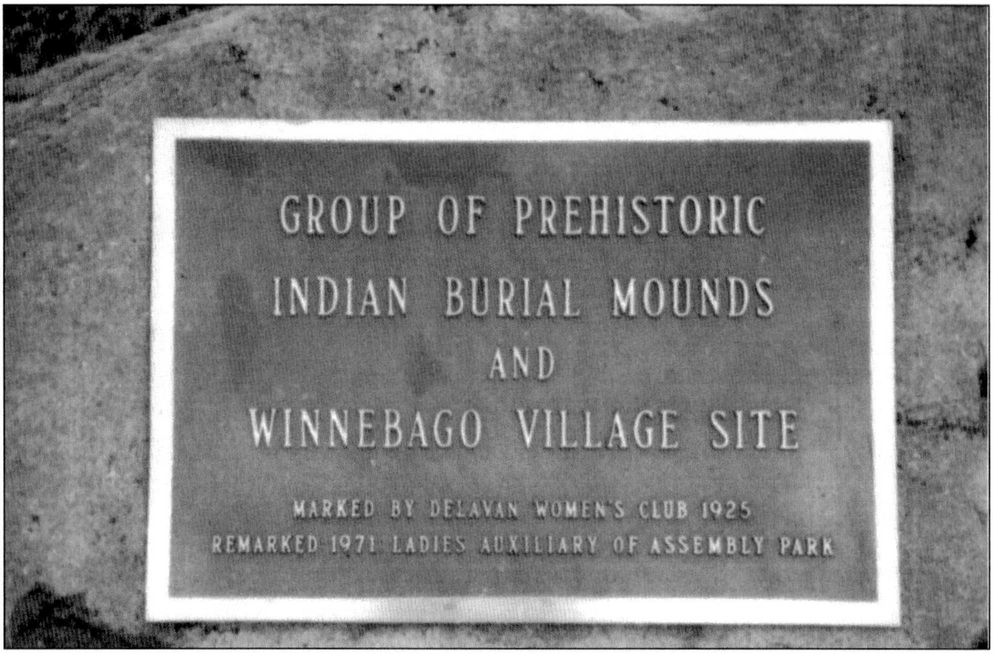

In 1925, the Delavan Women's Club placed a plaque at the site of the Indian Mounds located in Assembly Park, formerly known as Assembly Grounds. In 1971, the Women's Auxiliary of Assembly Park replaced the plaque. Of the mounds that survive around the lake, these are the only ones that are marked. Many mounds were destroyed during the early construction of Assembly Park. It is noteworthy to add that a survey of these mounds concluded that the three conical mounds were erected between 900 and 1050 A.D. by primitive mound builders who lived in this area before the Native Americans. The other small oval mounds were probably built by the Potawatomi Indians who lived at Assembly Grounds between 1480 and 1836 A.D. It is in this vicinity that Delavan founder Col. Samuel Phoenix spent his first night in a Potawatomi wigwam.

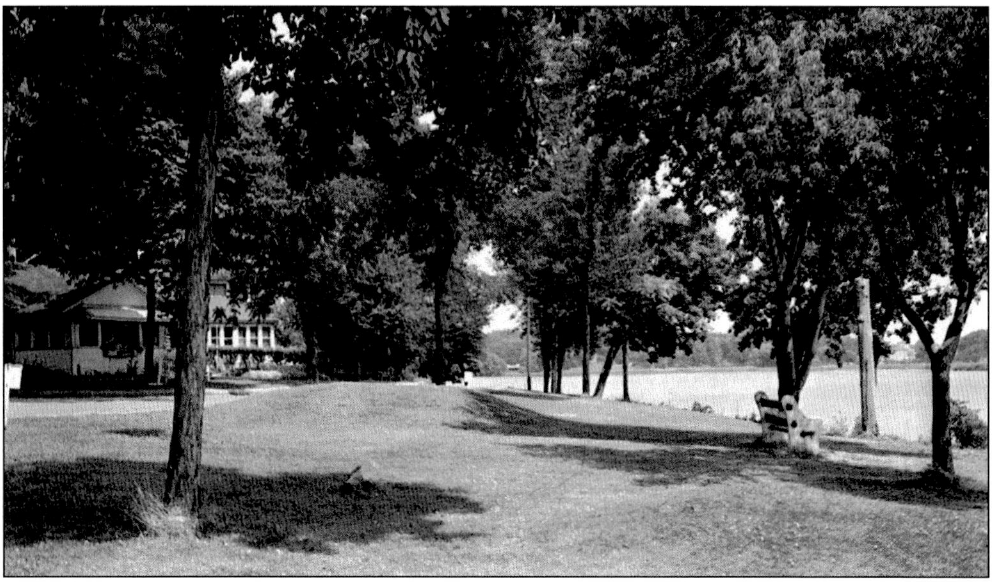

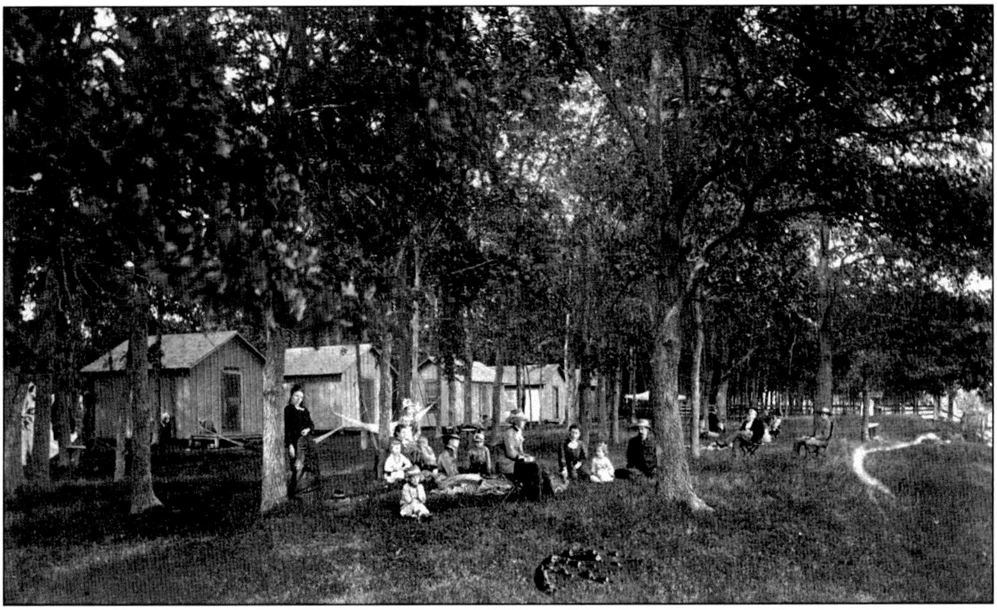

This very rare view, taken about 1880, is of the small cottages that made up Mabiewood on Delavan Lake. Mabiewood comprised some of the land now known as Assembly Park. Property around the lake was purchased by Edmund and Jeremiah Mabie when they chose Delavan for their circus quarters. In 1898, the 38-acre Mabiewood was sold to the Delavan Lake Assembly for $15,000 by the Mabie heirs.

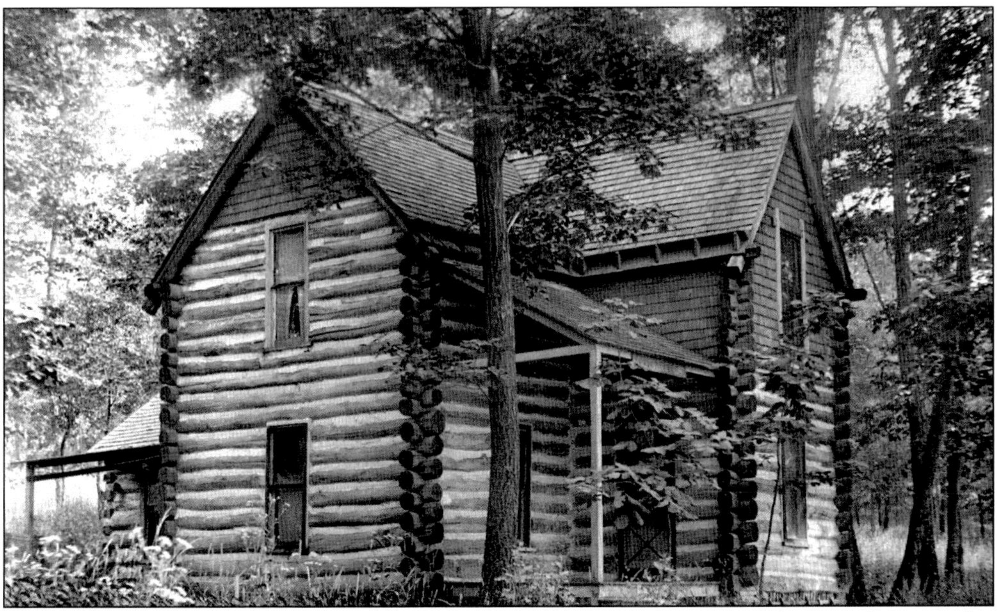

This postcard view shows the Old Kentucky Home on Assembly Grounds around 1912. This structure, although extensively remodeled, is still standing at 1611 Grant Avenue, according to the *Assembly Park Centennial, 1898–1998*. As the Assembly Grounds, or Assembly Park, grew, some entrepreneurs purchased and/or build several cottages and rented them out to vacationers.

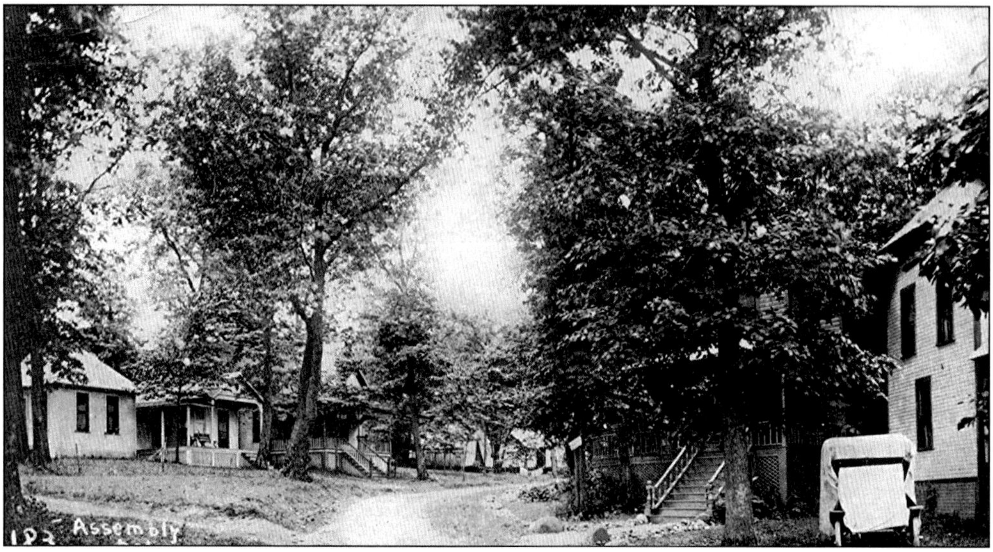

This postcard shows what Lincoln Avenue in Assembly Park looked like back in 1909. During the Chautauqua period (1898–1914), there were simply not accommodations for the thousands of people that would descend upon the Assembly Grounds during a program in the summer. Many of the attendees would pitch tents, staying there for two weeks for the sessions that began at the end of June.

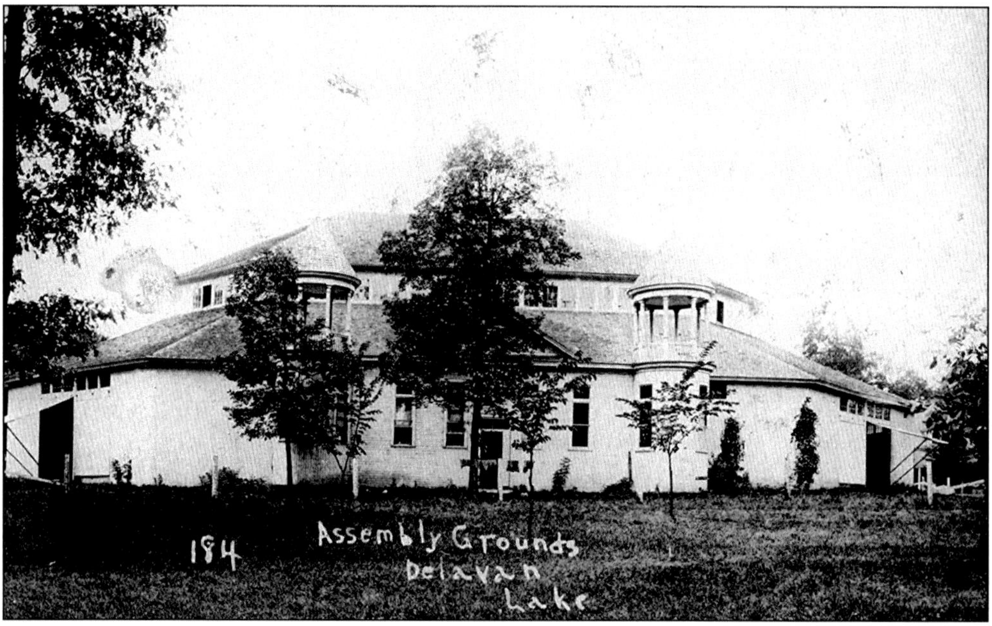

The Assembly Auditorium was completed in time for the 1899 season. Based on the ideals of the original Chautauqua in New York, the new auditorium would feature lecturers on religion, politics, society, art, science, and patriotism, whatever topics would "enlarge, refine, or ennoble the individual," according to Chautauqua Cofounder John Vincent. The auditorium would host up to 3,000 people a day during the two-week sessions. Crossed wires caused the fire that destroyed it in 1919.

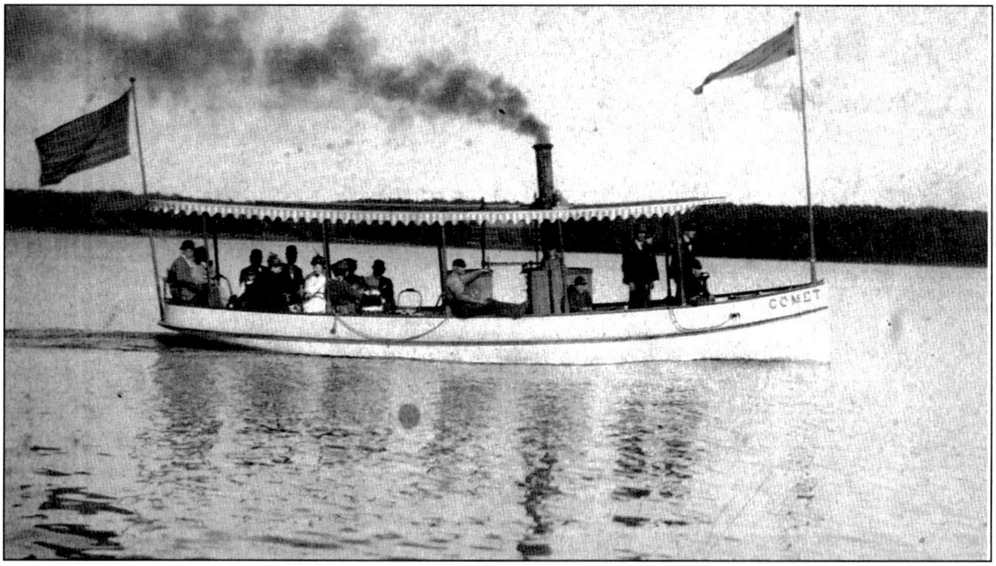

New to Delavan lake in 1891, the steamer christened *Comet* was a beautiful although small vessel that made fast time while transporting its 60 to 70 passengers to all the fundamental stops along the lake. In 1893, the *Comet* was purchased by Will Gabriel, who revamped its interior, gaining it more patronage. Despite being a favorite on the lake, in 1895 the arrival of larger boats drove the steamer to relocate on Brown's Lake in East Troy.

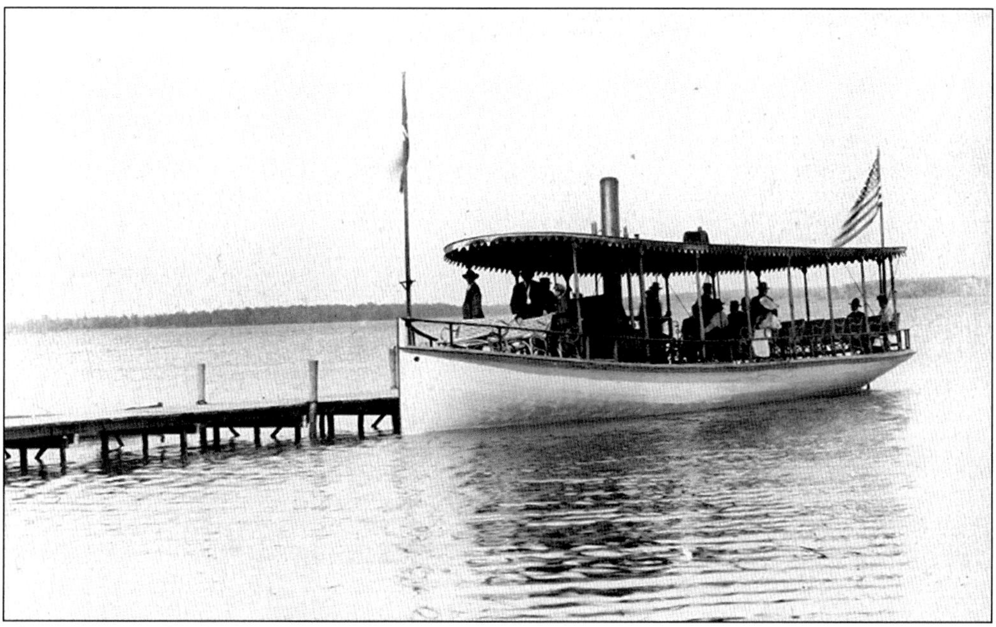

The steamer *Columbia*, owned by the Keefe brothers, made its headquarters at Highland Park. As of 1897, the Columbia was the largest steamer on Delavan Lake, leaving twice daily to transport her passengers from shore to shore. However, in June of that same year, the *Columbia* mysteriously burned while in dry dock at Highland Park. And although the steamer held $4,000 in insurance, only $2,000 was paid out because the engine and boiler were considered salvageable.

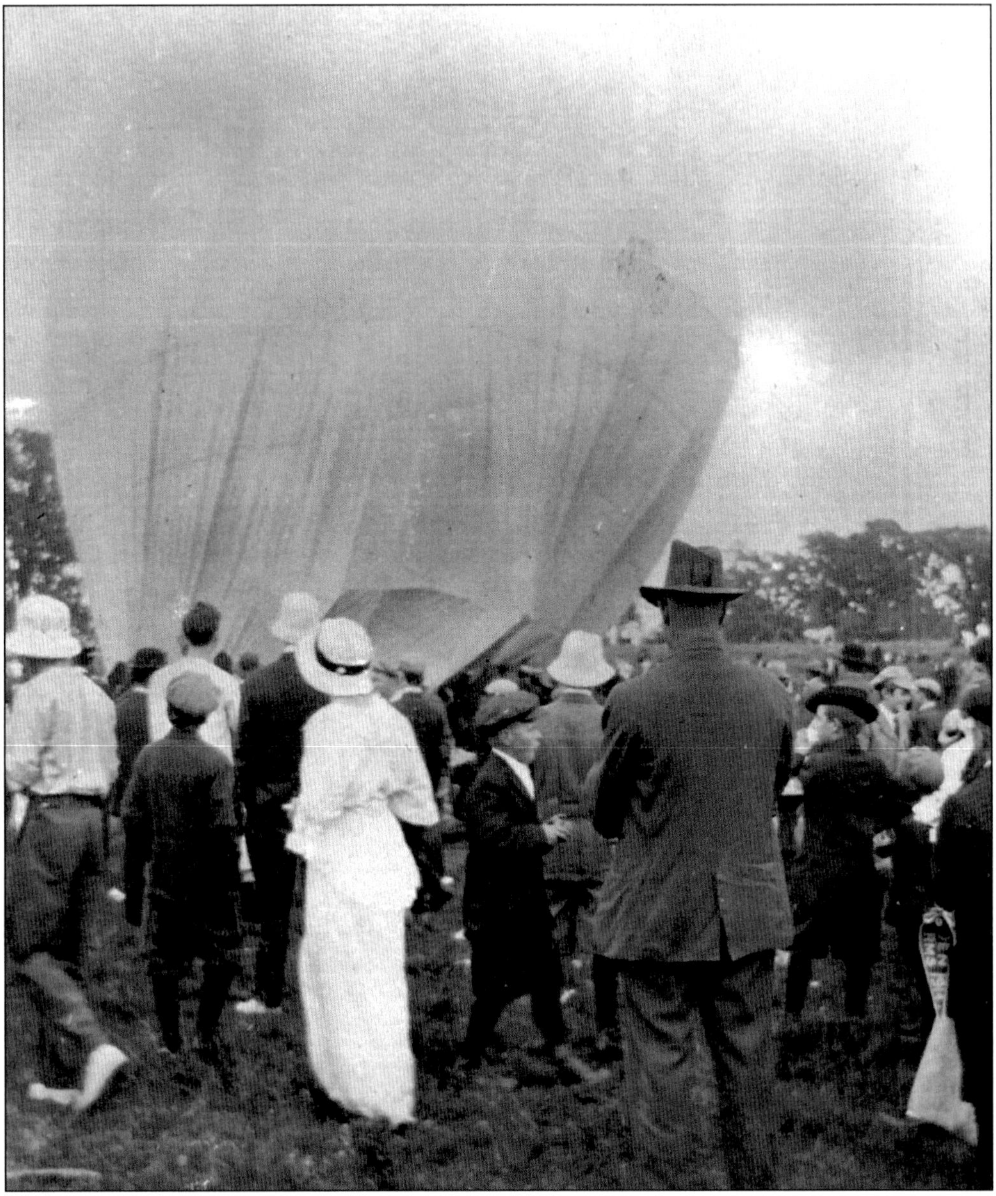

The children of Delavan had a magical benefactor from 1912 to 1914 in a man by the name of Edward Tilden. Mr. Tilden was born into a large Delavan family. It was before his birthday many years later in 1912 that he recalled an occasion when his family was too poor for him to see the circus. He vowed that one day he would put on a free circus so no child would have to pay to see it. Mr. Tilden was successful enough to accomplish this feat and for the next three years would host the parties that attracted crowds of people Delavan hadn't seen since the heyday of the Chautauqua assemblies. Mr. and Mrs. Tilden put an ad in the Delavan newspaper inviting every child to his birthday party held at Tilden grove, presently the site of the fourth and fifth holes at Lake Lawn Golf Course. Pictured here is Ed Hutchinson's balloon ascension at the 1914 Tilden Picnic.

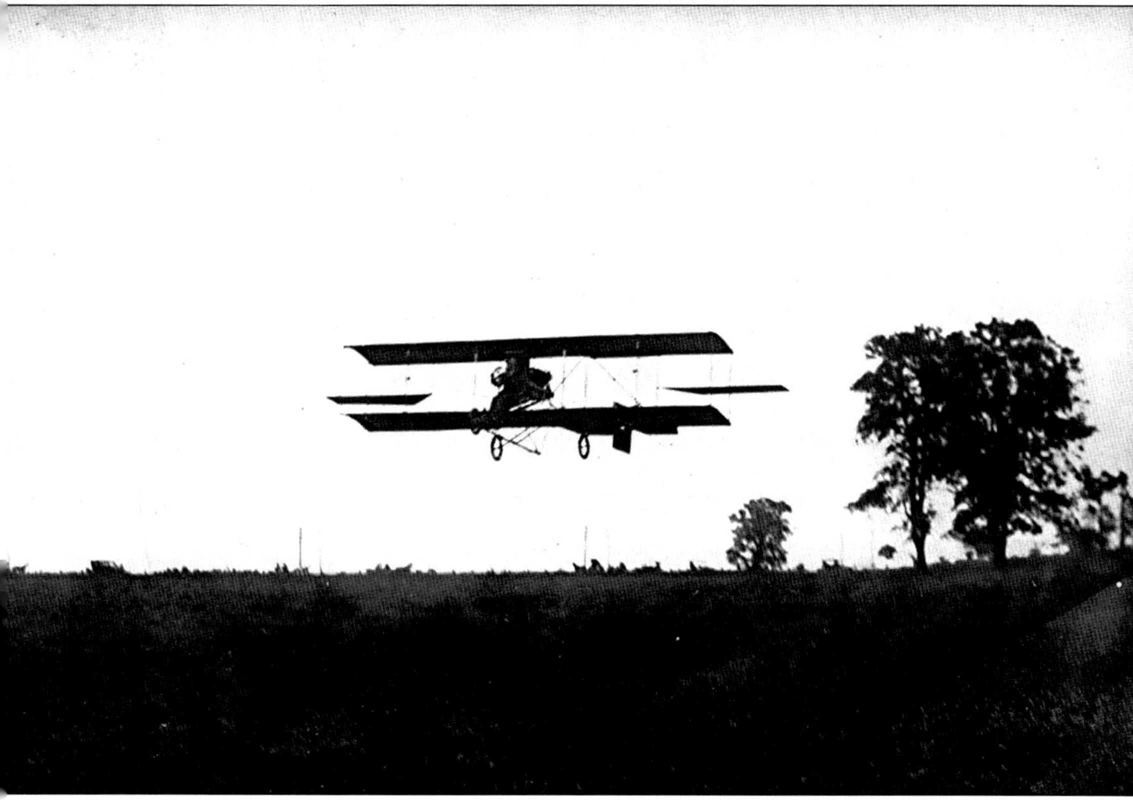

Jimmie Ward and his flying machine were the star attraction at Tilden's 1912 picnic. It is recorded as the first flight in Delavan. The plane was shipped in parts and reassembled not far from the party site. Children and adults watched in awe as Jimmie Ward soared above the crowd. Tilden was unable to provide a circus on such short notice, so instead he used his contacts to provide other activities. Along with Jimmie Ward, the Spanner Orchestra of Chicago, noted magician Henry Roethrig, and the famous Punch and Judy Show provided entertainment. The Tildens so enjoyed the party that they started planning another for the following year. Over 3,000 children and adults attended the 1912 celebration, at which they were fed and entertained for free. Horse-drawn transportation was provided for the partygoers, also free of charge. Children looked at Mr. Tilden in wonderment.

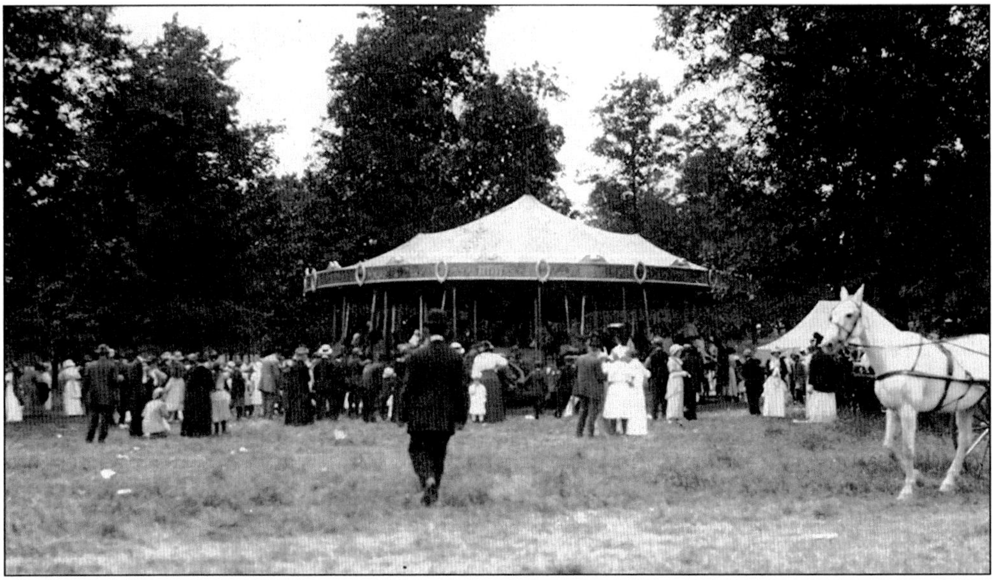

The June 1913 Tilden Picnic was even larger than the first one held in 1912, attracting over 5,000 attendees. This year featured a return engagement by Jimmie Ward and his flying machine, as well as the magician, but the biggest addition this year was a circus. Tilden had engaged the Rex Comedy circus to entertain the children. The 1914 picnic was even larger yet. These two views show the merry-go-round and the people arriving at the July 1914 picnic grounds. The Tildens wanted to plan the biggest party yet for 1915 to celebrate Mr. Tilden's 60th birthday, but sadly Mr. Tilden died in February of that year.

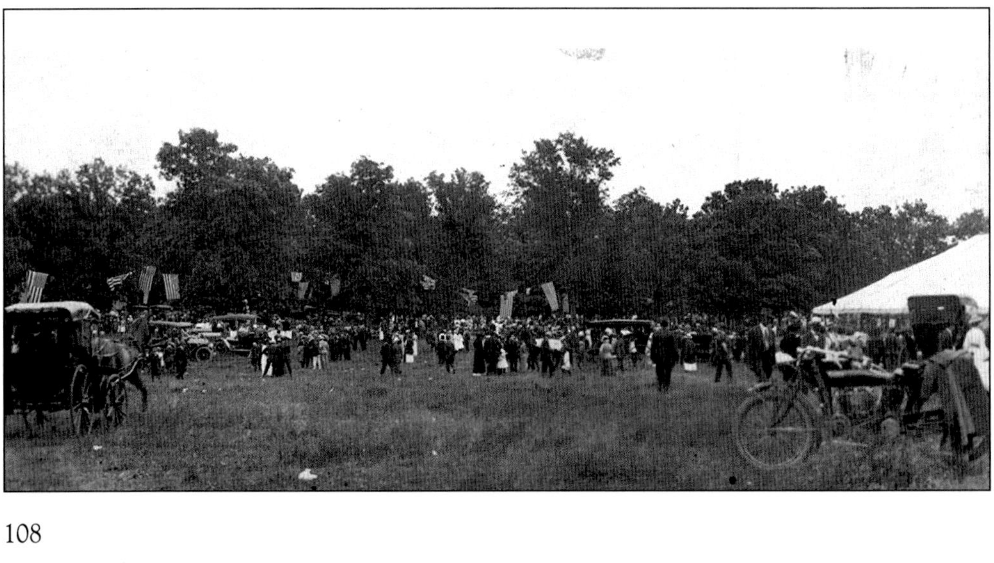

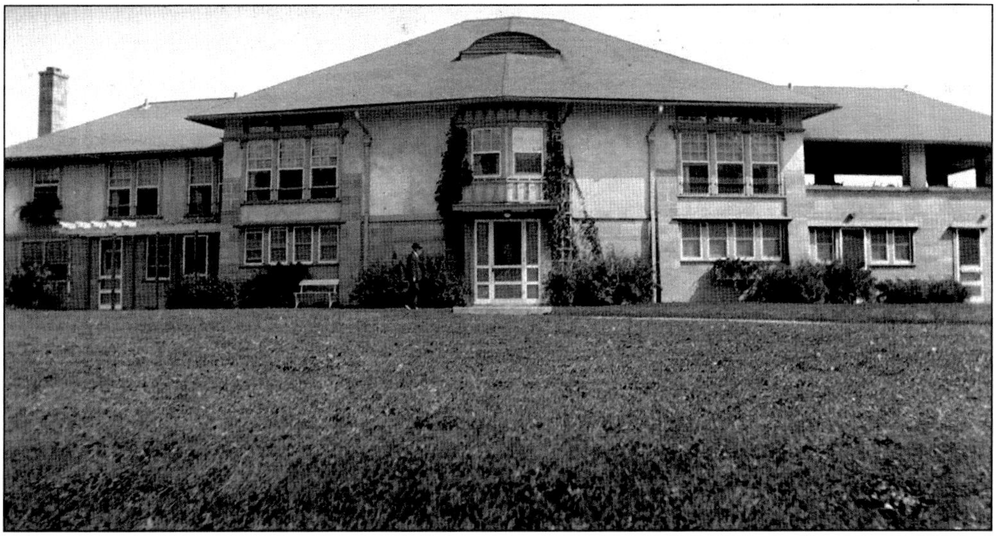

In 1913, the Delavan Yacht Club opened a nine-hole golf course at the corner of South Shore Drive and Lake Avenue, now Bailey Road. It was named the Delavan Lake Golf Course. In 1916, they consolidated the yacht club and the golf course to form the Delavan Lake Country Club and built a larger clubhouse on the property. It was expanded to 18 holes in 1923 after land was purchased from Joseph Buckles. The Depression hit the country club hard and the golf course ended up in a foreclosure sale in 1938. Despite the members' effort to buy it back, they were outbid and plans were drawn up for the Del-Mar subdivision. In 1941, the Delavan Lake Yacht Club procured a new home on Cedar Point.

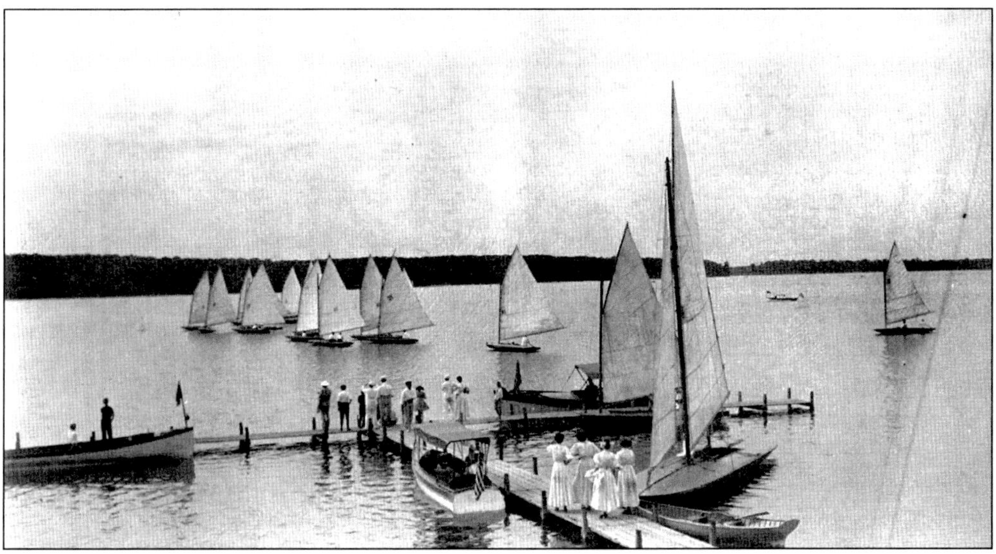

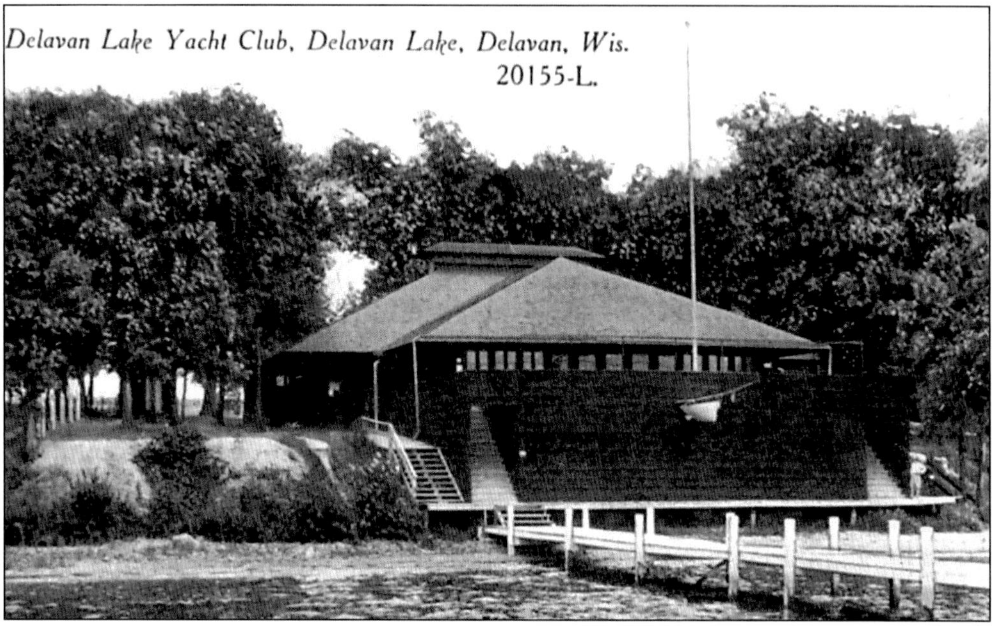

Although the Delavan Lake Yacht Club was established in 1892, their first clubhouse wasn't built until 1904—designed by Frank Lloyd Wright. It was located on the south shore of the lake, west of where the Del-Mar beach is today. The building was small but functional, and provided facilities for the club's functions. After building a new clubhouse across the street on the golf course, the clubhouse was moved in order to provide a park that would extend from South Shore Drive down to the lake. It was torn down in about 1916. Pictured below is the fireplace from the inside of the DLYC clubhouse.

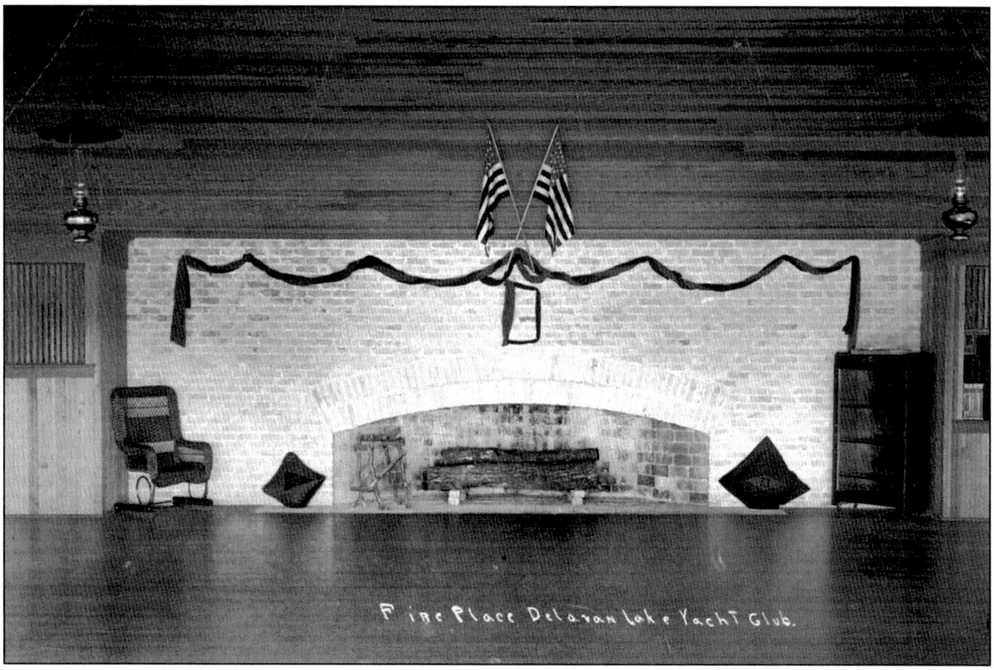

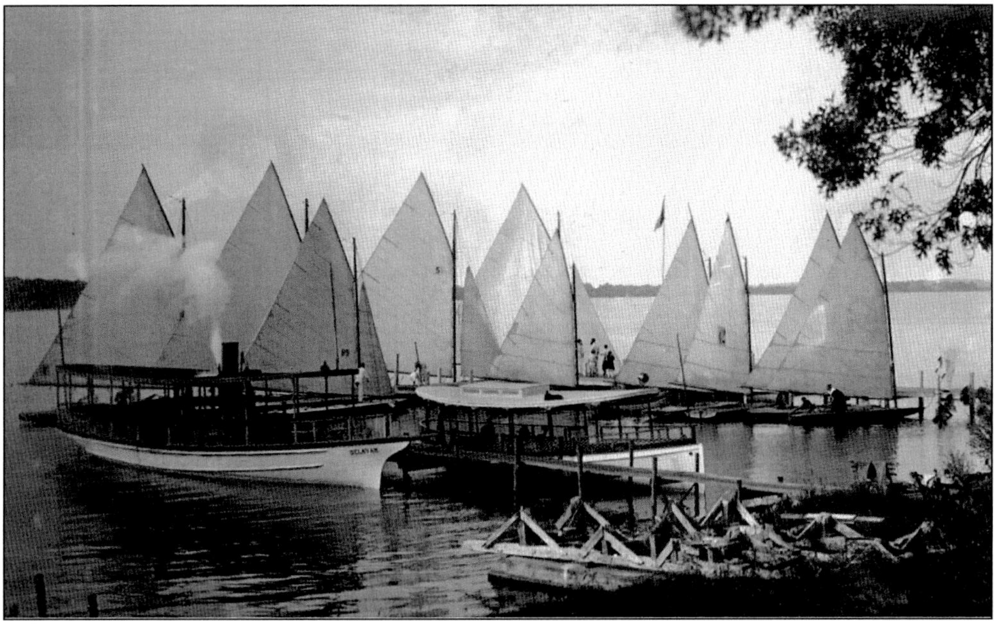

The 1911 image above was taken from the Delavan Lake Yacht Club pier on the south shore of the lake. It shows the sailboats lined up to race, while the steamers sit at the pier waiting to be boarded. The steamer on the left is the *Delavan* and the excursion boat on the right is the *Le Baron*. The photograph below, also taken from the south shore, shows launches secured to the pier on the left and sailboats tied up on the right. The people gathered at the end of the pier are awaiting the arrival of the barely visible excursion boat.

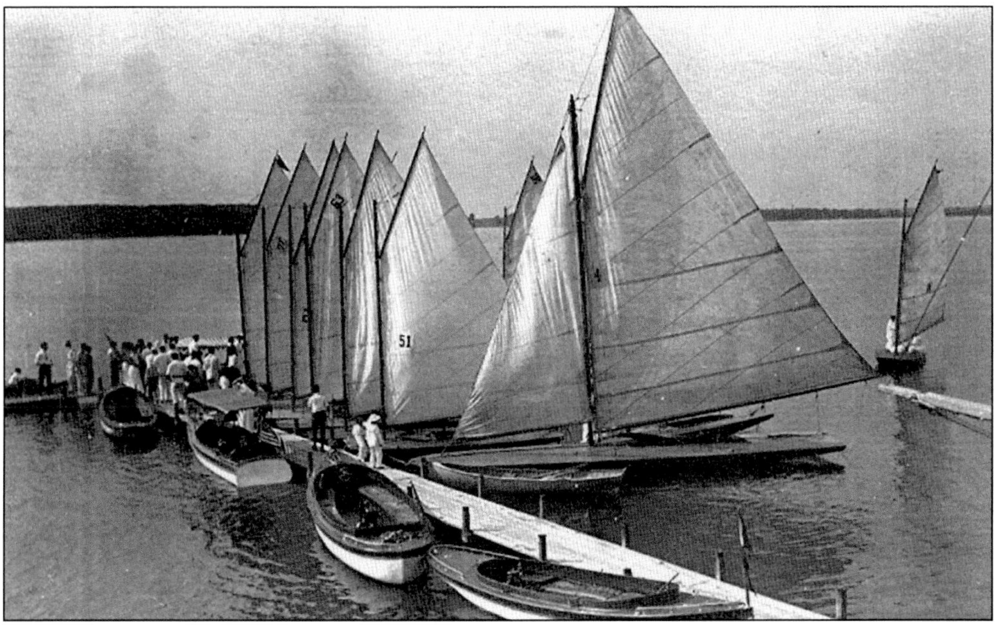

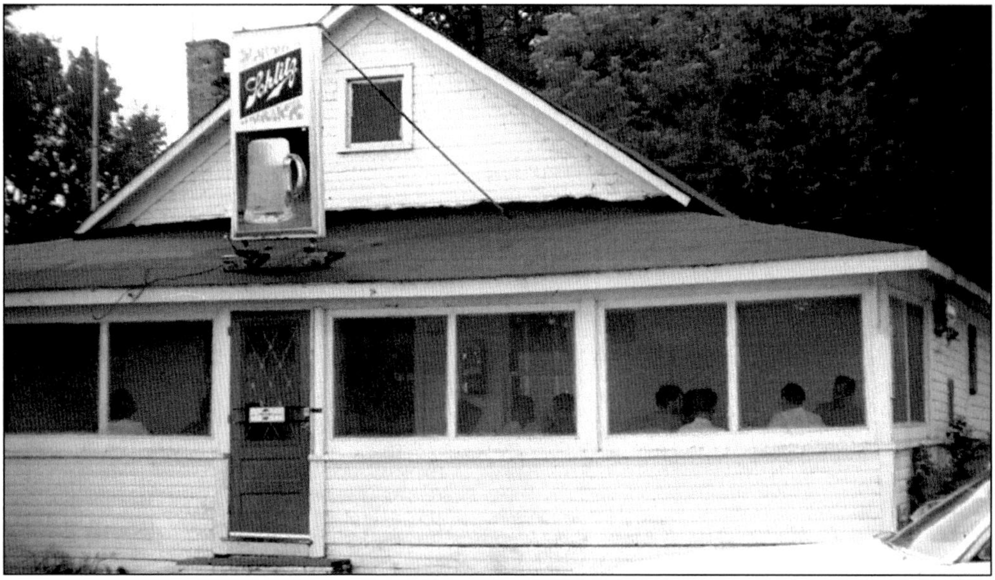

Fleming's Tavern on the north shore by Cedar Point was a great institution, well-loved by its patrons. Mentioning the tavern evokes memories of great hamburgers and the floor sloping dramatically downhill to the bar. Thomas and Katie Fleming operated the little fishing-boating resort until 1928, when they turned it over to their son William and his wife Ethel. For the next 41 years, Bill and "Ma" Fleming operated the tavern and were popular with the young and old alike. The bar in Fleming's came from Hollister's Log Cabin Resort. The business changed hands several times after the Flemings sold it in 1969. It was sold to the yacht club in 1982 and razed. The back bar from Flemings found a new home with the current Delavan Lake Yacht Club.

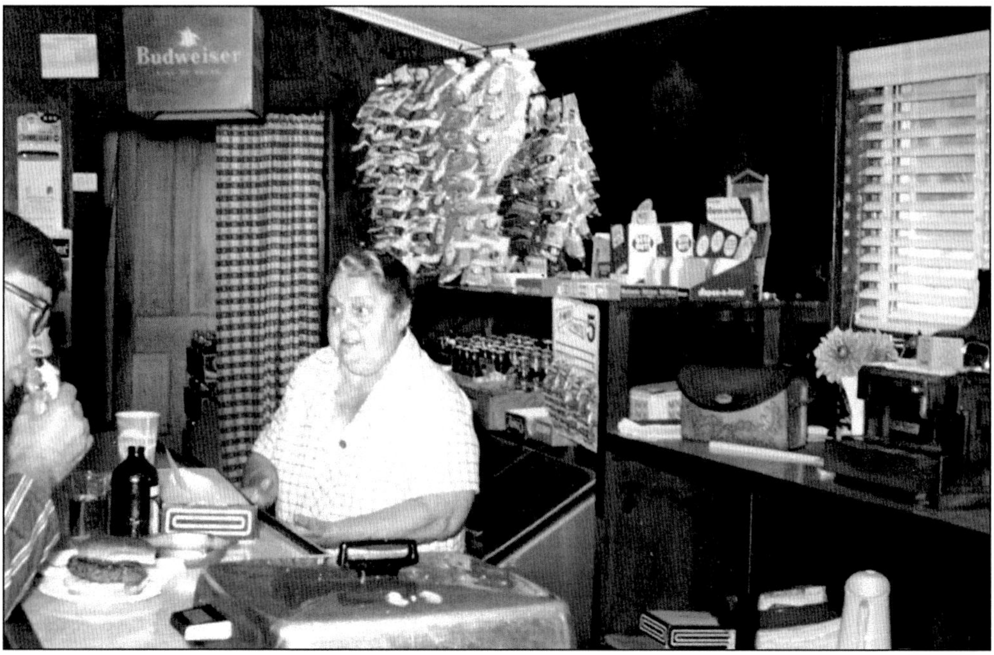

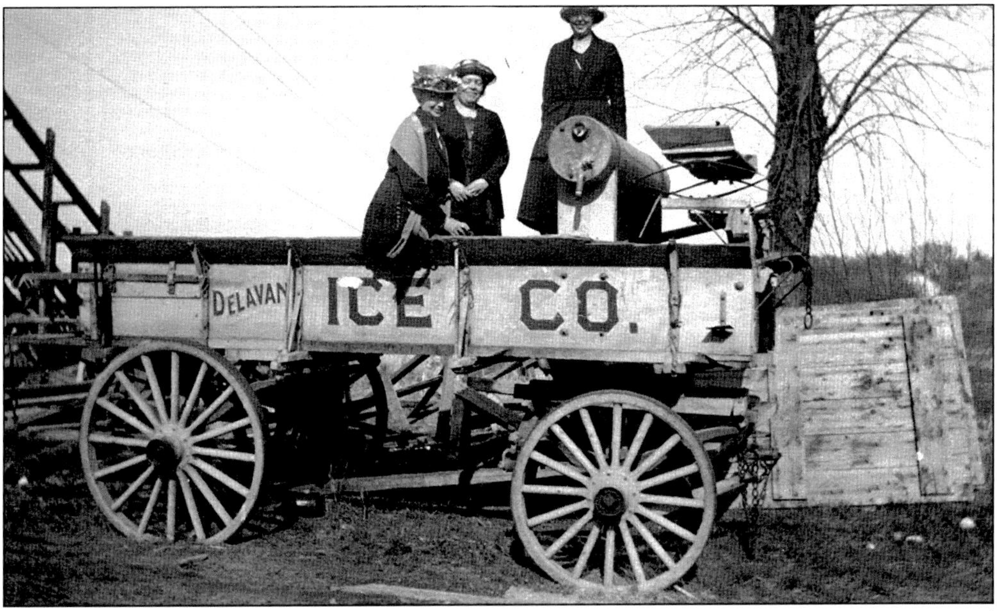

This wagon belonged to the Delavan Lake Ice Company, which in the early 1900s was owned by the Van Velzer brothers. The ice company was located at the outlet of Delavan lake, and although occupied by women instead of ice in this photograph, this horse-drawn wagon would deliver ice door-to-door. Some of the resorts had their own ice storage houses, which the Van Velzers filled.

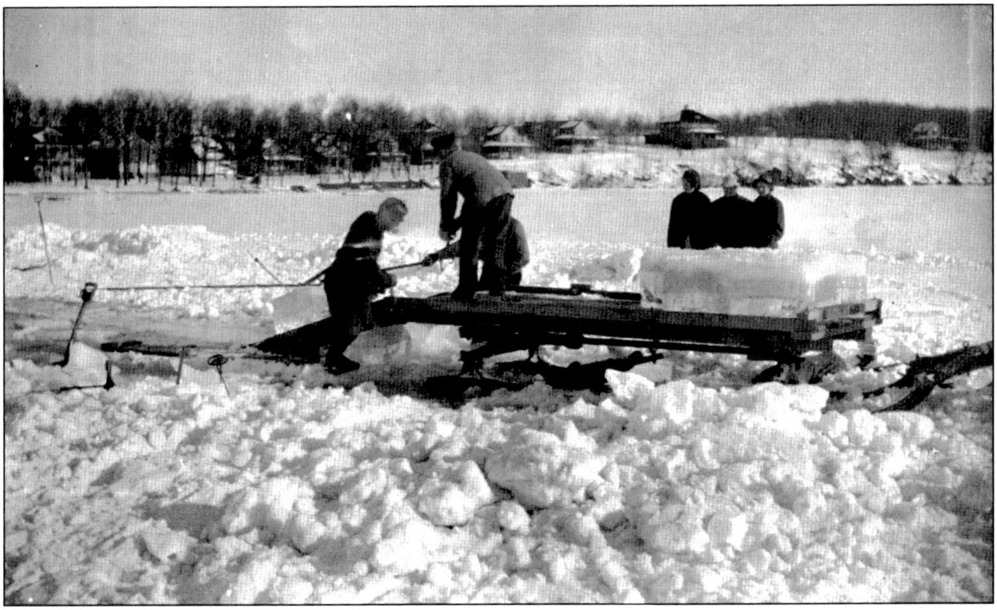

The ice harvesting shown above was probably being collected for the Van Velzer Ice Company, located at the outlet of the lake. It was the only ice harvesting operation on the lake. In order to get the best quality, the ice must be about 12 inches thick. After the ice was cut and the block freed, ice harvesters had to scrape or chisel the hardened snow off the top, which would leave them with a nice clear block.

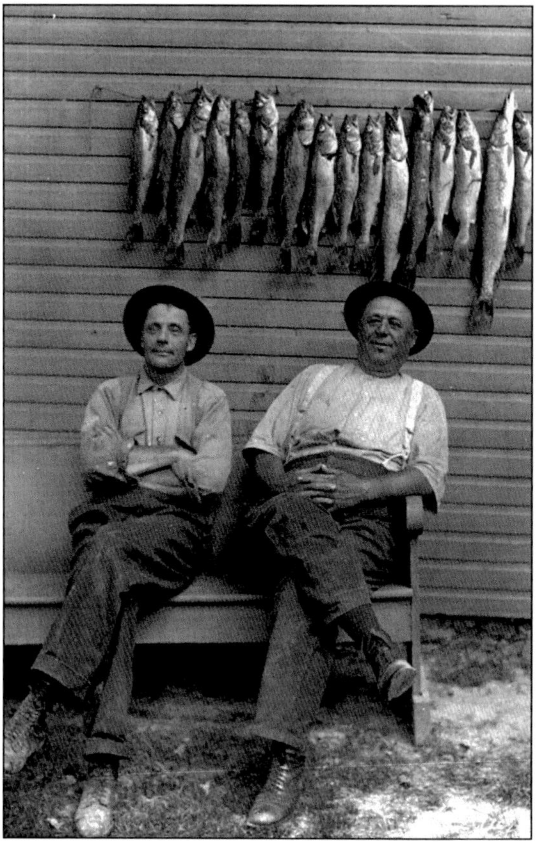

Delavan Lake has always been a great fishing lake. A booklet advertising Delavan Lake in 1895 boasts, "Delavan Lake is being fed by springs and the lake is very clear and home to many varieties of fish. It is restocked yearly and is a famous fishing ground. Pike, pickerel, or the gamy black bass, beloved of sportsmen, never fail to reward the patience of the angler." Red Winn and Gene Barker proudly exhibit their catch of pike. Below a 1908 photograph shows women displaying the efforts of their fishing expedition.

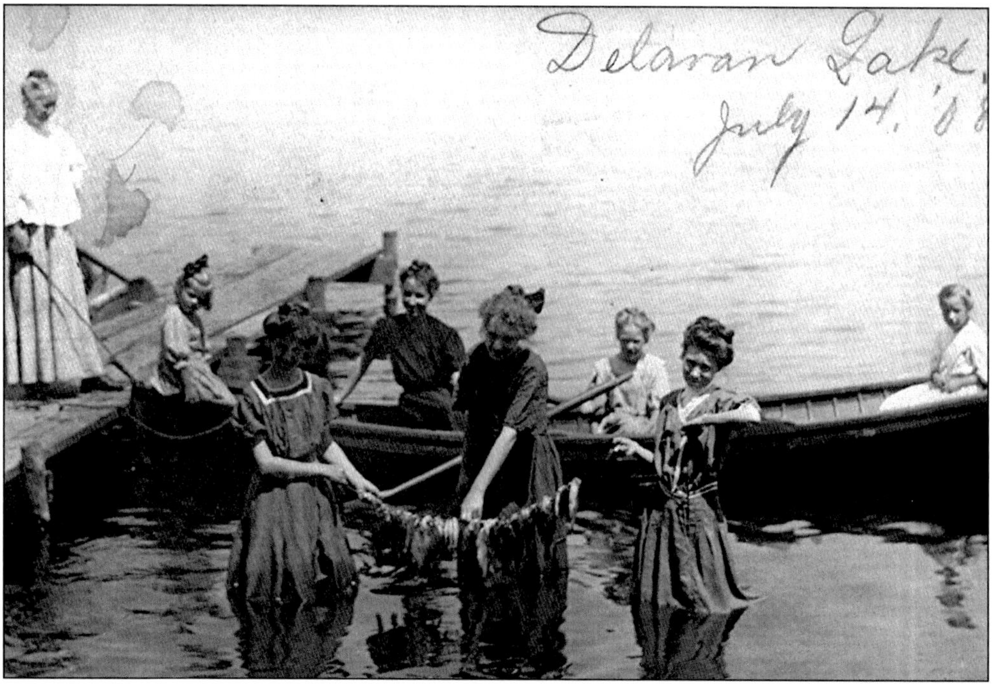

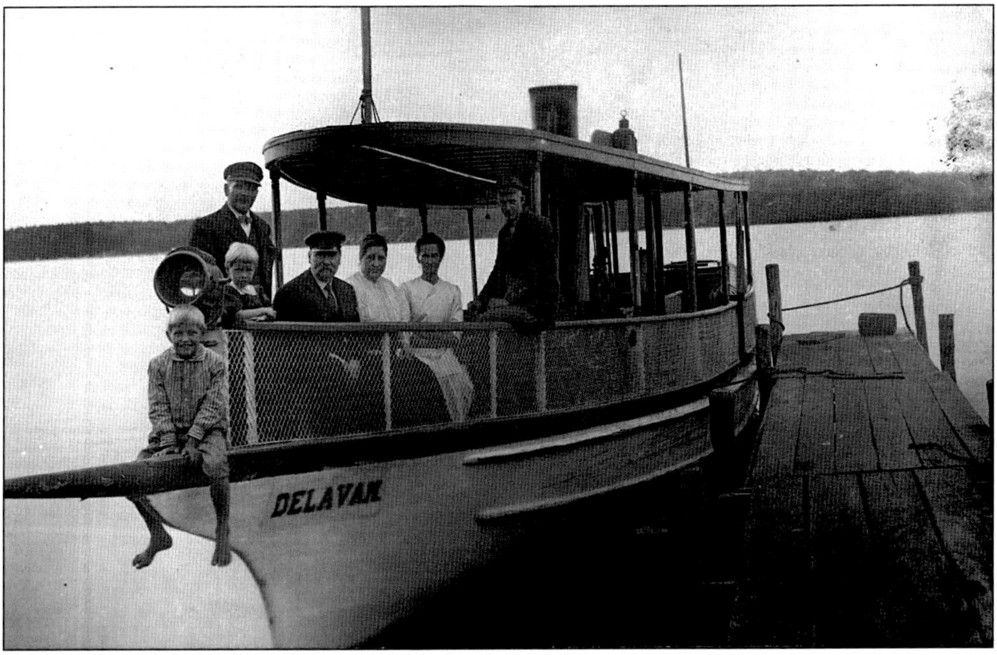

The steamer *Delavan* was an excursion boat that took passengers around the lake. The *Delavan* was launched in 1903, originally leaving from Mettowie. But after Mettowie burned down, it would leave from the highland pier and make scheduled stops at Woodlawn Bay, the Assembly Pier, Spring Lawn, and the Log Cabin. They would stop at other piers upon receiving a signal or by special arrangement. The *Delavan* was also available to charter for parties, dances, or special occasions. At dusk on August 30, 1908, the steamer accidentally ran into a rowboat, drowning a woman and her two children. The *Delavan* continued to tour the lake into the 1920s and was later scrapped.

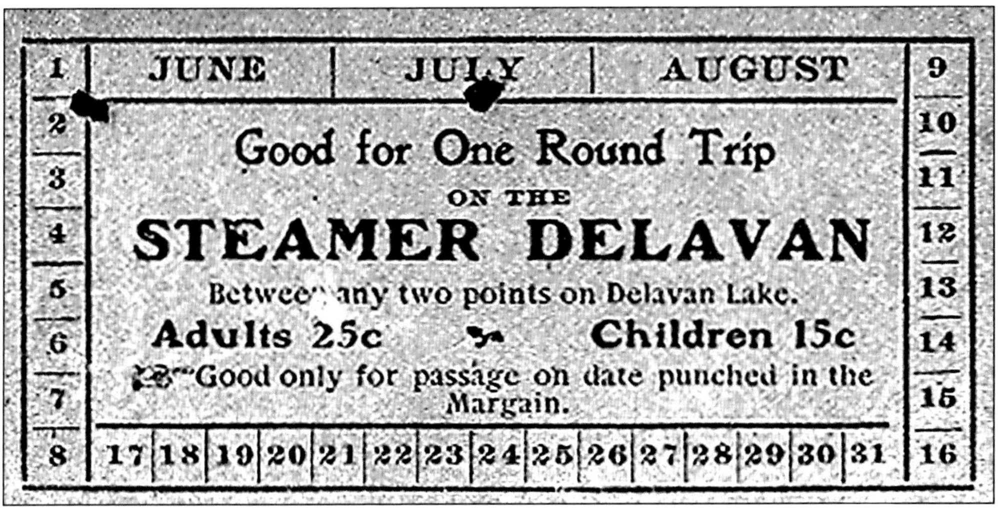

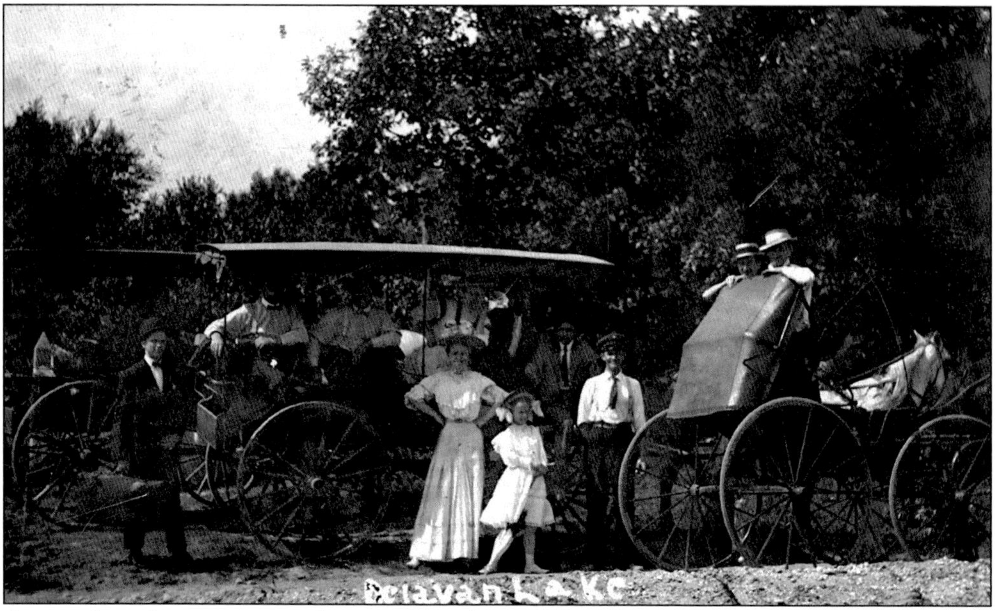

Captured in this rare image from 1908 is the Carpenter's Bus Line. Before the automobile became the norm, a bus like this one here had a scheduled route around the lake and into town. Some would assist in taking visitors from the train out to the lake. There were several bus lines running at the same time and several resorts had their own. Competition was stiff and some bus lines, like Carpenter's, didn't last very long.

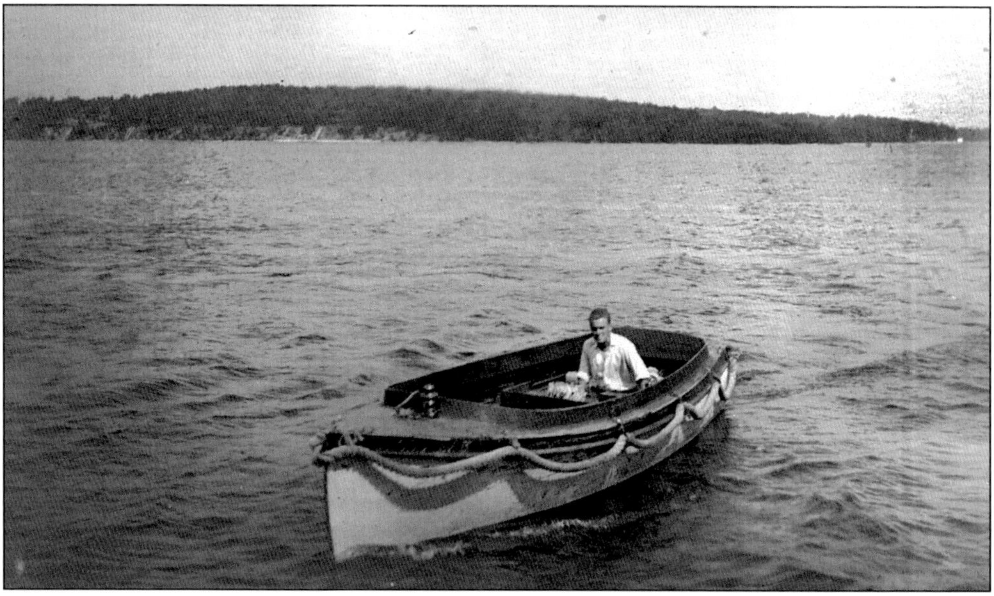

The marine mail carrier on Delavan Lake during 1912–1913 was Charles Beamsley. The marine mail route began in 1909 and was discontinued in 1957. Boats delivering the mail were contracted through the Delavan Lake Boat and Engine Company in early years. Marine mail service was implemented to relieve the regular postal carriers of the increased mail that occurred during the summer months, when the influx of visitors swelled around the lake.

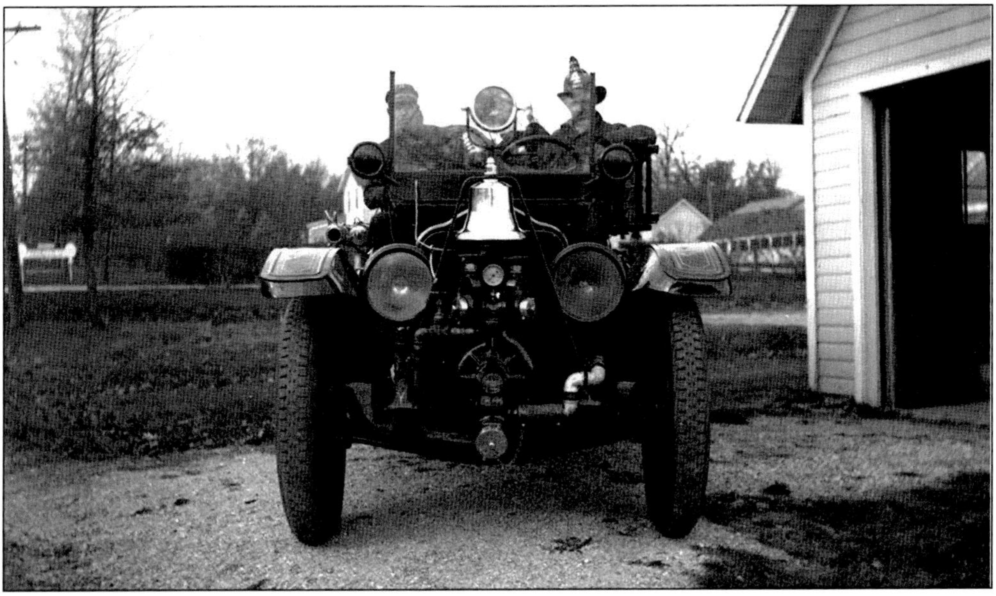

Dr. Cecil Bachelle was instrumental in the formation of the Delavan Lake Improvement Association's (DLIA) Fire Department in 1924. Before this time, there wasn't a fire department to battle the blazes that destroyed many hotels, resorts, and cottages around the lake. The Town of Delavan purchased the fire truck from the DLIA in 1963. The photograph above shows truck no. 2, a chemical truck that was housed in a specially built structure on the Buzzell Farm on the north shore of the lake. Below is the first hook and ladder shown at the Lake Lawn Lodge fire station, its normal station was at the LaBar farm.

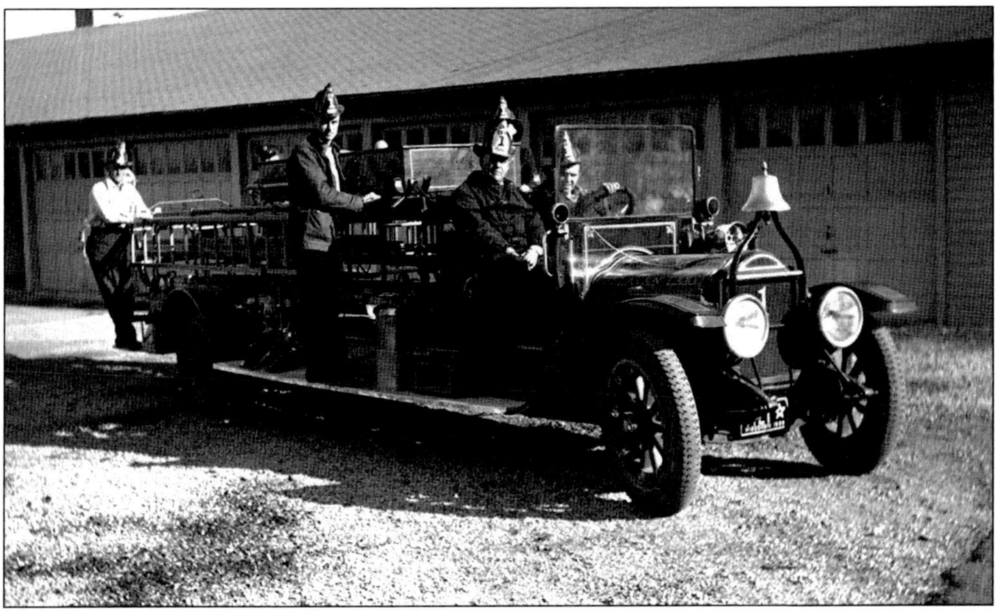

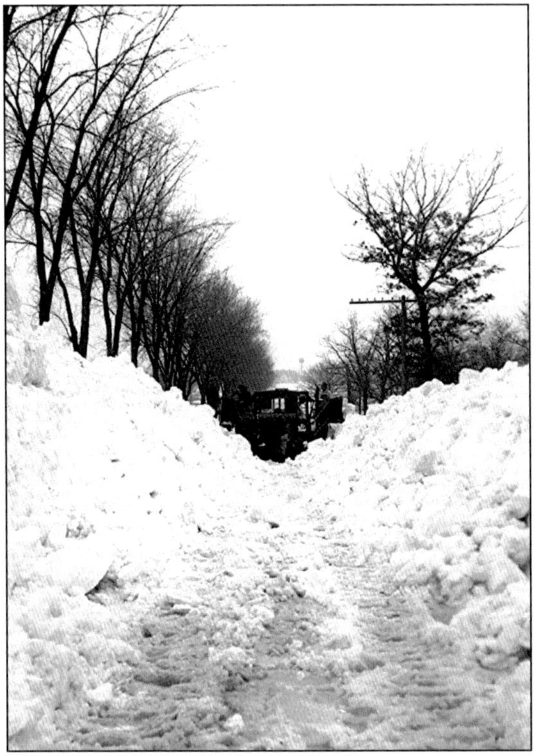

The snowstorm of 1936 reeked havoc on Delavan and the rest of the county. Kids were thrilled, at first, when they were out of school for the following six weeks—it was that long before the roads were clear enough for some teachers who lived in other communities to make it to Delavan. They were not too happy when they had to make up those snow days, keeping them in school until July. Shown here is the Town of Delavan highway department road crew opening the roads along the lake. Below are men shoveling the path for the snow plow to get through.

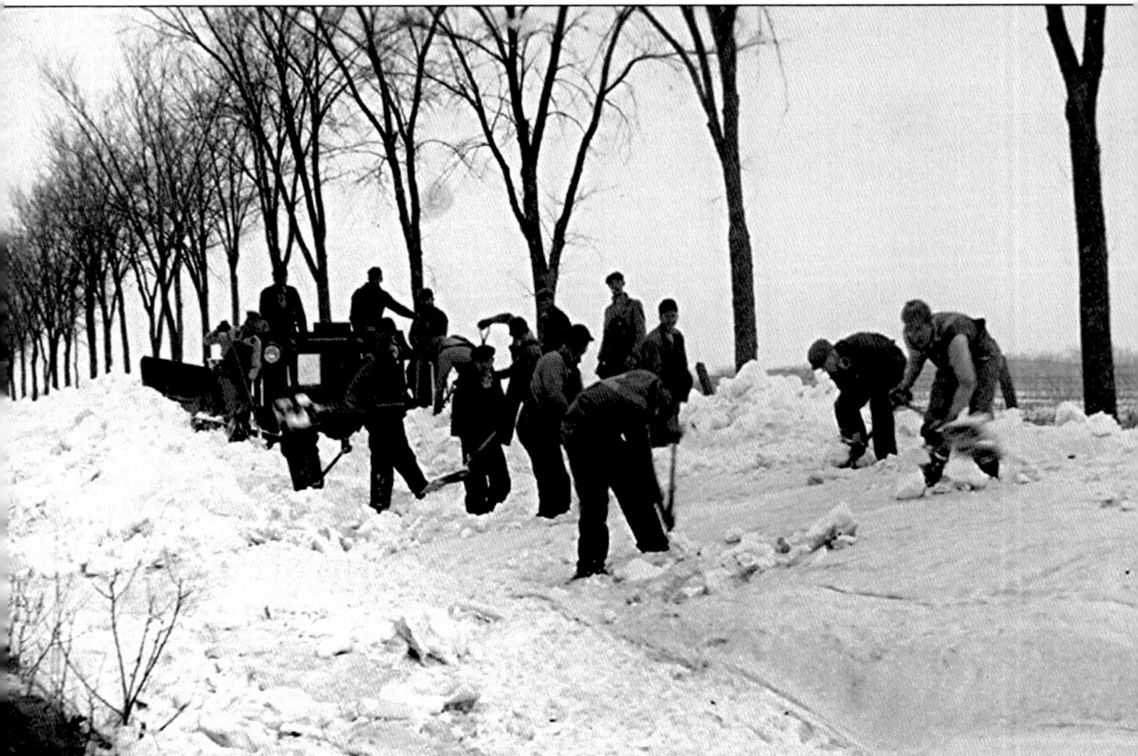

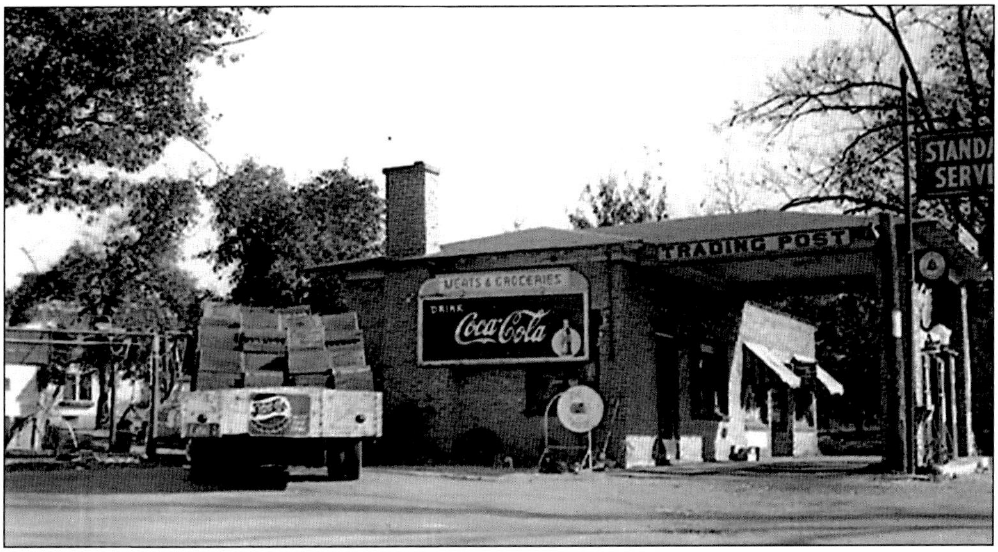

Jim's Trading Post opened at the southeast corner of Townhall Road and Highway 50 in 1931, operating as a refreshment and grocery stand. In 1937, he added a filling station and a brick addition to the existing structure. It was sold to Marshal Fouts in 1937, and then again in 1941 to George Proctor. Proctor carried a full line of meats and groceries, turned the station ito a Standard Oil, and offered minor car repair. He ran the business until his death in 1976.

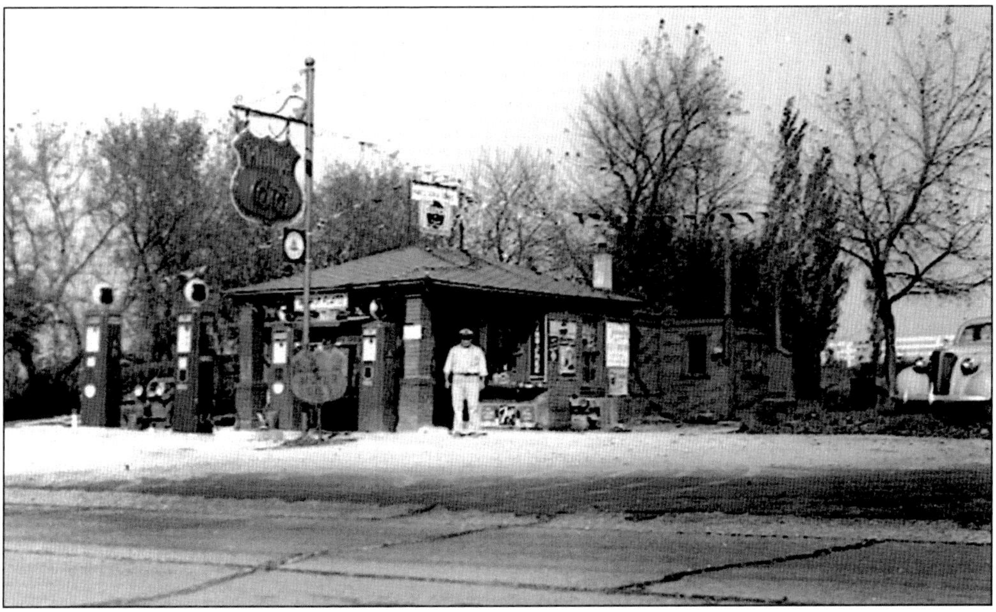

Harold Karlinski's Phillips 66 station was located in the Inlet on the northeast corner of Townhall Road and Highway 50. The original filling station at this location was built by George Humphrey in the late 1920s. Humphrey ran it as a Texaco station with a pop stand to quench the travelers' thirst. It has had numerous owners over the years.

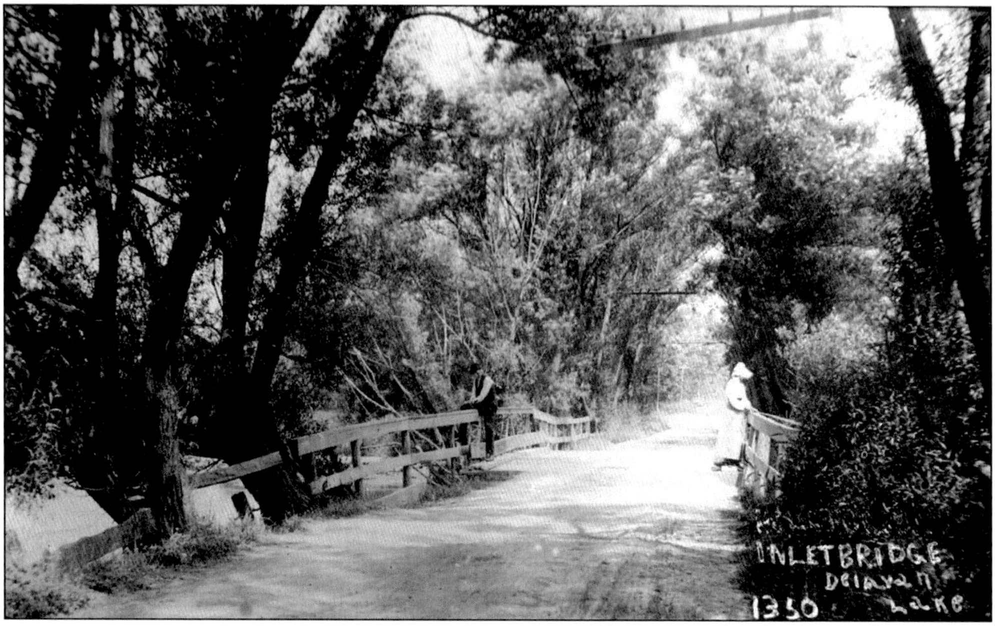

The bridges built over the inlet and outlet provided important access to both sides of the lake. The addition of these bridges cut down travel time around the lake dramatically. With road improvements these former one-lane bridges have evolved in to two-lane roads with ample shoulders. The photograph of the inlet bridge, taken about 1910, shows the growth of trees around the bridge. These trees aided in keeping the bridge in place and not collapsing into the water, as had happened previously. The road across the outlet, below, was built in 1900. The photograph below shows the interesting construction and displays a stenciled advertisement for W.W. Bradley Dry Goods.

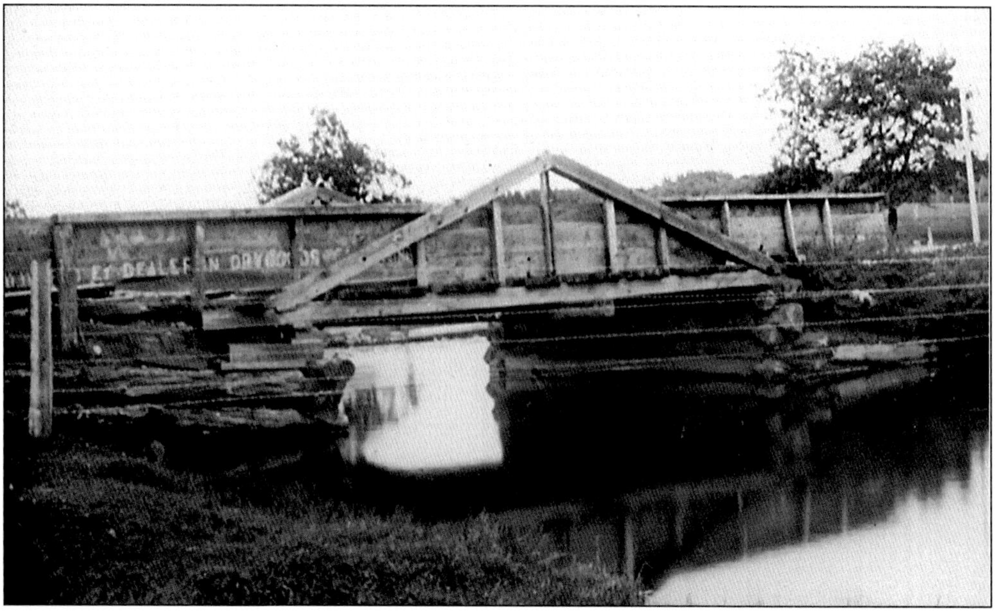

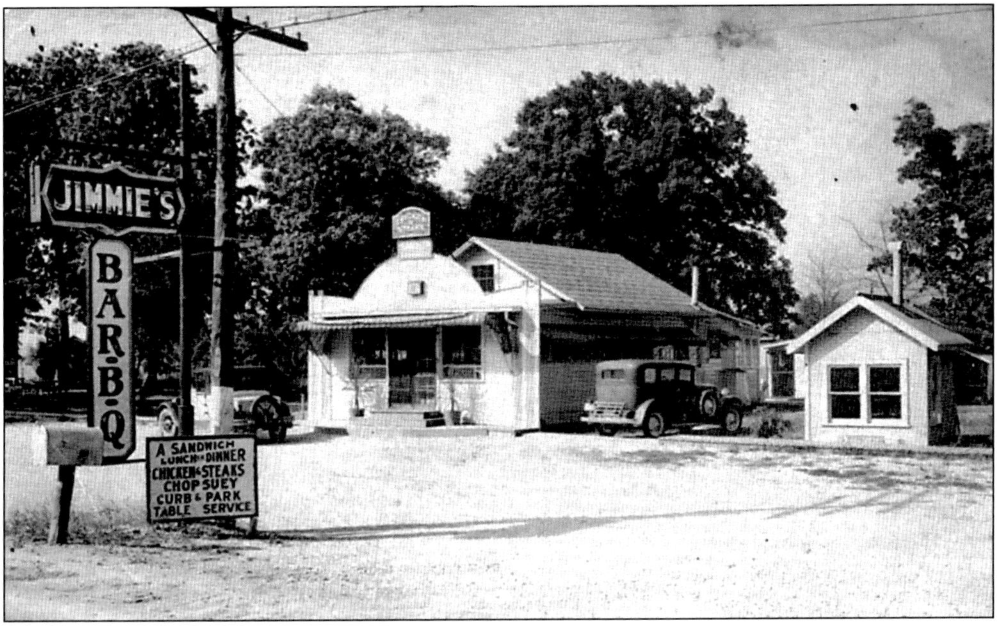

Jimmie's Bar-B-Q (pictured above), formerly known as Oaks Inn Bar-B-Q, was opened by James Drauden in 1928—the name changed in 1935. Drauden died in 1936 and his widow and nephew ran it until it closed in the mid-1940s. John Delaney open Delaney's, below, in 1924. He ran it until 1936 and then sold it to Lou Jackson, who operated it from 1941 until it closed. Both eating establishments were located in the inlet and enjoyed great success. Those old enough to remember may recall frequenting one or both of these places when the ballrooms emptied out at one o'clock in the morning. Both of these barbecue places enjoyed their heyday from about 1928 to 1947.

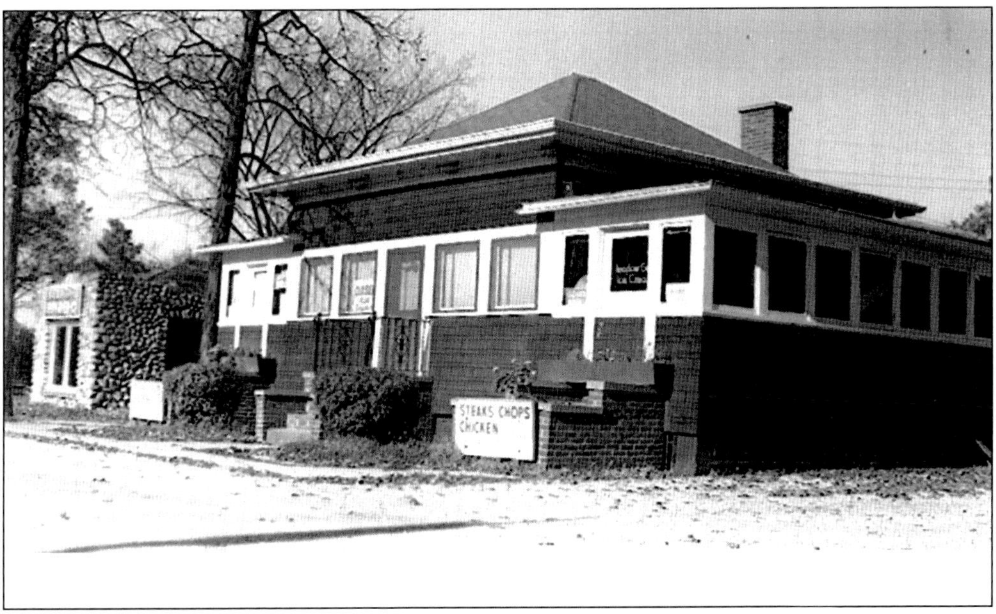

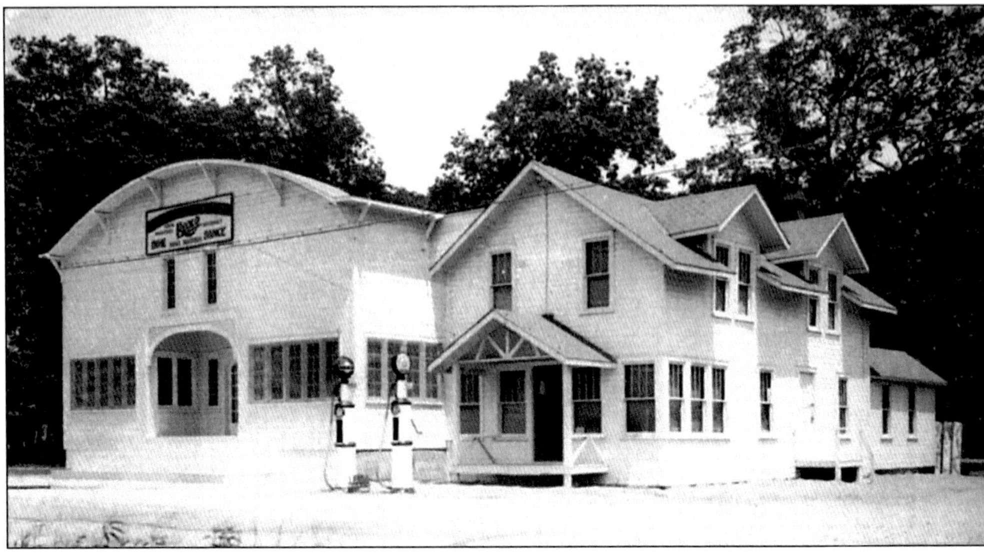

Bruce's Dance Hall and Tavern at the Inlet was owned and operated by Jerome and Margaret Bruce. It was run previously by Mr. Bruce's father as a refreshment stand during Prohibition. Bruce's Dance Hall was popular from the 1930s through the 1950s. It was adjacent to the Bruce Tavern, which later became Van Vleets and then the Branding Iron. The Branding Iron was destroyed by fire in 1982 and stood where the Ralph's Steakhouse parking lot is.

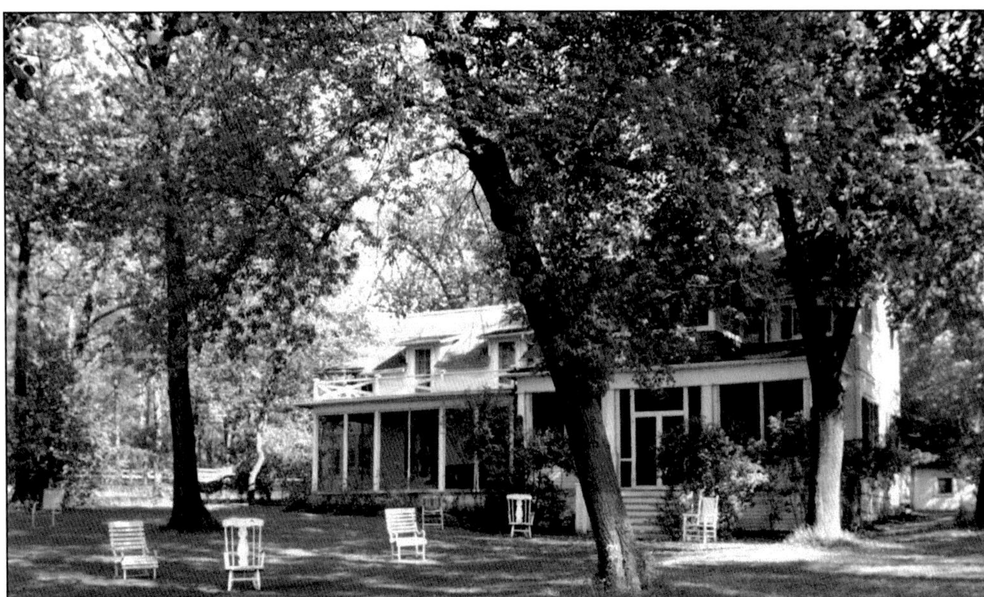

Orchard Rest is an example of one of the many private residences around the lake that built and rented out cottages to summer vacationers. Orchard Rest was located on South Shore Drive, about two blocks east of South Shore Manor. Cottages were continuously added to the property through the 1950s, but have since been removed. Between 1946 and 1966, Orchard Rest was owned by the Marsicano family.

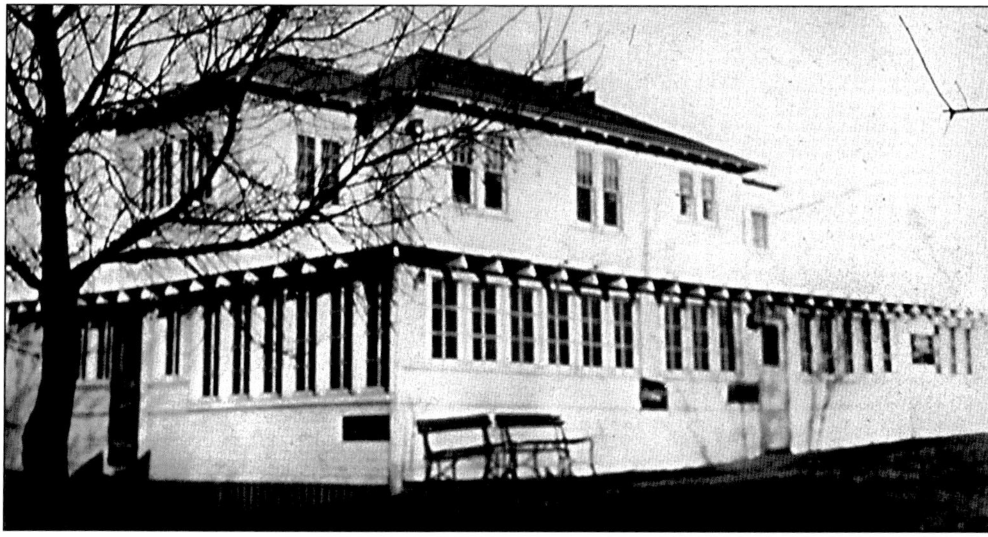

Blodgett's Resort, also known as The Pop House, was started by Albert and Ina Mereness Blodgett, who operated it from 1917 to 1945 on land that had been in the Mereness family since 1874. Located on South Shore Drive, just west of what is now the Community Beach, Blodgett's Resort, with its friendly atmosphere, provided ice cream and food for the hungry, boat rentals for the fishermen, and slot machines for entertainment. Swimming and lifesaving were also taught there by Arnold and Ruth Blodgett. When Al Blodgett was town board chairman from 1928 to 1934, several town meetings were held here.

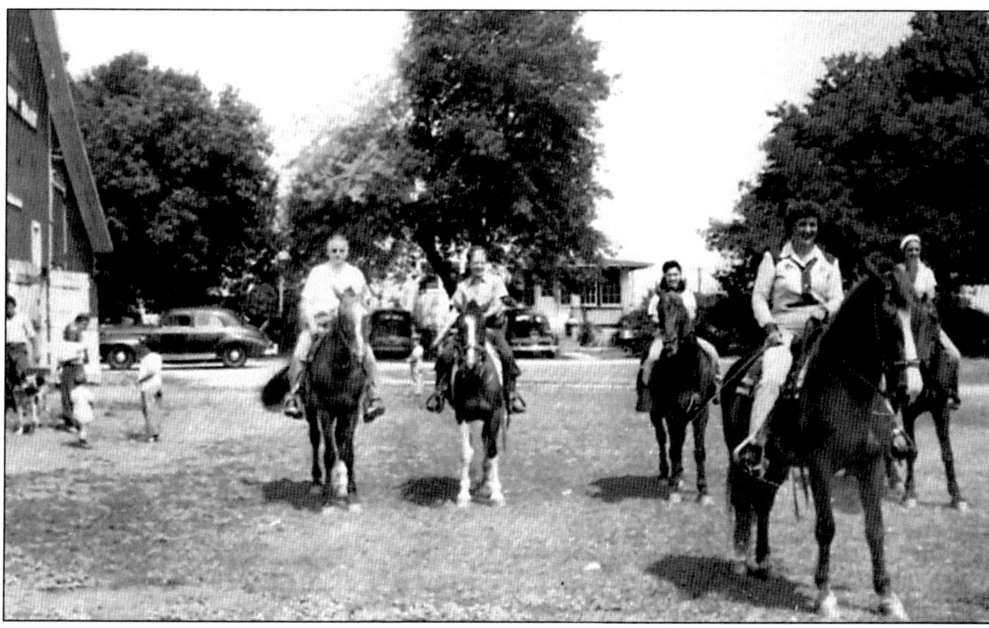

The Blodgett's also had a farm on County F, where they ran a room and board facility named Blodgett's Lake View Resort. Summer visitors would arrive by train in Walworth, then take a shuttle to the resort. Part of the farm, Melody Ranch, sheltered 17 horses and ponies that, guided by Pat or Joan Blodgett, took the guests for trail rides under South Shore Drive, through the creek, and down to the lake to swim.

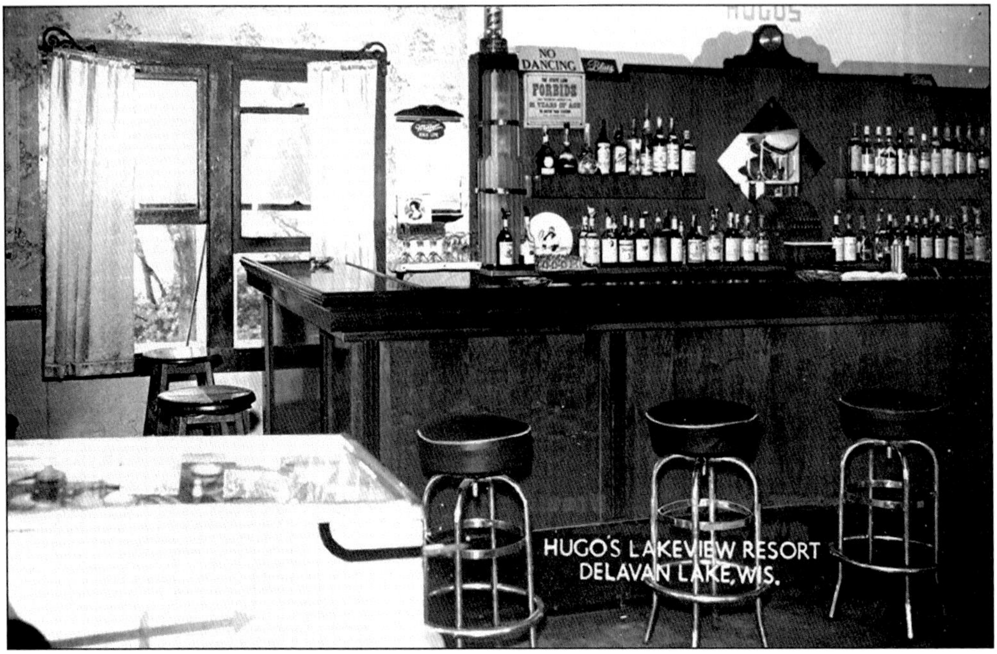

After remaining in the family for 71 years, Blodgett's Resort was sold in 1945 to Hugo Bolander, who operated under the name Hugo's Lakeview Resort. Bolander built cottages on the property and continued operation until 1966, when Emory and Helen Carlson purchased it and operated under the name Harbor Inn. The Carlsons would add gas pumps, boat slip rentals, and a pier service. Keefe Real Estate purchased the property in 1999 and razed the building to construct a condo/hotel, ending the life of a well-loved establishment.

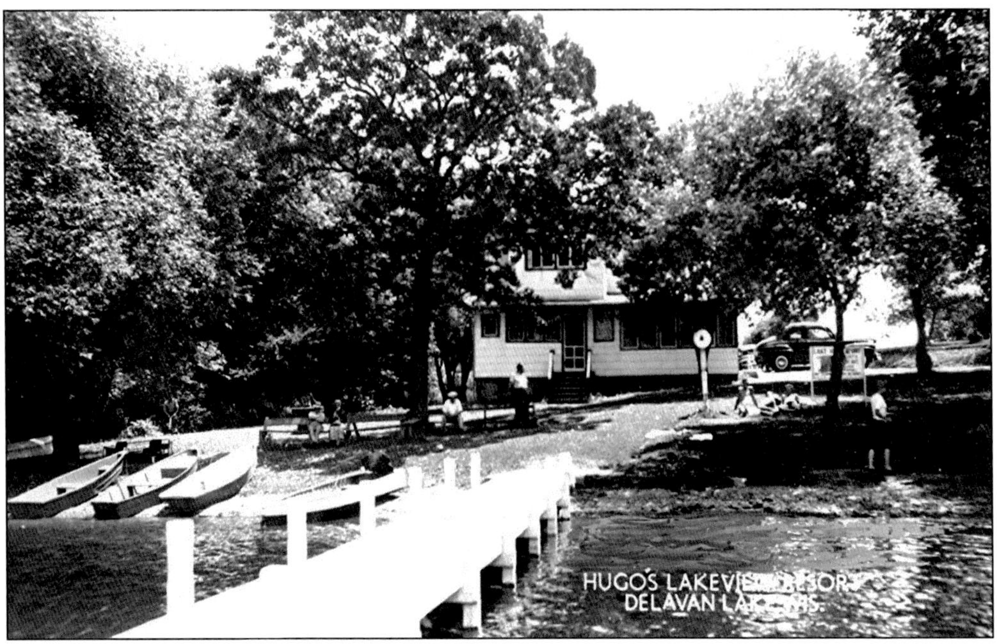

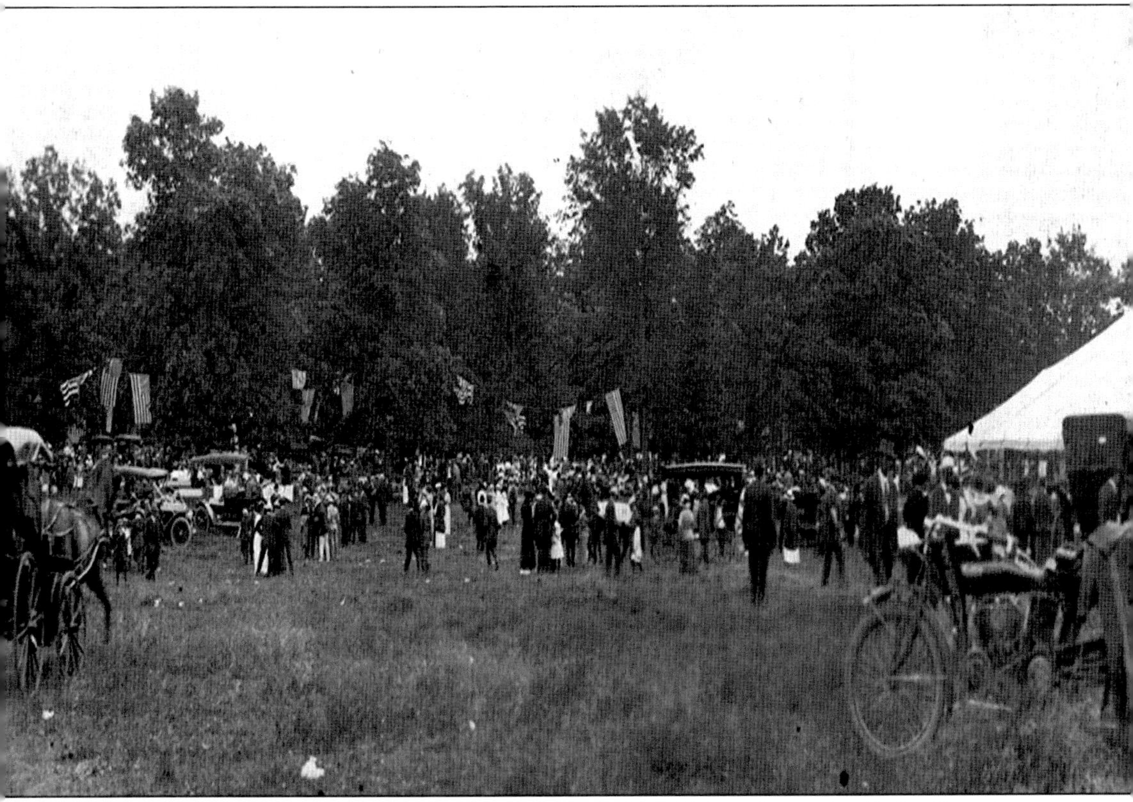

East Delavan was a thriving farm community as early as the 1840s and into the 1920s. Complete with post office, general store, harness maker, school, and church, it was located nine miles from both Delavan and Lake Geneva, and seven miles from Elkhorn. There was also a large building in East Delavan called Library Hall that held public meetings and dances. This is a view of the General Merchandise Store owned by F.H. Willey, taken about 1910.

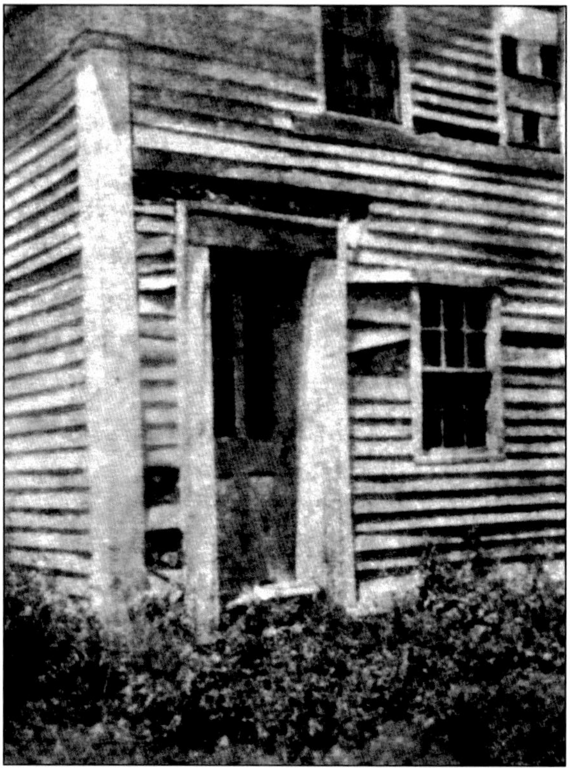

This stove wood house was located in East Delavan on what is now called Theater Road. When David Williams moved to East Delavan in the 1850s, building materials such as brick and stone were not available and log homes were the only houses in existence. Seeing the abundance of oak, William felled the trees on his land, cutting them into 10-inch pieces and packing them tightly with mortar like you would bricks. When finished nearly a year later, a pail of water placed in the window casement would not freeze on even the coldest of nights. The stove wood house was torn down in 1936.

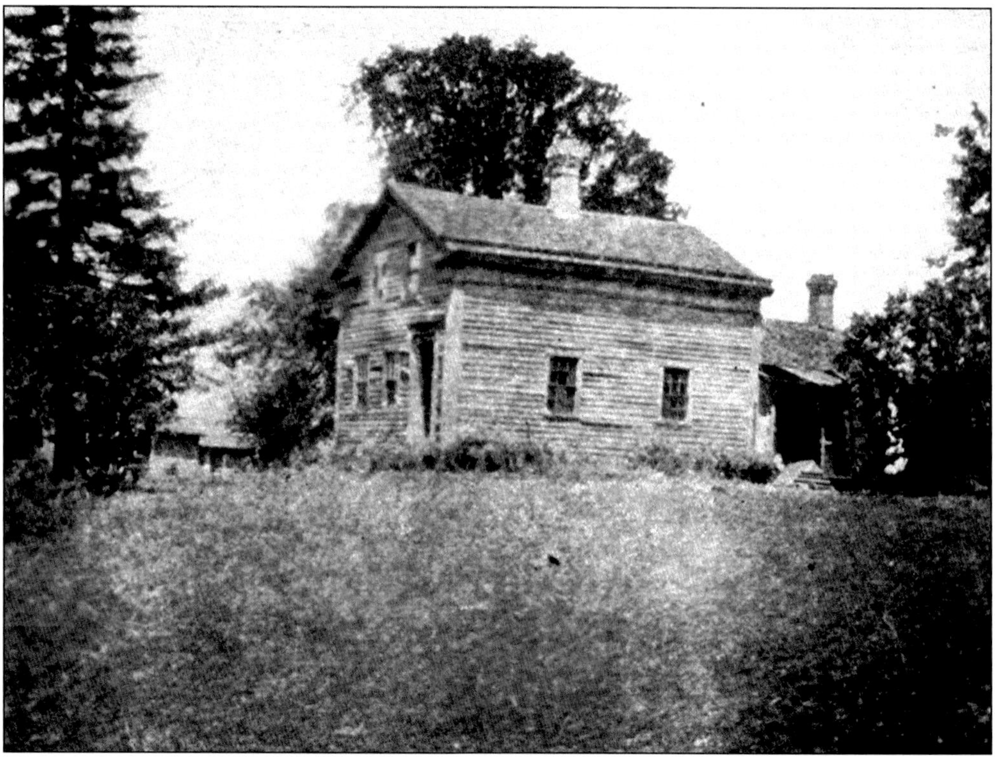

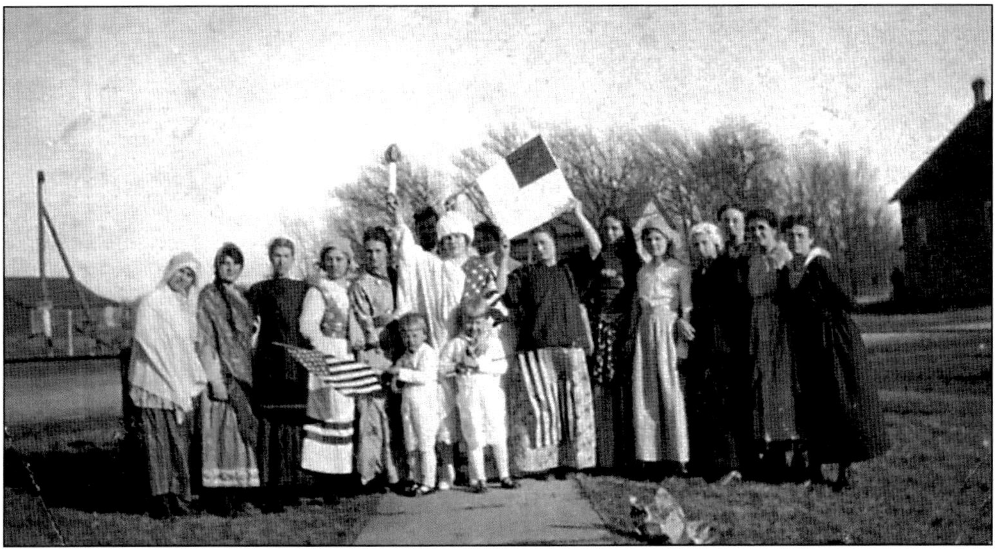

These are the ladies of East Delavan Baptist Church. The building on the right in the photograph is the general store. The East Delavan Baptist church was at first called the Delavan-Geneva Baptist church when it organized in 1845, due to its centralized location to both towns. They originally met in the schoolhouse until a church was built in 1848, when they also changed the name to the present East Delavan Baptist Church.

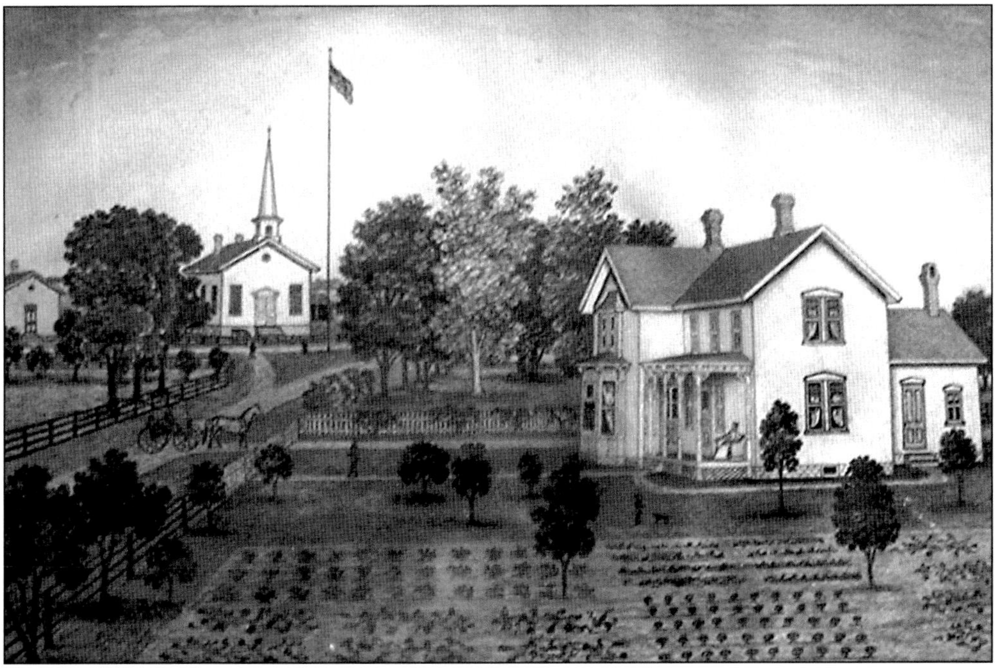

This beautiful pencil drawing by William Stanley in the 1890s depicts the residence of Henry Kirshner, Esq. This residence was located in East Delavan, where it still stands today. The artist spent much time in detailing the garden, the Kirshner family, and even their animals. In the distance he also captured the East Delavan Baptist Church and the East Delavan School.

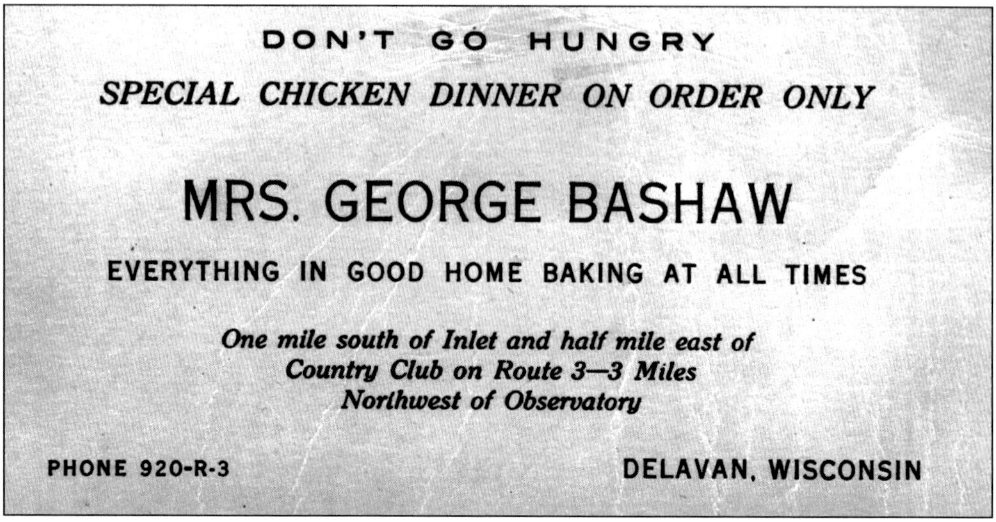

DON'T GO HUNGRY

SPECIAL CHICKEN DINNER ON ORDER ONLY

MRS. GEORGE BASHAW

EVERYTHING IN GOOD HOME BAKING AT ALL TIMES

One mile south of Inlet and half mile east of Country Club on Route 3—3 Miles Northwest of Observatory

PHONE 920-R-3

DELAVAN, WISCONSIN

Mrs. George Bashaw was a woman ahead of her time. In the early 1900s she ran one of the first carry-out food businesses in the township, right out of her kitchen. She was well-known for her great fried chicken dinners and mouth-watering pies. Pictured here is her pear filling recipe she shared with a friend while shopping at the general store in East Delavan, and also her business card. Note the Delavan phone exchange, with an East Delavan location and an Elkhorn mailing address on the stationary for the general store

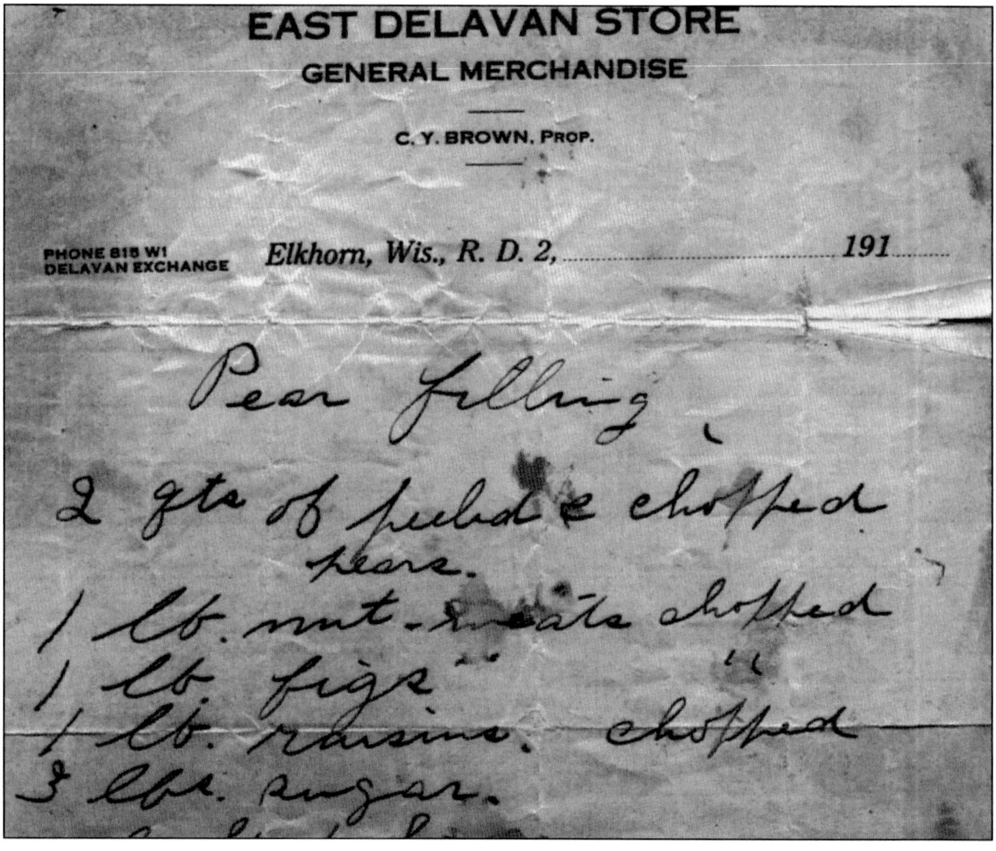

EAST DELAVAN STORE

GENERAL MERCHANDISE

C. Y. BROWN, PROP.

PHONE 815 W1
DELAVAN EXCHANGE

Elkhorn, Wis., R. D. 2, ... 191......

Pear filling

2 qts of peeled & chopped pears.

1 lb. nut-meats chopped

1 lb. figs "

1 lb. raisins. chopped

3 lbs. sugar.